The Encyclopaedia of Classic 80s Pop

DANIEL BLYTHE

First published in Great Britain in 2002 by
Allison & Busby Limited
Bon Marche Centre
241-251 Ferndale Road
London SW9 8BJ
http://www.allisonandbusby.com

A catalogue record for this book is available from
the British Library.

ISBN 0 7490 0534 3

Text design by Ben Yates, Tin Dog

Printed and bound in Great Britain by
Bookmarque Ltd, Croydon, Surrey

DANIEL BLYTHE was born in Maidstone in 1969. The first single he will admit to buying was 'Souvenir' by OMD, although the first single he actually bought was 'Making Your Mind Up' by Bucks Fizz. Daniel currently lives in Yorkshire with his wife and their small, noisy but loveable two children. He can often be found wandering the hills of the Peak District, musing on such life-affirming questions as how Heaven 17 got their name, which was the best Transvision Vamp album and who was really the most fanciable one out of Bananarama. He is also the author of two acclaimed novels, *The Cut* and *Losing Faith*.

◀» 'We were never really concerned with being cool. When you're younger, being cool is the most important thing, which tends to mean you just do what everyone else does.'

(Neil Tennant, Pet Shop Boys)

◀» 'The English may not like music, but they absolutely love the noise it makes.'

(Sir Thomas Beecham)

◀» 'Choose Life.'

(Popular T-shirt slogan, mid-1980s)

Introduction

Now That's What I Call The Top 100 Best I ♥ Class Of The 80s Nights Ever... Part 10

If you can remember the 80s, you were probably there. However, the chances are that you do your best to deny it.

You've destroyed the photo evidence, rolled up the Brother Beyond poster and taped over those chart compilations. You gave away the snood, the leg-warmers, the mirror-shades and the shiny jacket (with Don Johnson rolled-up sleeves) to a grateful branch of Save The Children in 1991. You're convinced, too, that you've recently seen that same shiny jacket on sale for £75 in the window of Reflex, the 80s retro shop which has just opened up where your bank used to be. Nostalgia re-invents itself – first as farce, then as tragedy.

Since the boom of the retro industry, those who market memories would like us to believe that our lives were a succession of perfect moments. In an ideal world, we all fit the demographic, we all live synchronicity. We sat on leather Habitat sofas, twisting Rubik cubes while watching the Royal Wedding. We programmed ZX-81s while our older brothers and sisters played the Human League loudly upstairs. We saw Bucks Fizz win Eurovision, their ripped skirts held aloft, just before Mrs T. appeared on the news, hectoring and bouffanted, a cue for Dad to have a moan about the state of the nation. Spandau Ballet's 'True' was the song during which you finally got to snog Gemma from 4D at the legendary school disco. Everybody listened to 'Ghost Town' in their heads while watching the pictures from the Brixton riots, while – at the other end of the decade – 'Wind of Change' accompanied the fall of the Berlin Wall. You are important, you are inextricably linked to the icons of your age. In the words of a Number 7 hit from 1989, 'You're History'.

The truth, of course, was far more horrible. Most of us stumbled through the decade without being trendy, a word which destroys itself by its own definition (brief flashback of Suzanne Ross from *Grange Hill* dressed as Boy George, getting an earful from Mrs McCluskey in the corridor). In a haze of sexual frustration and insecurity, in embarrassing trousers and bad haircuts, we hoped it would all soon end and that there would be something bigger and brighter just around the corner. If only we'd known that the future had *Eldorado*, automated call-centres and Mr Blobby lying in wait for us.

Retrospectively, far too many people try to claim that they were cool, that they were there, that they saw it all – not only were they at the epicentre of every trend, but they also were blessed with profound political and moral insight at the age of 13. Um, I don't think so. At 13, anyone vaguely normal is obsessed with at least three of these four things: surviving school, rampant hormones, some kind of sport, pop/rock music. So, like Drew Barrymore in *Never Been Kissed*, here's your chance to do it all again. And to get it right this time.

A Classic Case

The 80s – the last great decade for the single. It was the last era in which the Top 40 was an event, something which actually seemed to matter to the young as a whole, rather than just to seven-year-olds and a navel-gazing coterie of DJs.

I should, at this point, insert some notes for anyone under the age of 21 who has wandered in from the DVD section. In the 80s, a '7-inch vinyl single' was the standard pop medium, rather than a variety of sex toy available from the Internet. A 'climber' was a record which went up in the charts after its release, and not an illicit street drug. And your 'garage' was a place to keep all those boxes of old records, not an anodyne clattering noise overlaid with some bloke boasting through a Vocoder about his unlikely sexual conquests.

As soundtracks to teenage angst go, the 80s serve one well. A huge range of styles was in evidence. We had New Wave and New Romantic, synth-pop and ska, the last days of disco and the fag-end of punk, the growth of indie-guitar and the big intake of breath as dance emerged, blinking, into the light. Classic melodies, harmonies and lyrics were still valued. Even manufactured bands made a show of playing their instruments.

It's no coincidence that the more likeable of today's disposable pop acts – such as A1, Atomic Kitten and S Club – are drawing unashamedly on 80s influences, even covering 80s 'classics'. A great song, a 'classic', doesn't have to be particularly good, but it is one which transcends its medium to become something memorable. It can only be a matter of time before the sons and daughters of thirtysomethings are asking: 'Dad, were you alive when S'Express were at Number One?'

Pop Goes...?

As Nick Hornby memorably pointed out in *High Fidelity*, the written word can't do justice to the sheer contempt with which people of a certain age say the word 'pop'. For them, it is stupid and immoral, and therefore must be said a) with scorn, as if it epitomises everything simply dreadful about society, and b) as if one were slightly mentally defective.

If, however, you were born at the dawn of colour television and had a Milk Monitor in your class at primary school, then you'll be of an age to defend Pop. If you bought your first Madness or OMD single from the racks at WH

Smith and you can remember your mum cooking those Vesta packet meals, then Pop may mean something shiny, indefinable, even loveable. And if you ever got drunk enough to dance to 'True Blue' or 'I Think We're Alone Now' at your end-of-term disco, it may be something you feel guilty about liking.

Pop, for the purposes of this book, can mean anything which was regularly played on Radio 1, although in those days Radio 1 was allowed to admit that previous decades existed. (It started to go downhill when they scrapped the Golden Hour, but we won't go there now...) It can mean the sounds which were showcased on *Top Of The Pops* and in all manner of publications from the *NME* to *Smash Hits*. It can mean a musical genre whose main form of distribution was the 7-inch single. It covers a multitude of sins, and a plethora of virtues. And yes, pop did, as one band of visionaries predicted it would, eventually eat itself (the process began with the overkill of sampling). Today, the public consumes the results.

For a few people, the word will forever be associated with the phrase 'Cheggers Plays'. They are often found running pub quizzes in which they divide participants into teams called The Reds and The Yellows. These people are harmless, and should be tolerated.

And finally... this is an Encyclopaedia?

Frank Zappa once said that writing about music was like dancing about architecture. And let us not forget that it was also the estimable Mr Zappa who once called music journalism 'stuff written by people who can't write, about people who can't speak, for people who can't read'. Well, this isn't the place to come if you are looking for an academic dissection of the water-imagery in the *Ninth Wave* sequence of Kate Bush's seminal 1985 concept album *Hounds Of Love*, even though the beauty and quality of Ms Bush's work is indisputable. And if you want to trace the influence of expressionist electro-pop from Kraftwerk through to 808 State and rave – you might do it at home, but don't do it here. This is, to be honest, a none-too-serious book with a serious name.

Many people have been anxious to collar me and ask some kind of variation on the following: 'Are you going to put Marvelsprocket in? They had a no.55 hit in 1987, you know, on the Katalog label. Hugely influential band. The indie-dance revolution couldn't have happened without them.' Um, well, you can't please everyone. Just to note a few points:

◀ Some may sniff at the omissions, but it didn't seem right to include people with long-running careers not *substantially* linked to the 80s, such as Kate Bush, Pink Floyd, Prince, David Bowie and Queen. You'll find plenty about these people elsewhere. On the other hand, fans of (for example) Depeche Mode and Wet Wet Wet may protest that those acts' inclusion spits in the face of their longevity. They may be right.

◀ A subjective process of selection went on. Please don't send me outraged letters scrawled in pig's blood because I haven't included Blue Rondo A La Turk, Oran 'Juice' Jones or The Tweets. Ask nicely, and your pet omission may get to go in any future edition (but only if you can persuade me they are interesting enough).

◀ It's also fair to say that the truly awful is celebrated here alongside the great and the good, which is how it should be. The existence of crimes against music is sometimes used as the sounding-board for a little rant. It's my party, and I'll cry if I want to.

◀ Entries are conveniently arranged in alphabetical order – like any sensible person's record collection. (All right, any sensible *man's* record collection.) Inevitably, some sections sport more entries than others. I've very good reason to be grateful to XTC and ZZ Top.

◀ Individual artists are listed according to last name. There may be some dispute over the location of Terence Trent D'Arby, but then that's what he gets for being so pretentious as to have two surnames. Danny Wilson, however, were a band and not a person, hence their inclusion under D and not W – anyone wishing to argue about this should see me outside. Ditto for Matt Bianco.

So who is this book for? It's for you – if you ever bought a ticket to the world and have now come back again, if you liked the sound of a club where the drinks were free, or if you thought that working as a waitress in a cocktail bar sounded a glamorous way of escaping your humdrum existence. It's a book for you if you knew there wouldn't be snow in Africa this Christmas, or if you sometimes stood alone at parties. Or if you went way too fast and were going to crash, or if you had the sun in your hair, the moon in your eyes and you just didn't give a damn. Or, indeed, if you would sell your soul for a tacky song like the ones you heard on the radio.

It's a book for you if you were ever convinced that 'La Isla Bonita' had a line about a 'young girl with eyes like potatoes'. If you ever wanted hair like Robert Smith. If you smile wryly at the memory of the All About Eve single 'Martha's Harbour' playing on *Top of the Pop*s while Julianne Regan sat there like a lemon, not miming. And if you recall a certain impudent question to Five Star on Saturday morning TV.

And finally, it's a book for you if you ever felt, like Mr Roddy Frame of Aztec Camera – who will forgive me for not quoting directly, as I don't wish to cost my publishers several hundred pounds – that although one can't buy time, one can sell one's soul, and that the closest thing to heaven might be to rock and roll.

The Memorability Guide

Purely subjective and possibly quite cruel, but it's written in the stars. Less about quality and more about how well-remembered they are.

★ ★ ★ ★ ★ Eternal Flame

Essential. You can't write the history of the 80s without them. Still played, still enjoyed, their songs are covered by new bands, and they are even on the road from time to time.

★ ★ ★ ★ (Keep Feeling) Fascination

Well-loved. Destined forever to appear in those 80s retrospectives, and really none the worse for it.

★ ★ ★ Don't You (Forget About Me)

Solid, solid as a rock. Compilation regulars. *TOTP2* has played them, albeit with very sardonic captions by Steve Wright.

★ ★ What Have I Done To Deserve This?

Hard to recall them... May still be writing and producing, but the ID parade on *Never Mind The Buzzcocks* was a bit humiliating.

★ Fade To Grey

Let's face it, that hit record was a long time ago. And not much good.

Key To Categories

⊚ **Name And Number:** Cunning disguises – other hit names for the same act.

♪ **The First Picture Of You:** First UK chart single, and the year in which that record peaked.

🎧 **Radio Romance:** Bite-size listening: best singles, essential collections.

💣 **It Ain't What You Do, It's The Way That You Do It:** The top pop moment…era-defining actions and feats.

✔ **Is There Something I Should Know?:** Trivia – go and win a pub quiz.

🔊 **Speak Like A Child:** Can you believe the things they say, and do they echo what you fear?

♥ **Victim Of Love:** Unusual covers, wacky tribute bands and resonances…

⏭ **(Forever) Live And Die:** So where are they now – still cutting the discs, or washing the dishes?

rewind

play

avant-garde beatbox noises

ABC ★★★★

Northern soulfulness

These days, people will do anything to be first in a pop book, including calling themselves flagrantly unfair things like A and A1. Before such gamesmanship was rife, you'd always find ABBA there in prime position, followed by ABC.

But that was in the old days – which, as their fellow Sheffield popsters **The Human League** have noted, can't have been that good or they would have lasted. And how different Sheffield was in the early days of ABC. These days, England's fourth city has re-invented itself as a 21st-century Babylon of tourism, hedonistic clubbing, sleek European trams and 'quality shopping' (whatever the hell that is). It's looking smart these days, but is still full of utilitarian-chic, over-priced coffee bars, all staffed by homogenous twenty-year-olds in stretchy tops who know all about the 80s because they go to the retro nights at the Roundhouse. (When you tell them that you lived through it the first time round, they laugh nervously and look over your shoulder in the hope that the next customer will be a little less like their dad.) A recent single by The All-Seeing I called 'First Man In Space' (featuring none other than Phil Oakey on vocals) brilliantly encapsulates the kind of culture-shock which might be felt by any returning Sheffielder today. All of which, admittedly, doesn't really tell you much about the band under discussion, but I thought I would start as I meant to go on.

Martin Fry's group were purveyors of glamour and style in an age which seemed to have lost it. The clichés of industrial South Yorkshire didn't inform the music of this lot, thankfully, as you might expect from a man in a gold lamé suit. *The Lexicon Of Love* is their classic album, encapsulating their polished production sound, melodic pop tunes and witty lyrics. A mammoth 150-date tour accompanied it, after which Martin Fry became seriously ill and put the group on hold. However, 1987's 'When Smokey Sings' was a memorable comeback single, recapturing their classic sound for another foray into the Top 20.

- ✔ The name was apparently chosen because the first three letters of the alphabet are known throughout the world.

- ✔ In the late 1970s, Fry edited a fanzine called *Modern Drugs*, and he met the other members of the initial ABC line-up when he interviewed them about their band Vice Versa.

Adam and the Ants ★★★★

♪ **'Dog Eat Dog'** (1980, no.4)

If your earliest pop memories involve a man with a white stripe across his nose and your prototype experiments in fashion involved painting two strokes of lipstick on your cheek, or you were ever seized with a desire to jump down the stairs to the school dinner-hall and swing on the lampshade above the assembled multitudes – don't worry, you are not alone. For this and much more, you have to thank the missing link between punk and New Romantic, the irrepressible Stuart Goddard, known to all in the early 1980s as Adam Ant.

Adam's band appeared in the 1978 film *Jubilee*, and early recordings saw them briefly involved with Malcolm McLaren, who stole the band for **Bow Wow Wow**. It was 1980's *Kings Of The Wild Frontier* which saw the birth of the classic 'Ant Music' sound, best described as a fusion between punk, glam rock and African drumming. They were one of the first 80s groups to be strongly associated with the visual medium; it's hard to hear 'Stand And Deliver' without picturing Adam leaping out of a tree in his highwayman gear and taunting the gentlefolk, all filmed endearingly on cheap-looking OB videotape. (If you're one of these frustrating people who can't see the texture difference between film and videotape, and you're not bothered that *Brookside* is now on 'filmised video' and looks awful, then don't worry. You probably spent the 1980s going out and having fun.)

If 'Prince Charming' goes on late enough at an 80s night, several people will immediately start doing the hands-crossed-above-head dance – proof that all you need for an enduring legacy is one simple, memorable image.

💣 At a Plymouth gig in 1979, Adam managed to cut his head open and needed 6 stitches … Adam's 1985 comeback tour had to be cancelled, as he wasn't able to get himself insured. I've no idea if these two events are related.

🔊 'It's about time we had 80s nostalgia … it's about time they paid homage to the greatest period of pop artistry ever. The best dressed, suited and booted, verse-chorus-verse-chorus period since ABBA.' So says Adam in 2002.

♥ There was a tribute band called Adam & the Antz (note the subtle difference in spelling) but they split up in 2000.

⏭ Adam Ant disbanded the group in 1981, but continued to work with guitarist and songwriter Marco Pirroni for his solo career, which included the Number One hit 'Goody Two Shoes'. In 1990, Adam recorded *Manners and Physique* with former Prince producer André Cymone, preceded by Top 20 come-back single 'Room at the Top'. Since then he has done the odd acting role and one further album, 1995's *Wonderful*. He has re-emerged for revival tours, and seems to be well despite some well-documented 'incidents' reported in the press during 2001.

The Adventures ★★★

♫ **'Broken Land'** (1988, no.20)

Harmonious Celts

At times like this, you realise just what 'under-rated' truly means. The Adventures were a beautiful, melodic six-piece whose status as one-hit wonders does them no justice at all. Their struggle for success proves once again what a bunch of dullards the British public could be when confronted with real talent.

Founder members Terry Sharpe and Pat Gribben were originally in the Belfast punk band The Starjets, and got The Adventures together in London in the early 80s. Their early work was on Chrysalis Records, and if there was any justice, 'Another Silent Day' would have been a massive hit in 1984. However, they had to wait for a move to Elektra before they got anything approaching recognition. 'Broken Land', a powerful, heartfelt and melodic piece of pop-rock about the Irish troubles, scraped into the Top 20, but it just cried out to be a Top 5 single – and if you don't like it, you have no soul. Their first Elektra album *The Sea Of Love* (1988) is packed full of such excellent songs: chiming gui-tars are surrounded by brilliant harmonies and lush synth sounds, most notably on 'When The Rain Comes Down', 'Heaven Knows Which Way' and the oh-so-nearly-a-hit, 'Drowning In The Sea Of Love'.

So what on earth happened to 'Your Greatest Shade Of Blue', from the next album *Trading Secrets With The Moon*? And what about 'Raining All Over the World', another great hit-in-waiting in 1992? Radio 1, to their credit, played it all the time and the band did all the summer roadshows, but to no avail. Well, at the end of the day, people just preferred New Kids On The Block. And that, frankly, is their loss.

🎧 Do please go and get hold of *The Sea Of Love* if you haven't heard of this band!

✔ The full line-up: Terry Sharpe (lead vocals), Eileen Gribben (vocals), Gerard 'Spud' Murphy (vocals), Pat Gribben (guitar), Tony Ayre (bass), Paul Crowder (drums).

✔ Debut album *The Adventures* was re-released for the US market as *Theodore And Friends* in 1988.

✔ Among those providing backing vocals on *The Sea Of Love* were 70s singer Katie Kissoon and fellow Irishman Brian Kennedy – an aside on the sleeve notes presciently reads 'your time will come', and indeed Kennedy would emerge as a hit artist in his own right in the 90s, starting with his album *The Great War Of Words*.

🔊 *Billboard* magazine review of *The Sea Of Love*, 1988: 'Class-A offering from UK pop band sounds like a can't-miss proposition for radio. Spectacular, widescreen production by [Pete] Smith enhances melodic, guitar-charged tunes sung by potent triumvirate of vocalists...' (A case of some great reviews not translating into great sales. I know the feeling.)

A-ha ★★★★

♫ 'Take On Me' (1985, no.2)

Norwegians would

There are some things the Scandinavians just seem better at than the English: sex, philosophy, minimalist furniture, managing our football team, speaking grammatical English … In the 1980s you could easily have added 'boy bands' to the list.

Once the trio of Morten Harket, Pal Waaktaar and Magne (Mags) Furuholmen had signed to WEA, 'Take On Me' became a hit in the UK after the third attempt – a chance most bands just wouldn't get these days. It caught the imaginations of teenagers with its keyboard solo and clever video, which showed Morten and the boys coming to life from a girl's comic. 'The Sun Always Shines On TV' was a Number One, helping the album *Hunting High And Low* into the Top 10, while *Scoundrel Days* cemented Pal Waaktaar's reputation as a songwriter. James Bond movie theme 'The Living Daylights' helped their credibility along further, as did the soaring ballad 'Stay On These Roads', and they popped up a few more times in the 90s.

✔ Mags and Pal's first band was called Spider Empire. They came up with the name A-ha as it is an expression recognised in different languages all over the world. (So they could just as easily have been called OK, Taxi, Computer or Mmmm-hmmm.)

🔊 Today the pop industry takes advantage of kids who are barely in their teens, who'd do anything to be stars. We were like that when we first made it, we signed every contract there was. And that's why we became pin-ups, why nobody cared that we also wrote songs. It's only now that the powers that be

30

who looked down on us before have begun to say that A-ha always was a good band.' Morten Harket in 2002.

♥ Noughties boy-band A1 covered 'Take On Me', updating the imagery for the video: where A-ha combined live action and animation, A1 were fighting computer viruses in cyberspace.

▶▶ Mags moved into the art world, while Pal formed his new band, Savoy. In 2000, A-ha got back together for their first new album in seven years, *Minor Earth Major Sky*, which has done well for them (although not in the UK). There are quite a few sites out there, a lot of them devoted to raising awareness that the band are still going. Just to be perverse, here's a link to a German one: **www.a-ha-mems.de**

All About Eve ★★★
♫ **'Wild Hearted Woman'** (1988, no.33)

Best described as folky goths (but see below) this band was formed by Julianne Regan, formerly bassist in Gene Loves Jezebel, and guitarist Tim Bricheno, later to join the **Sisters Of Mercy**. The mystical, hippie-esque quality of their work struck a chord and their single 'Martha's Harbour' was a Top 10 record in 1988, even after a disastrous *Top Of The Pops* performance. Their albums *All About Eve* and *Scarlet (And Other Stories)* sold well in the UK.

Later work such as 1992's 'Phased EP' seemed the baffle the critics, with one music paper remarking of the latter: 'What year is this?' They disbanded in the 1990s, but later re-formed to tour with The Mission. Well, there's nowt so queer as folk. Except possibly goths.

31

In the 1980s, *Top Of The Pops* would occasionally go out 'live' rather than pre-recorded, but most of the acts still chose to mime. This resulted in an unfortunate incident when All About Eve performed at the BBC studios in Birmingham. Thanks to an engineering cock-up, Regan couldn't hear sound of the record coming through and so didn't start 'singing', but all the time her vocals were playing. She just sat there staring into space as party balloons floated down around her. You had to feel sorry for them. They got invited back the following week to do it properly, so no harm done.

All About Eve had a close association with The Mission throughout their career. Regan sang backing vocals on their debut album and The Mission's lead singer Wayne Hussey co-produced All About Eve's single 'Our Summer'.

'We were just tarred with that brush [Goth]. OK, maybe we did wear black clothes sometimes. We played with Fairport Convention for a while so we were dubbed folkies and then we were known as the poor man's Fleetwood Mac.' Julianne Regan.

Marc Almond: see **Soft Cell**

Altered Images ✮✮✮

♬ **'Happy Birthday'** (1981, no.2)

The very mention of the name Clare Grogan is enough to make most thirtysomething heterosexual males go all misty-eyed and thoughtful. We're probably also likely to have a minor 'Homer Simpson Moment' too: 'Mmmmmm … Clare … Gro-gan!' Who else could do so much with a layered fringe and a bit of pouting? (Well, okay, *apart* from Boy George.)

She was already known from the film *Gregory's Girl*, and now here she was fronting her very own group. Originally a new-wave band with a darker feel, and produced by **Siouxsie and the Banshees**' Steve Severin, Altered Images broke into the Top 40 with a more poppy sound. The first single, one of those relentlessly perky ditties which everyone remembers, stayed in the charts for 17 weeks, and 'I Could Be Happy' and 'Don't Talk To Me About Love' were also Top 10 hits. These days, Clare concentrates on her acting career.

Apparently there were some chaps in the band too. I'm sure they were very nice.

Amazulu ★ ★

♫ **'Excitable'** (1985, no.12)

In the fickle world of popular music, home to so many desolate dreams and lost causes, it's probably wisest not to invite sarcastic comments from the compilers of irreverent reference works. These might go something like: 'had a no. 5 hit with a Chi-Lites cover, the optimistically-entitled "Too Good To Be Forgotten" in 1986.' Oh. Too late.

Cheap jibes aside, their sunny reggae-pop wasn't bad and earned them five hits. Large-dreadlocked, raffishly-attired and rather attractive girls, they had an early break in 1984, when they had one of the musical slots on anarchic comedy show *The Young Ones*. It's season 2, episode 4 ('Time'), if you want to check it out, and the song they performed was 'Moonlight Romance'.

✔   The name 'Amazulu' means 'the people of Heaven'.

- ✓ They were recently cited as an influence on the 2001 single 'Romeo' from awfully-hip techno duo Basement Jaxx. So, not forgotten at all.

Aneka ★★

♫ 'Japanese Boy' (1981, no.1)

Big in Japan?
The second most memorable 80s hit with the word 'Japanese' in the title (the first, of course, being 'Turning Japanese' by The Vapors). Mary Sandeman – a Scottish singer whose normal speciality was Gaelic folk music – decided to dress up in a kimono, don a glossy black wig and heavy make-up and perform this little ditty.

The song's pleasant enough with its wistful tone and chiming Eastern chords, and has one of the most recognisable intros ever. Her follow-up 'Little Lady' stalled at no.50, and Aneka went back to being plain old Mary Sandeman again.

- ✓ Interestingly, she did a little better in Germany, with 'Japanese Boy' getting to no.3 and 'Little Lady' to no.10 in 1981, plus 'Ooh Shooby Doo Doo Lang' making no.18 in 1982.

Art of Noise ★★★

♫ 'Close (To The Edit)' (1984, no.8)

Eclectic musical jackdaws and futuristic sound-pioneers led by producer Trevor Horn, who had been responsible for The Buggles and **ABC**. Their avant-garde beatbox noises caused a stir on both sides of the pond in the mid-80s. Best-known tracks are 'Peter Gunn', featuring the guitar of Duane Eddy, and the collaboration with Tom Jones on his cover of Prince's 'Kiss', on which Tom manages to make the declaration 'Think I'd better *dance* now!' sound truly terrifying.

▶▶   Former Noiser Anne Dudley has gone on to provide orchestral arrangements for Pulp and Boyzone, among others.

The Assembly ★★

♪ **'Never Never'** (1983, no.4)

Short-lived collaborations don't come much better than this. Vince Clarke of **Yazoo** got together with Feargal Sharkey of The Undertones for the one-off electronic ballad 'Never Never'. And that's about the size of it.

Clarke has therefore had top 5 hits with four different acts (the others being **Depeche Mode**, **Yazoo**, and **Erasure**). Trust me, this comes up in pub pop-quizzes all the time. You can have it for free.

The Associates ★★★

♪ **'Party Fears Two'** (1982, no.9)

Scottish band whose core was the duo of Billy McKenzie and Alan Rankine. They began by playing David Bowie covers in working men's clubs. 1980 album *The Affectionate Punch* gained a lot of critical praise, and was re-recorded and remixed in 1982. *Sulk*, an album sometimes pigeon-holed into the glamour-revival led by the likes of **ABC**, gave them some hit singles: the most famous, 'Party Fears Two', was apparently based on a couple of characters McKenzie knew who used to go round gatecrashing parties. It was also used as the theme tune to the satirical radio programme *Week Ending*.

🎧   Early singles compilation *Fourth Drawer Down* is a favourite with fans.

🎙️   Billy McKenzie was found dead in a potting-shed at Auchterhouse, Dundee in January 1997, two months before his 40th birthday. With a sad irony, his death came just as he had signed a new deal with Nude Records.

🔊   'Chasing after the shadow of David Bowie, singers of a post-New Romantic persuasion roar to the heavens of arriving for a forced grandeur that invariably reeks of overblown tack.' Original *Melody Maker* review of *Sulk* from 1982.

🔊   On the other hand: '*Sulk* is arguably the least influenced album of all time – it has few if any precedents – and also the least influential. Nobody save maybe Prince on "If I Was Your Girlfriend" or Bjork on "Venus As A Boy" has been able to rival its emotionally overwrought (compliment!), "out of this world" music.' *Melody Maker* in 1994. What a difference a decade makes.

Rick Astley ★★★

🎵 **'Never Gonna Give You Up'** (1987, no.1)

Public dancer

The man who confused quite a few people in the music business by sounding like Isaac Hayes and looking like that scrawny ginner in your class at school who always got picked on, Rick Astley had the last laugh when he shot to phenomenal success in the latter part of the decade. And then he just as quickly (or so it seemed) disappeared.

Born in Warrington and brought up in Newton-le-Willows (possibly the least rock'n'roll sounding place on the AA Road Map), Rick showed early promise in the school choir. The legend goes that he was **Stock, Aitken and Waterman's** teaboy (and presumably that he was heard practising as he sauntered through the studio dispensing camomile and lemon to **Bananarama** and refilling **Hazell Dean's** frothy cappuccinos). Sadly, it's only partly true. Rick did work at the studio while he was being 'groomed' – but as a tape operator, and after he'd already been spotted by Waterman in a Warrington social club, singing with soul band FBI.

'Never Gonna Give You Up' was one of the best-performing debuts any artist could wish for – it spent 5 weeks at the top, was in the charts for 18 weeks in total, became the biggest single of 1987 and was also huge in the US, Australia and Germany. An upbeat, melodic pop song about simple devotion, it somehow manages to transcend its formulaic origins and has become a classic.

Then came a bad idea. After the similarly poppy follow-up 'Whenever You Need Somebody', Rick had to do the Christmas ballad thing, and the song which was chosen for him was 'When I Fall In Love'. Oh dear. You could hear people wincing all over the land before they'd even heard it. Only the prospect of Motorhead performing 'When A Child Is Born' could have seemed more disastrous. In the event, Rick did a decent job – the song let his voice shine through – but with perfect timing, the Nat King Cole original was re-released for Christmas 1987 as well. The tabloids got the perfect 'race for the top' they always desired, but inevitably the sales of Rick's version took a knock and the **Pet Shop Boys** eventually got there. It's still hard to forget the rather uncomfortable video in which Rick, resplendent in long winter coat, stands beside an wobbly mock-up of a log cabin, trying to appear serious and wistful beyond his 21 years while some unconvincing fake snow makes it look as if he's got an especially gruesome case of dandruff.

A couple more hits, a 15-country world tour in 1988, and then it all went quiet. Where had Rick Astley gone, and what was he doing? In 1991, the answer seemed to come: he'd been in the studio, growing his hair along with his musical stature. Having parted company with the terrible trio, Rick made his comeback with the rather pleasant, soul/gospel-tinged single 'Cry For Help', a perfect showcase for his uncannily rich and deep voice. The Top 10 album *Free* followed, and he then seemed to slide back into obscurity – but two further albums were issued in the 90s and beyond, *Body & Soul* and *Keep It Turned On*.

- Rick's *Greatest Hits* album was released in 2002 in the UK and Europe.

- Rick on *Top Of The Pops* doing 'Never Gonna Give You Up' proved therapeutic to everyone who had ever felt embarrassed at not being able to dance. Now that a major pop idol made it cool just to twitch your arms and legs in a self-conscious way, it perhaps wasn't so bad after all.

- Rick apparently doesn't want to be famous in Britain again. Astley sightings have become almost as legendary as those of the Loch Ness Monster, but a still-youthful Rick was spotted promoting his single 'Keep It Turned On' in Germany and Eastern Europe in 2002. It's estimated that he's earned £10m, and he lives quietly in Surrey with his Danish wife Lene and their daughter. We wish him well.

Aztec Camera ★★★★

♫ 'Oblivious' (1983, no.18)

Essentially the project of Roddy Frame, backed by a succession of anonymous types, and responsible for some of the most tuneful guitar-pop of the 80s. Roddy was something of a prodigy – he formed the band in his teens and the debut album *High Land Hard Rain* came out in 1983 when he was just 19. Founder members Campbell Owens and Dave Mulholland had inexplicably deserted the group before the album's release, leaving Roddy as something of a one-man show, a role which he seemed happy to fill for the rest of the decade.

'Oblivious' made the Top 40 on the second attempt, and remains an early-80s classic with its edgy guitars and shuffling beat. But 'Somewhere In My Heart' is the one everyone knows, a joyful and uplifting single which, by virtue of being released in the middle of the uninspiring 1988, just screamed 'proper pop song with guitars and a chorus and everything!' at you. The album *Love*, from which this hit came, was a conscious attempt to be more commercial, and it seemed to work. 1990's 'Good Morning Britain', with Mick Jones of The Clash, is a storming wake-up anthem, too.

◀)) 'I remember the first time I went to America. I arrived in San Francisco minutes before this TV show… I hadn't changed or shaved for a couple of days, I had oil on my hands and stuff. I arrived at the television studio and straight away they said, "And now Roddy Frame from Aztec Camera!". I walked on, and it was like a little discotheque situation with glitter and tinsel hanging behind me. The kids in the audience didn't know what to make of me. They were all wearing designer suits and I was standing there manky in the middle of this showbiz thing.' Roddy in *Record Mirror*, 1988.

▶▶ Roddy records solo now and continues to put out excellent stuff like the recent 'Reason For Living'. Have a look at **www.killermontstreet.com**, which even attempts to instruct you in Roddy-style guitar playing...

pause

ß

being exploited in a hothouse

Bad Manners ★★
♫ **'Ne-Ne Na-Na Na-Na Nu-Nu'** (1980, no.28)

'Ah,' remarked my slightly camp music teacher to someone sporting a cluster of badges, 'you've earned your badge for **Madness**! How lovely. I saw someone last week with one for Bad Manners.'

You'd think that a large bald man in a frilly dress dancing the Can-Can would be a somewhat specialist taste, but this escapade gave Bad Manners their biggest hit in the summer of 1981. For years after their initial success, the ska group, featuring the large and unmistakable Buster Bloodvessel (real name Douglas Trendle) were favourites of the student ball circuit with favourites like 'Special Brew', 'Can Can' and 'Lip Up Fatty' and it's easy to see why – they were just a fun, singalong, put-on-a-show band. Their success at the time is not to be sniffed at – only Madness spent more weeks on the chart in 1980. If you've got badges for both, hang on to them.

- ✔ They changed the lyrics of 'My Boy Lollipop' to 'My Girl Lollipop', presumably to keep it heterosexual...

- ✔ Buster Bloodvessel became the owner of a theme park in Margate, and also owns Margate FC.

Bananarama ★★★★
♫ **'It Ain't What You Do, It's The Way That You Do It'**
(1982, no. 4, with Fun Boy Three)

The Spicier Girls
This is what we like. A band where the question 'What was their best single?' must be secondary to the pressing matter of 'Which one did it for you?'

Let's be honest for a moment. If you were a red-blooded teenage male in the 1980s, then Siobhan Fahey, Keren Woodward and Sarah Dallin had to be plastic pop's most shaggable trio (leaving aside the dungarees and the dodgy hair-gel phase as parodied by Tracey Ullman). Oh, and don't forget Jacquie O'Sullivan, who joined in 1988. To maintain an artificial, unwarranted air of suspense during this item, the author will not reveal which Banana he most fancied until the end.

Although they were superb *Smash Hits* fodder and the template for today's girl-power bands, they didn't need manufactured 'characters', unfeasibly large trainers or celebrity boyfriends – just their look and a clutch of catchy tunes was enough.

DJ Gary Crowley started them off, helping them to get a deal with Decca in 1981, and Sex Pistols member Paul Cook produced their first single 'Ai A Mwana'. It only got to no. 92, but then singing in Swahili was never a great move commercially. Then they got noticed by Terry Hall, at the time the blond-quiffed leader of the Fun Boy Three. The girls ended up doing backing vocals on the shuffling no. 4 hit 'It Ain't What You Do, It's The Way That You Do It' (that title really needs brackets). By the time the second Bananarama single 'Really Saying Something' came out on London Records, Terry and his amusing boys were doing the girls' BVs instead.

Throughout a succession of hits, including big US single 'Cruel Summer', the girls had a reputation for taking their pop career less than seriously – but there was still one further leap to make. In a piece of true synergy, the perfect commercial girl group found, it seemed, the ideal producers in **Stock, Aitken and Waterman** in 1986. Their first SAW single was the upbeat 'Venus', a cover of Shocking Blue's US Number One from 1970 which the girls had actually been singing for four years. It made no.8 in the UK (the same position as Shocking Blue, chart trivia watchers!) and gave them their first and only American Number One. More hits followed in the same vein, but by the time 'Love In The First Degree' came out, it's fair to say that people were starting to shake their heads a little at the ubiquitous 'sound' of **Stock, Aitken and Waterman**. By the end of the decade, Bananarama had changed direction once again – Siobhan discovered heavy eyeliner, married the **Eurythmics**' Dave Stewart and escaped to form the scarily different Shakespear's Sister. Keren and Sarah carried on with Jacquie in place and new producer Youth, even bringing back a few guitars into the mix for 1990 single 'Only Your Love'.

Oh, and it was always Keren, of course.

- ๏ I'd guess 'Robert De Niro's Waiting' is the classic for most people, but the cheesy 'Venus' has a certain charm. Two greatest hits collections are available, one from 1988 packaged in a glamorous triptych of Vogue-style images, and the most recent from 2001 in a lovely pink box.

- ✔ Theirs was not the only cover of 'Venus' to be a Top 40 hit. A band called Don Pablo's Animals had a go in 1990, but it doesn't really count as it's a dance record which just samples the intro over and over. (Trust me, I think it's particularly boring, and I like 'Pump Up The Volume'.)

- ✔ Julie Burchill's always loved them. Don't let that put you off.

- ✔ And the only act to appear on both the versions of the **Band Aid** record is…? Ah, you're ahead of me. That pub quiz cup is yours for the taking.

🔊 Keren claims that 'there are a few tracks you don't even know about, that I hope never see the light of day, but I know are going to be hanging around the vaults at PWL somewhere...'

♥ There's a tribute band out there called Mangowango ... A German band called The Boonaraaas, best described as 'girly garage-pop-punk', have done versions of 'Cruel Summer' and 'Robert De Niro's Waiting'.

⏭ Sarah and Keren, who both turned 40 at the start of the millennium, continue to record as a duo: **http://clubs.yahoo.com/clubs/bananaramaclub** will keep you updated.

Band Aid ★★★★★
♫ **'Do They Know It's Christmas'** (1984, no.1)

Feeding the world
The only five-star one-hit wonder in this book, and deservedly so. And you simply can't take the piss out of this. Sorry. That roll-call in full: **Bananarama**, Bob Geldof, **Culture Club**, David Bowie, **Duran Duran**, **Eurythmics**, **Frankie Goes to Hollywood**, **Heaven 17**, **Human League**, Kool and the Gang, Marilyn, Midge Ure, Paul McCartney, **Paul Young**, Phil Collins, **Spandau Ballet**, Status Quo, Sting, The Style Council, **U2** and **Wham!**

The facts: Bob Geldof was watching TV in October 1984, saw the news reports from Ethiopia and used his contacts to get people together. The technicalities: It was recorded on November 25th 1984, produced and remixed by Trevor Horn. Midge Ure was the co-producer, who gave the record its unique sound through some use of sampling. The song was released that same month, and went straight to Number One in the UK – it topped the American charts two weeks later. The reason: because it had to be done. Because, as Bob Geldof said at Live Aid the year after, 'There are People. Dying. Now.'

The first relief shipment of over £30,000 worth of food and medical supplies to Ethiopia arrived on 11th March, 1985. The rest is history. And the question is, could it ever happen in quite the same way again?

- ✓ A dodgy 1989 remix was filled with the likes of **Kylie**, Cliff Richard, **Wet Wet Wet** and **Chris Rea**. Only **Bananarama** appeared on both. But then you'll know that if you've been paying attention.

- ✓ Bono of **U2** had severe qualms about singing the line 'tonight thank God it's them instead of you', but he was talked round.

- ✓ Bowie, McCartney and **Frankie Goes To Hollywood** were unable to attend the studio session, but they recorded messages of support on the B-side.

- ✓ The American response was 'We Are The World' by USA For Africa, featuring Michael Jackson, **Lionel Richie**, **Cyndi Lauper**, Bob Dylan and Willie Nelson.

The Bangles ★ ★ ★

♫ **'Manic Monday'** (1986, no.2)

The fact that The Artist Who Seems To Have Decided He

Is Once Again Known as Prince could write a fantastic pop song like 'Manic Monday' has always been enough – well, nearly enough – for me to forgive the purple poser his more irksome antics. That it started the career of the 80s' feistiest female foursome is the icing on the cake.

The Bangles were formed in 1981 by drummer Debbi Peterson and her bassist sister Vicki. Originally they were called Colours, and then The Supersonic Bangs. And then just The Bangs. Wa-hey. Major totty factor, particularly that of the awesomely luscious lead singer and guitarist Susanna Hoffs, will have shifted units, but it was probably also an impediment to their being taken seriously. A shame, as there are many great musical moments to savour: the harmonies of 'If She Knew What She Wants', the great blink-and-miss-them lyrics of 'Walk Like An Egyptian' with its immaculate whistling bit in the middle and a zestful cover of Simon and Garfunkel's 'A Hazy Shade Of Winter'. In 1989, after their most successful album *Everything*, The Bangles parted company.

✔ One Bangle was called Michael Steele. That makes her the most attractive woman to be called Michael that I can think of. Okay, who else is there? Princess Michael? Oh, there's some woman in *ER*, apparently.

✔ When Prince Rogers Nelson wrote 'Manic Monday', he was known as 'Christopher'. Well, it's better than that twiddly ankh-like thing (the type-setters' nightmare).

✔ A challenge – find the missing link between the Bangles and **OMD**. Answer elsewhere.

♥ Irish band The Saw Doctors sing affectionately of their respect for Ms Hoffs and co. in their subtle tribute, 'I'd Love To Bang The Bangles'.

▶▶ Susanna Hoffs enjoyed a solo career, which included a minor hit with the **Lightning Seeds** song 'All I Want' and a cover of David Bowie's 'Boys Keep Swinging'. The Bangles then re-formed in 2000.

Toni Basil ★★

♫ **'Mickey'** (1982, no.2)

One of the liveliest early-80s pop records was made by a cheerleader and choreographer with a Kate-Bush-like line in arm-waving and eye-popping. Most people will know the exuberant chorus to 'Mickey', but few will admit to liking it until they have had a few pints.

Toni was born Antonia Christina Basilotta, but her date of birth is a matter for some speculation – estimates seem to veer between 1943 and 1950. She made an appearance in the film *Easy Rider* in 1969 and was the choreographer for *American Graffiti*, among others.

✔ The song, written by Mike Chapman and Nicky Chinn, was originally to be called 'Kitty', and to be sung by a man to a woman.

✔ Although Toni never had any more chart hits, she directed the video for Talking Heads' 'Once In A Lifetime'.

✔ America's king of parody, Weird Al Yankovic, recorded a version called 'Ricky'. Apparently you have to be bothered about the programme *I Love Lucy* to find it funny. I'm not. I didn't.

♥ The song was a hit all over again when it was covered by every 21st-century Humbert Humbert's favourite manufactured popstrel, Lolly.

Beastie Boys ★★★
♫ '(You Gotta) Fight For Your Right (To Party)' (1987, no.11)

Not big or clever

White rappers lend themselves so easily to cheap jibes – look at Vanilla Ice (no, on second thoughts, don't bother). The Beasties seemed to have realised this by treating it all as one big joke to begin with, but some of the media wanted to take them more seriously than they deserved.

They all had comedy rap names – Ad-Rock, Mike D and MCA – although their mums knew them as Adam Horovitz, Michael Diamond and Adam Yauch respectively. It seemed in 1987 that there had never been so much *Daily Mail* outrage about the (alleged) activities of three young American men, what with their inflatable phalluses, supposed misogyny, Volkswagen-badge-stealing and staged Sex-Pistols-lite swearing at press conferences. All of which, in truth, was far less offensive than their fashion sense. Whatever possessed *anyone* to think that turning your baseball cap back-to-front and sporting the logo of an old-fashioned car firm around your neck on a toilet chain could be seen as cool? Beats me. And the shiny blouson jackets... oh, it brings me out in a rash just to think about them.

The basic musical premise was actually quite innovative. Take some sampled Aerosmith and Led Zep guitar riffs, weld them to a backing beat and, well, sort of shout over them. In an adolescent way. Thus was created 'Fight For Your Right', one of the most memorable party tunes ever. It's hard to listen to 'No Sleep Till Brooklyn' without thinking of the **Morris Minor** version ('No Sleep 'Til

Bedtime'), but the album *Licensed To Ill* actually trod more diverse ground, some humour coming out on tracks like 'Girls' and the guitars getting seriously crunchy on their biggest hit, 'She's On It'. They re-emerged in 1989 with a different agenda, mixing samples in a subtler and more eclectic way for *Paul's Boutique*. They continue to be active, promoting their other interests in clothing (snigger) and magazines (presumably not the ones which their mums threw out in 'Fight For Your Right').

You still see the odd E-reg Volkswagen driving round without its badge today. Makes you wonder.

💣 In Liverpool in 1987, Adam Horovitz was charged with actual bodily harm when he allegedly hit a girl in the audience at the Royal Court. He was later acquitted.

✔ The guitar solo on 'No Sleep Till Brooklyn' was provided by Kerry King of the metal band Slayer – who, I am reliably informed, cheerfully ignores the key of the rest of the song.

⏭ The Beasties returned to the UK charts in the late 90s with the single 'Intergalactic'.

The Beautiful South ★ ★ ★

♫ **'Song For Whoever'** (1989, no.2)

Acerbic vignettes

I'm sorry, I did try, but it is impossible to summarise the early career of the Beautiful South without using the word 'quirky' at some point. Just thought I'd warn you.

Fair enough, the 90s brought them their greatest success, with the oft-quoted statistic that one in seven households became the owner of a copy of their Greatest Hits album, *Carry On Up The Charts*. But we should at least note their origins at the end of the 80s.

As the brainchild of former **Housemartins** Paul Heaton and Dave Hemmingway, their manifesto was to smuggle political lyrics in under jaunty, singalong tunes, and to sneak acerbic commentary on domestic violence and emotional angst into the charts wrapped in pop-friendly melodies. And it worked like a charm.

'Song For Whoever', surely a contender for best no.2 record of the decade, is about a songwriter exploiting his relationships for the sake of Performing Rights cheques and songs that will get into the charts; after a while all the women blur into one and he forgets their names. It's a total pop masterpiece, featuring the triad of complementary voices which was to be the South's trademark – Heaton, Dave Rotheray and Brianna Corrigan.

'You Keep It All In', a bouncy ditty about emotional repression, was a good follow-up. Everybody in the band then expected poignant rejection ballad 'I'll Sail This Ship Alone', re-recorded for the single, to be a Number One, but instead it barely scraped into the Top 40, just showing again that the Great British Public don't know classic songwriting when it leaps up and snogs them. Other notable compositions on the debut album *Welcome To The Beautiful South* were the Housemartins-style 'From Under The Covers', a breathy cover of **Pebbles**' 'Girlfriend', the wry chart commentary 'Straight In At 37', the delicately macabre 'Woman In The Wall' and the quirky (hooray!) final track 'I Love You (But You're Boring)', which sounds like Morrissey, but with more humorous self-awareness.

More albums followed – *Choke*, *0898* and *Miaow* spawned a few more hits each. The band always managed to sound fresh and innovative, even when returning to favourite themes like relationships going sour, media exploitation and sexism.

♫ There are just too many good songs to choose from ... the best thing I can do is just say go and buy *Carry On Up The Charts* if you can still find it, preferably the version with the additional B-sides CD so that you get mini-masterpieces 'In Other Words I Hate You' and 'Woman In The Wall' too. There's a rare 'faulty' pressing which includes the Jacqui Abbott vocal version of 'Let Love Speak Up Itself' instead of the single version which Heaton sings on... A more recent overview, *Solid Bronze*, takes in some of the later hits but inevitably misses out some earlier ones.

♫ 'Prettiest Eyes' and 'One Last Love Song' are the South at their most tender, but listen to 'I Think The Answer's Yes' from *Choke* if you want what Ben Elton used to call 'ooh, bit of politics'.

♠ Some shops wouldn't stock the debut album, because it features a picture of someone smoking and someone with a gun in their mouth. Ever the wry commentators, the Beautiful South released a nice, fluffy version for these sensitive souls to put on the shelves, sporting a cute teddy and an ickle bunny wabbit. If you've got one of these, it's probably worth a bit.

♠ Paul Heaton's profile has certainly helped: in a notable appearance on *Question Time* he advocated the evacuation and destruction of the House Of Lords...

✔ Brianna Corrigan left the band, apparently amid a dispute over the song '36D'. She was replaced by Jacqui Abbott, who then couldn't join them on tour anyway because she was expecting a baby.

The Beloved ★★★

♫ 'The Sun Rising' (1989, no.26)

Slipping quietly in at the end of the decade in chart terms, they went on to bigger things in the 90s, but are worth a mention here because this success was the result of building – and rebuilding – a reputation.

The original four-piece of Jon Marsh, Steve Waddington, Tin Harvard and Guy Gausden formed in 1984 as a jangly indie 4-piece who, if memory serves correctly, wore parkas and sang about flowers and stuff. Their credibility even survived Jon Marsh's eight-day residency as *Countdown* Champion in 1987, where he became the quiz-show's top seed and was knocked out in the quarter-finals. (I'm sorry, is that too much information?) The cutting-edge wit of Richard Whiteley produced the assertion that Jon had not allowed himself to get 'too *bogged* down'. And yes, if you have never seen *Countdown*, this is fairly typical of its humour. As far as we are aware, the only other pop star to have submitted himself to the *Countdown* challenger's chair was the guitarist from little-known Scottish duo The Motorcycle Boy, although **Toyah** has turned up a few times in Dictionary Corner. (Now, if they could just get Sarah Cracknell...)

Anyway, back (briefly) to The Beloved. By 1988 they had slimmed down to the duo of Marsh (guitar/vocals) and Waddington (guitar/keyboards). Experiments with dance rhythms on their groundbreaking single, the celebratory morning-after-the-rave-before anthem 'The Sun Rising', led to the trippy album *Happiness*. After Steve Waddington left for pastures new, Jon – now paired with his lovely wife Helena – took the band to even greater success, 'Sweet Harmony' becoming a Top 10 hit in 1993. Jon is now a successful DJ.

Berlin ★★

♫ 'Take My Breath Away
(Love Theme From Top Gun)' (1986, no.1)

In 1982, a self-produced EP called 'Pleasure Victim' earned US band Berlin a deal with major label Geffen. They weren't known in the UK, though, until 1986 – by which time big power ballads were the order of the day. The success of the Tom Cruise/Kelly McGillis movie *Top Gun* pushed this one to the top – Berlin were, by then, a trio comprising Terri Nunn, John Crawford and Rob Brill. We pause only to have a cheap laugh at someone in a middle-of-the-road band being called 'Brill', which is a bit like being a rapper called 'Def Wicked'.

The hit was also helped by a rather strange video which nobody understood at the time, which was meant to be about the ghost of a dead pilot haunting an airfield. The song sounds sufficiently spooky, especially with its well-timed (if cheesy) change of key.

With her vampiric mascara and two-tone hair making her resemble the bastard child of **Toyah** and a badger, singer Terri Nunn certainly had an image to play with. However, the second hit 'You Don't Know' only got to no.39 in 1987, failing to capitalise on their success, and another single 'No More Words' didn't do the business either, despite a quite lunatic person bouncing up and down on BBC2's pop roadshow *No Limits* to proclaim it 'the best song ever!' Four years on, a re-issue of 'Take My Breath Away' was back in the charts.

▸▸ There were signs of activity in 1999, and a mixture of studio material and some live performances made up *Berlin Live: Sacred And Profane* in 2000, essentially the work of Terri Nunn and some new musicians. She also sang on *Anonymous Messiah*, a 2001 tribute album to Marilyn Manson. New album *Voyeur* came out in 2002.

Big Fun ★

♫ **'Blame It On The Boogie'** (1989, no.4)

Prototype boy-band who were chiefly memorable, if that's the word, for the above pop-by-numbers cover and their other Top 10 hit, 'Can't Shake The Feeling'. Big Fun perhaps ought to have been sued under the Trades Descriptions Act, as they were not even particularly medium-sized and about as much fun as a cold Pot Noodle. Three cloned blond boys with shiny bomber jackets and earrings, Phil, Jason and Mark looked and sounded like **Bros's** less interesting younger brothers. The music was the same old jaunty, insipid stuff from Pete Waterman, obviously aimed at the usual markets – namely a) hormonal preteen girls and b) well-dressed bachelors with good taste in fabric and a season ticket to Barbra Streisand. They were last seen teaming up with **Sonia** and the amusingly-named Gary Barnacle on a charity version of James Taylor's 'You've Got A Friend' in 1990.

Despite their dreadfulness, they opened the door for countless **Bros** and **Brother Beyond** imitators in the subsequent decade. Remember Bad Boys Inc, OTT, Upside Down, Worlds Apart, 911 and Point Break? No? Lucky you.

✔ The cult 1989 film *Heathers* features a song called 'Teenage Suicide (Don't Do It)', by a band called Big Fun. Disappointingly, it's a fictitious group and not this lot.

◀» The band in *Smash Hits*, 1989: 'We haven't written anything that's nearly as good as **Stock, Aitken and Waterman**.' Phew, that's all right then.

Black ★★★

♪ 'Sweetest Smile' (1987, no.8)

The band were called Black, he dressed in black (turtleneck tucked into black trousers!) and the record sleeves were always in monochrome. You could make a pretty good guess that Liverpudlian singer-songwriter Colin Vearncombe wasn't going to be a purveyor of jaunty, feelgood melodies. Or was he…?

Vearncombe was one of the 80s' most accomplished songwriters and, a brace of Top Ten hits aside, his project was seriously under-rated by the public. It took him most of the decade to get his pop career up and running, despite bringing in guitarist and keyboardist Dave Dix, a support slot with **The Thompson Twins** and a deal (which ultimately fell through) with the WEA label. By 1986, three singles – 'Human Features', 'More Than The Sun' and 'Hey Presto' – had all failed to engage the buyers' attention sufficiently. Things looked black for Black. (Sorry.)

However, the fantastic 'Wonderful Life', released on a small label called Ugly Man, turned out to be the breakthrough song, and Vearncombe's subsequent deal with A&M produced the first Black LP. It's a classic album, veering from atmospheric introspection to funkiness and the occasional up-tempo rock moment ('Everything's Coming Up Roses' and 'Just Making Memories'). Vearncombe's smooth voice is complemented by sax breaks, lush keyboards and controlled guitars. Backing singers The Creamy Whirls give admirable support, especially on the track 'Finder', and the whole album has a seamless, well-produced feel. Perhaps this doesn't always help – it's arguable how much the rather sterile drum loop lends to the otherwise excellent title track, for example.

Third single 'Paradise' was given the kiss of death when someone at Radio 1 enthused that it had Number One written all over it – it turned out to have no.38 written all over it, and Black never saw chart action again. Subsequent albums *Comedy* and *Black* didn't sell as well, and *Are We Having Fun Yet?* (1993) was released on a mail-order basis on the band's own label, Nero Schwartz. How appropriate.

🎧 'Wonderful Life': forget the fact that it's been used on a life-insurance advert, and enjoy an outstanding 80s pop tune which never seems to date. But 'Sweetest Smile' is great too if you're in mellow mood, and even 'Paradise' towers over much of the dross from the chart that week.

✔ At the age of 16, Colin was in a punk band called The Epileptic Tits. (Look, I don't make these things up, honest.) He also looks a bit like **Billy Bragg**.

🔊 'Everyone always thought my songs were too gloomy. So I gave one of those gloomy songs a positive title, "Wonderful Life", and suddenly the reactions changed. That does say something about how people tend to listen to their music. Personally I feel it's ridiculous that songs always have to be upbeat. In a music journal they once wrote about me that I would probably sing a line like "Everything's coming up roses" as an announcement of my suicide. I liked that. I like a certain ambiguity.' (Colin Vearncombe).

🔊 Colin continues to write songs and, although Black is officially 'dead' as a band, he still performs as a solo artist. He prefers playing solo, saying it helps him to focus on the strengths of particular songs.

Black Lace ✶

♪ 'Superman (Gioca Jouer)' (1983, no.9)

Holiday, celebrate...

Summer favourites, immortalised by Spitting Image as 'two wet gits with girly curly hair'. Colin Routh and Rob Hopcraft were the gentlemen in question, although Mr. Hopcraft bailed out some time ago, leaving Routh and his two new backing singers to appear at a Butlins near you somewhere this summer. Fellow founder-member Alan Barton, who left to join the band Smokie, died in a car-crash in the 1990s.

The sound of summer in 1984 was the truly terrible 'Agadoo'. However, when judgement day comes, I would expect them to plead for the, ahem, hilarious 'El Vino Collapso' also to be taken into consideration. And the final damning evidence is their part in propagating the song most eligible to be banned under international arms treaties – that ultimate cringe on wax, that staple of second-rate wedding DJs everywhere, the excruciatingly *awful* 'I Am The Music Man'.

Times change, but customs remain the same, and nobody prevents the import of dreadful holiday songs. For some reason it seems like a good idea to buy that 'wicked' record you heard in Benidorm or Ibiza – whether it's Whigfield, the 'Macarena', or some dodgy Euro-dance version of 'Smells Like Teen Spirit' – and inflict it on people who are sensible enough not to holiday in these places.

Look, let's be honest here. Most of us will, at some point, have had a holiday romance, right? And the problem with holiday romances is this. That person may have looked dead fit with a tan, in a black lycra swimming costume, basking in the warm glow of the Mediterranean sunshine and your sangria-goggles. However, they're a rather less attractive proposition in the cold light of day back home, standing in the Lottery queue at Kwik-Save, pale, pimply, shell-suited and giving a snotty child a clip round the ear because it's whingeing for a McDonald's for the umpteenth time. So imagine, just then – as you scurry for cover, wheeling your squeaky trolley past the frozen peas, contemplating your boring job and your dreadful friends and your crap town – the supermarket sound-system starts to play 'Agadoo'.

Moral: context is everything. Stop bringing novelty records home with you. *Please*.

- ✔ 'Agadoo' was written by two Frenchmen; Black Lace and their manager heard it in a club in Derby and sealed its fate by adding the 'amusing' dance movements.

- ✔ 'Agadoo' was voted 4th most annoying song of all time in a poll by the Dotmusic website. Aqua, The Teletubbies and The Tweets were all considered worse...

- ✔ The unconnected Canadian rock duo Black Lace, who recorded the album *Get It While It's Hot*, must get very puzzled by the European fans shouting for 'Do The Conga' and 'I Speaka Da Lingo'.

Blondie ★★★★★

♫ **'Denis'** (1978, no.2)

Another one where the phwooargh-factor of the lead singer more or less erased all memory of the rest of the band. How many walls did Debbie Harry adorn? How many fevered dreams did the pink dress from the sleeve of *Plastic Letters* inspire?

Debbie was formerly a Playboy Bunny waitress, as well as vocalist in folk-rock group Wind In The Willows. The classic Blondie line-up was formed in 1975, and the big breakthrough came with the international hit 'Denis' from the aforementioned *Plastic Letters* and the subsequent album *Parallel Lines*. A pop-rock crossover with a hint of punk was their winning formula, and trading on the looks of Ms Harry certainly helped – even when she was wearing a silly silver wig like something out of *The Tomorrow People*.

They had five Number One singles in the UK and four in the US – 'Heart of Glass', 'Call Me' and 'The Tide Is High' all scored the double, and while 'Atomic' only made no.39 in the States, the UK No.5 hit 'Rapture' was another chart-topper over there in 1981.

💣 In 1982, rhythm guitarist Frank Infante sued the band, claiming he was being excluded from their activities. An out-of-court settlement was reached and he remained a member...

📢 'I had a basic outline of all the different ingredients of what would make a good, entertaining rock group – or character – just from observing people that were successful, seeing what I admired and seeing what I thought I would like if I saw myself....Being treated as the character Blondie and then being whoever else I am was very frustrating for a while. At first, I was surprised and didn't know what to do. Then I got afraid and then I got angry. I just had to drop that for a while...There were some problems from the fans... A lot of them felt I was deserting or killing off Blondie by going brown-haired... Having this fear thing going on. It's strange.' Debbie on the fan reaction to her temporary 'Brownie' look on the *Koo Koo* album cover.

▶▶| Debbie had sporadic success with her solo singles, most notably 'French Kissin' in the USA' in 1986 and 'I Want That Man' in 1989, the latter rather prematurely announcing the advent of the 21st century in its lyrics. In 1999, to everyone's amazement, Blondie were back on top of the singles chart with the new classic 'Maria'. Across the country, thousands of thirtysomething men had idly turned on *Top Of The Pops* to see what kind of soulless pap the kids were buying these days, only to find themselves gazing in awe at the greying, middle-aged woman who had been their prime adolescent fantasy. They were suddenly struck by the shock of the passing years and the weight of their mortgages and their proper jobs, and they wept for the passing of their feckless youth.

The Blow Monkeys ★★★
♫ **'Digging Your Scene'** (1986, no.12)

It's time for a little trivia quiz to keep you on your toes.

1. 'Blow Monkeys' are:

a) Simians trained in the art of safe explosives handling, often employed by crack bomb-disposal squads in Northern Ireland.
b) Studio runners employed to fetch bands their drugs.
c) Australian aboriginal didgeridoo players.

2. The band's first album was entitled :

a) *Animal Magic*

b) *Jackanory*
c) *Newsround*
d) *Play School*

3. Dr Robert, lead singer – and wearer of quite remarkable M&S pullovers – was neither medically nor academically trained. Born Bruce Robert Howard, he gained his nickname at boarding-school because:

   a) He was a fan of *Doctor Who*
   b) He liked to play 'Doctors and Nurses' behind the cricket pavilion before prep
   c) He was a good listener
   d) All of the above

4. Their first hit single 'Digging Your Scene' was:

   a) About AIDS
   b) About £1.40
   c) About four minutes long

5. Released in May 1987, the single '(Celebrate) The Day After You' was initially banned by the BBC because:

   a) It contained the word 'fuck'
   b) The lyrics were overtly political
   c) Mike Read thought it was obscene
   d) Dr Robert sported an offensive jumper on the sleeve

6. 'You Don't Own Me' was a song on the soundtrack to which film?

   a) *Dirty Dancing*
   b) *Three Men And A Baby*

c) *Wall Street*

d) *Amadeus*

7. In 1989, Dr Robert recorded a duet as Robert Howard with which songstress?

a) Kim Wilde

b) Kym Sims

c) Kim Appleby

d) Kym Mazelle

Answers: 1:c, 2:a, 3:c, 4:a, b and c, 5:b 6:a 7:d.

Well, it was different, but I think I would prefer to hold over any similar ideas for *The 1980s Pop Puzzle Compendium*. This may contain such gems as the **Sinitta** Join The Dots Challenge, the **Kajagoogoo** Wordsearch and the **Proclaimers** Spot the Difference Corner.

Betty Boo ✫✫✫

♫ 'Hey DJ – I Can't Dance (To That Music You're Playing)'

(1989, no.7, with the Beatmasters)

It's become well-known that Betty Boo was, in fact, a young lady by the name of Alison Clarkson – and she was recently the subject of a question on *University Challenge*. Performing what could probably be called a pop-rap hybrid, Betty first stormed into the charts with the Beatmasters in 1989 after being in bands called The She-Rockers and Hit'n'Run.

Now, normally it's one of the Five Rules Of Pop (I'll think of the other four later) that any song with the word 'DJ' in it is going to be a pile of untreated sewage. However, it seems likely in retrospect that Betty's tongue was some way into her cheek when recording her debut single. Subsequent 90s hits 'Doin' The Do' (her theme song) and 'Where Are You Baby?' featured similar levels of flippancy, with Betty/Allie sporting a space-age silver catsuit in the latter. Furthermore, she's the only artist in this book to rhyme 'tissues' with 'serious sub-issues', for which she deserves recognition. And she is – if you will indulge me – dead fit.

✔ Copyright problems prevented Alison from being known as Betty Boop, so she just knocked the last letter off.

▶▶ Ms Clarkson is now a jobbing songwriter, and doing pretty well for herself – she's written Number One hits for Hear'Say, among others. But the Do is not yet Done: she's purchased a studio in Oxfordshire and is recording some new material of her own…so stand by for the Betty Boo Comeback. In the meantime, the 2001 compilation *Doin' The Do: The Very Best of Betty Boo* is available in all good record shops. And no doubt one or two mediocre ones as well.

———

Bourgeois Tagg ★ ★
♫ **'I Don't Mind At All'** (1988, no.35)

With a name like that in the late 1980s, you'd think they were going to be a politically angry group with a chip on their shoulder about middle-class values. It's quite disappointing to discover that the moniker merely comes from sticking together their surnames. (See also **Climie Fisher**.)

American duo Brent Bourgeois and Larry Tagg's 'I Don't Mind At All' stuck out like a smooth thumb among the plethora of injured members in the charts in early 1988. A haunting acoustic ballad with intriguing lyrics, it gathered an unexpectedly large amount of airplay on Radio 1. Inevitably, the great British public failed to do the decent thing and make it a Top 10 hit. It's fair to say the song wasn't representative of the rest of the album *Yoyo*, which mixes rocky MOR with **Level 42**-style pop-funk.

✔ Brent Bourgeois released a solo album, *A Matter of Feel*, in 1992. He got to work with Robert Palmer, who'd liked Bourgeois' work ever since the 1988 single.

Boy George: see Culture Club

Bow Wow Wow ★★

♪ **'C30, C60, C90, Go'** (1980, no.34)

Tape That

Malcolm McLaren, variously described as a 'pop svengali', a 'pop guru' and a 'bit of a prat', made some interesting decisions in his career. When the Sex Pistols self-destructed at the end of the 70s, the man credited with taking them to fame launched this new outfit. McLaren chose to front them with the half-Burmese teenager Annabella Lwin, whose look seemed rather disturbingly modelled on that of a Third World child prostitute. Other members Matthew Ashman and Leigh Gorman came from **Adam and the Ants**, with whom Bow Wow Wow shared their frantic 'Burundi beat' sound.

Raucous and frenzied, Bow Wow Wow exploded on to the radio with their endearing first hit, a paean to the joys of home taping, at a time when the technology must have seemed fresh and exciting. (Pause for thought – how many people under the age of 25 have ever seen a C30 tape?)

Continuing the chromium oxide theme, 'Your Cassette Pet' was a Christmas 1980 release, featuring a handful of tracks available only on the likeable stretchy medium – quite a commercial risk at the time, as this was well before the late-80s boom in 'cassingles'.

Annabella appeared nude on the original cover of the debut album, the pithily-titled *See Jungle! See Jungle! Go Join Your Gang! Yeah, City All Over! Go Ape Crazy!* (yes, really). Ms Lwin's mother, who had apparently always had her doubts about McLaren, objected strongly – although I'm not sure whether it was to her daughter appearing in the buff or to her band's album having such a crap title.

The singles 'Go Wild In The Country', and 'I Want Candy' both saw the band briefly visiting the Top 10 before they split amid tensions in 1983. Lwin went her own way, and the remaining members formed The Chiefs of Relief.

◁» 'I was a girl coming away from her family and friends, leaving everything behind and joining this rock group that was like *The Muppet Show* almost. It was a very lonely and distraught and distressed kind of lifestyle on the road.' (Annabella Lwin.)

▶▶| Annabella had a solo deal with Sony in the early 90s, which didn't come to anything much after the single 'Car Sex' flopped. She later became a Buddhist. Guitarist Ashman, who had turned down a deal to re-form the band in the 90s, died in 1995. However, the reunion eventually happened in 1998, Lwin and Gorman getting back together to promote *Wild In The USA*, a collection of remixes and live performances.

Billy Bragg ★★★

♪ 'Between The Wars (EP)' (1985, no.15)

Labour of love

Carrying the chip on his shoulder more cheerfully these days, Billy comes across as one of the UK's most sincere – if occasionally over-earnest – songwriters. Motivated by a genuine and witty political sensibility rather than cheap point-scoring, he has been the face and voice of protest pop for the last two decades, largely unaccompanied on the electric guitar. He had a very unlikely Number One without ever getting any airplay, as his version of 'She's Leaving Home' was the official AA-side of **Wet Wet Wet's** version of 'With A Little Help From My Friends'.

He is the milkman of human kindness, he will leave you an extra pint, and as long as he continues to write great songs like 'Sexuality' he's all right by us.

✔ Billy was in the punk group Riff Raff in the late 1970s. He then joined the army, but bought himself out shortly afterwards.

✔ Billy recently won a special musicians' edition of quiz-show *The Weakest Link*. His prize money went towards the relief of victims of torture (or fans of **Milli Vanilli**, as they are more commonly known).

Bros ★★★

♪ 'When Will I Be Famous?' (1988, no.2)

Brothers beyond the pale

How naff were Bros? Checking them off on the 80s naff-o-meter produces ticks in lots of boxes: shiny jackets with tacky slogans on, blond highlights, squeaky/growly voices, false macho posing, extravagant spending sprees. And yet they had more in common with **Duran Duran** (talent aside) than the boy-bands of today, as they at least pretended to be a proper band with proper instruments.

Salvaged from obscurity by manager Tom Watkins, brothers Matt and Luke Goss and their friend Craig Logan were the top teen sensations of 1988. Bros-mania outdid the fanatical devotion which **Wham!** had inspired earlier in the decade; in fact, some said it was like Beatlemania all over again (only with three Ringos). Brosettes, as the fans called themselves, took to hanging around every venue where the boys were known to be appearing, as well as stalking them outside their houses. Some of the more cunning (the Provisional wing of the Brosettes) found out which shops they bought their jeans in and slipped tantalising notes into the pockets. These presumably said things like 'Gemma loves you, Matt and Luke! Phone her on 01 etc' (if they were bold), 'kelly wonts to hav your babees luk and mat so her mum can get off the social' (if they were honest), and 'Deodorant, hairspray, Clearasil, Marathon' (if they had put their shopping list in by mistake).

The eager fanbase also caused one of the biggest embarrassments in Radio 1's history. One of the station's annual 'best ever' polls (which could usually be relied upon to put Queen's 'Bohemian Rhapsody' snugly and predictably on top) declared 'I Owe You Nothing' to be the greatest pop song in the history of the universe. 'Oops' is putting it mildly. Hindsight may be a wonderful thing, but it was obvious that it didn't even qualify as the best Bros song. You could almost see the producers' heads in their hands as they wailed 'What have we done?' into their BBC coffee.

Matt and Luke enjoyed a busy schedule of posing, grinning and lapping up the adulation of teenage girls. Tediously, they sometimes had to have a break from this in order to do a bit of work on their records. Once they had arranged not to be too involved with this side of things, they were free to get back to what they did best, namely zipping off and spending all the money they had made (plus a lot which they hadn't). Craig decided to get out while he could, abandoning thousands of poseable Craig dolls to the sad fate of being melted down for Frisbees. Although he seemed a veritable Ridgeley at the time, this turned out to be the most sensible decision of his career.

A severe case of Second Album Syndrome was to afflict Bros – somebody, somewhere decided to let the Aryan brothers write all their own material for the new record, which left Tom Watkins rather lost for words when he heard what they'd actually produced. There was 'Too Much', a dull attempt to rock things up. There was 'Madly In Love', the same song under a different name. And there was the excruciating 'Sister', a supposedly moving tribute to a departed sibling, which is still used in some parts of the Secret Service as a weapon to get recalcitrant traitors to confess all.

And so Bros went the way of all boy-bands, leaving the inevitable trail of weeping pre-pubescent girls. They would now be sensible women in their late twenties and early thirties, who may well be reading this – with, I hope, some degree of shame.

Both Matt and Luke attempted to launch solo careers with limited success, even sprouting facial hair in a desperate attempt to emulate the success of **George Michael**. It was never going to work. Craig, meanwhile, took the brothers to court for his missing earnings and left them near-bankrupt.

✔ The nostalgia industry seems to want to erase the Bros Years from its collective memory, as their songs hardly ever turn up on 80s retrospectives.

◀)) 'We could be dismissed as three good-looking haircuts and I'm sure we frequently are. But when you can sing, dance and play as well as we can and you're still this side of 21, who cares anyway?' Matt Goss, perhaps over-estimating public opinion of their haircuts in 1988.

▶▶ Luke has been furthering his film career in the likes of *Blade 2*. Matt moved to America and spent several years resting and writing new songs. Craig now runs his own successful production and management company, and in 2002 he got engaged to that foxy little minx, Dannii Minogue. He probably has to resist the urge to chuckle maniacally at the irony of it all.

Brother Beyond ★★

♫ **'The Harder I Try'** (1988, no.2)

Remembered mainly as the putative rivals to **Bros**, this clean-cut foursome were, in many ways, more of a template for today's boy-bands than the Goss brothers. They sang! They danced! They... did interviews with *Smash Hits!* And, unlike the decade's previous pretty-boy groups such as **Duran Duran** and **Spandau Ballet** – and, crucially, unlike **Bros** – not one of them even pretended to be able to play an instrument. This was the future.

Their first single, on EMI, flopped. So did their next two on Parlophone, the highest making only no.56 – in today's hit-or-bust market they would have surely been dropped. The summer of 1988, though, was notoriously a time where people would buy anything, and, sure enough, the perky and Motownish 'The Harder I Try' reached no.2. More hits followed, including 'He Ain't No Competition' and a remix of earlier miss 'Can You Keep A Secret', but with crushing inevitability, the chart placings got lower and they vanished around 1991. However, chief Brother Nathan Moore re-surfaced briefly in the early 90s in another boy-band, Worlds Apart.

✔ Before he was in Brother Beyond, Nathan once had a job in a garden centre, where he apparently made £5 a day and was fired after a brief time. Still, being exploited in a hothouse, hawking piles of manure and surrounding himself with vegetables – it must all have been excellent training for a pop career.

🔊 Damning With Faint Praise corner: Nathan once stated that the band has 'gone down somewhere in history, but not too indelibly'. We like that.

Bucks Fizz ★★★

♫ **'Making Your Mind Up'** (1981, no.1)

Douze Points

Yes, it's 'The Fizz', as anyone who has seen Matt Lucas and David Walliams' *Rock Profiles* parody is inevitably going to call them.

Winning the Eurovision Song Contest, and all the kitsch baggage that brings with it, has not always been a guaranteed route to chart success. This lot – comprising Mike Nolan, Bobby Gee, Cheryl Baker and Jay Aston – managed it, taking their easy-listening, hi-NRG pop style far enough to have a few hits in the 80s. They must have wondered for a bit, though, especially after 'A Piece Of The Action' failed to get any (stalling at no.12) and ballad 'One Of Those Nights' only just scraped into the Top 20. Fortunately for The Fizz, more chart-toppers followed – the classic (if silly) 'The Land of Make-Believe' and the more average 'My Camera Never Lies'.

It seemed that the two boys with mullets and two gorgeous blonde girls could do no wrong. However, in 1984, more than their fair share of troubles began to beset them: Jay Aston (the feisty one) left under a cloud, and then a nasty car crash left Mike Nolan with serious injuries and Cheryl with some broken bones. But The Fizz pulled through, and with chirpy new member Shelley Preston on board, they hit the top 10 again in 1986 with 'New Beginning (Mamba Seyra)'. Unfortunately, 'New Beginning' didn't turn out to be one, and they struggled for further chart recognition, returning for a while as a trio *sans* the lovely Shelley.

Somewhere along the line, David 'Burger' Van Day of former rivals **Dollar** (don't laugh, I'm sure it was the Blur v Oasis of the age) got involved, and started touring as Bucks Fizz. The country faced the agonising spectacle of tours by two rival factions with the same name, rather like the product of one of those horrible transporter accidents in *Star Trek* (and surely the only thing Bucks Fizz have in common with heavy rockers Saxon). Mr Van Day was last seen rather sadly trying to update 'Making Your Mind Up' with a couple of gyrating (and worryingly young) ladies. The dispute has just been resolved and Bobby G's band is the official Bucks Fizz: the website **http://communities.msn.ca/BucksFizzGoldenDays** is the home of their current Bobby-plus-three-lissom-things incarnation.

💣 I'm sure quite a few young men can pin their sexual awakening down to the exact moment when Jay and Cheryl were divested of their skirts on Eurovision.

✔ Cheryl Baker had already been a member of hit band Co-Co in 1978 – they'd been unsuccessful at Eurovision.

- Sadly, nobody from Bucks Fizz appears to have had an Embarrassing Punk Era Name. However, Bobby Gee's real name is Bobby Gubby.

- 'Making Your Mind Up' is the UK's fourth biggest-selling Eurovision song, after Brotherhood of Man's 'Save All Your Kisses For Me', Sandie Shaw's 'Puppet On A String' and Gina G's 'Ooh Aah… Just A Little Bit'.

- Obviously the prototype for clean-cut acts like the 90s group Deuce and the more recent Steps and S Club. 'The Land of Make-Believe' was covered, in a not-unpleasant Noughties fashion, by telegenic boy-girl band AllStars in 2002.

- Cheryl Baker became a TV presenter – most notably, of course, on *Record Breakers*.

pause

cute little catch

Belinda Carlisle ★★★

♪ 'Heaven Is A Place On Earth' (1988, no.1)

Ms Carlisle was born Belinda Jo Kerzcheski on August 17th 1958 in Hollywood, California. I'm not sure she loves being described as a former Go-Go girl, but she did indeed go solo when that particular band of Californian party-girls dissolved in 1985. 'Mad About You' was a US Top 3 hit in 1986, and Belinda toured as support to Robert Palmer. Her first encounter with the British charts was at the tail-end of '87 with 'Heaven Is A Place On Earth' (the accompanying video was directed by actress Diane Keaton) and she took the top spot in the New Year when the usual battle for the Christmas Number One had died down.

Sporting fabulous cheekbones, a voice with a cute little catch in it and an impressive range of variations on the exclamation 'Whaa-ooh!', Belinda's sound was MOR rock with girlie vocals, and it worked. Belinda had quite a few more hits, including the ballad 'Circle in the Sand' and the storming 'Leave A Light On' from the consistent *Runaway Horses* album. You can always spot the chorus coming a mile off in a Belinda Carlisle song. Go with that, it's part of the fun...

- ๏ A 1992 compilation was optimistically-titled *The Best Of Belinda Volume 1*, although there have been other retrospectives since.

- ✔ Crazy Punk Incarnation corner – ready for this? – Belinda was first in The Germs, then in Black Randy & The Metro Squad, and was also known as Dottie Dànger.

- ✔ Fellow Go-Go Jane Wiedlin had a hit with the chirpy 'Rush Hour' in 1988.

♥   Asia's biggest boy-band Bazooka'n'Tulips, known to their legions of fans as the Zooka (no, this is not a joke) started their career by covering Belinda Carlisle songs. (Point of order: so why don't our boy-bands have quirky names which can be abbreviated in an amusing fashion? Nobody's going to call Westlife 'the Life', are they? Or Boyzone 'the Zone'? And as for A1…)

►►   After her 1993 album *Real*, Belinda cut her hair in a *gamine* style and rejoined the re-formed Go-Gos (that's re-formed as in got back together, rather than reformed as in acquired a new sense of moral uprightness) but has since been touring as a solo artist again, most notably on 2002's 'Here And Now' Tour. And she's still gorgeous.

Neneh Cherry ★★★

♫ **'Buffalo Stance'** (1988, no.3)

D'ya know what I mean?
One of the few artists able to put equal conviction into both singing and rapping, the medallion-swinging, lissom Neneh (jazz trumpeter Don Cherry's stepdaughter) was born Neneh Mariana Karlsson in 1964 in Stockholm, daughter of percussionist Ahmadu Jah from Sierra Leone and Swedish artist Moki Cherry.

Music obviously ran in the family – Don Cherry's children from his first marriage, Jan and David Cherry, became jazz performers, while Titiyo, Neneh's sister on her father's side, is a pop star in Sweden. However, family relationships have apparently become so complex through divorces and remarriages that even Neneh and little brother Eagle-Eye have difficulty agreeing on how many half-siblings they have... Neneh started off in Bristol's indie-funk-hip-hoppers Rip, Rig & Panic. I'm not quite sure which one she was meant to be. Anyway, she first bounced on to our TV screens in the zooming, cartoon-like video for pop-rap crossover 'Buffalo Stance', in December 1988.

She was infamous initially for going on *Top Of The Pops* while very obviously pregnant, which caused a bit of huffing at the time. However, exposure in the womb to Simon Bates, lots of flashing lights and **Bros** probably caused her daughter Tyson rather less lasting discomfort than being named after a boxer with a criminal conviction.

The album *Raw Like Sushi* also featured the sublime and mysterious-sounding 'Manchild', a ballad with interesting rap inserts and full string section, plus assorted orgasmic noises in the background – it was to be her next (and best) hit, but was to provide her last visit to the Top Five in the 1980s.

She returned in 1994, duetting with Yossou N'Dour and his putative Senegalese dialect (which actually didn't mean anything at all) on '7 Seconds'. She contributed to the 1995 Comic Relief single 'Love Can Build A Bridge', and rocked up her sound with a full-throttle backing band for her 90s hits like 'Kootchi'. A singular artist with zest and charm – interesting to see what she does next. The medallion was a bit much, though.

- ✔ What on earth is a Buffalo Stance? It's a reference to the streetwise fashion 'look' of styling team Buffalo. Originally recorded as a B-side by 80s band Morgan McVey – one half of whom, Cameron McVey, later became Neneh's husband.

- ✔ One of Neneh's more unusual and little-known performances is on a 1998 version of Guns'n'Roses 'Sweet Child O'Mine' by the band Acacia, on which she performs the lead vocal. It's not a bad version. Different, anyway...

◀ᵢ On that *TOTP* performance: 'The cameraman kept on shooting my bump... I wouldn't have gone there if I felt I would get embarrassed. I felt really proud of my little bump, right? Mind you, it looked huge! I was sitting watching it back home thinking "I look enormous, man!"...'

▶▶ Eagle-Eye has visited the charts recently, and he and Neneh duetted on 'Long Way Around', featured on his 2000 album *Living In The Present Future*.

China Crisis ★★★

♪ **'Christian'** (1983, no.12)

Often touted, though rarely in the big time – but China Crisis did make it on to the covers of *Smash Hits* and *Number One* magazines. The core of the group was vocalist/keyboard player Gary Daly and vocalist/guitarist Eddie Lundon, who formed the group in Liverpool after leaving school in 1979. First releases 'African and White' and 'Scream Down At Me' were on the small local label, Inevitable, but a signing to Virgin followed. Their chart fortunes fluctuated, but high-points included the thoughtful ballad 'Christian', the sublime top 10 single 'Wishful Thinking', and the more upbeat 'King In A Catholic Style'.

Difficult Shapes And Passive Rhythms was the 1982 debut album, while *Working With Fire And Steel* and *Flaunt The Imperfection* consolidated their reputation. 1986's *What Price Paradise* was released to what they tend to call 'mixed reviews', and *Diary Of A Hollow Horse* went down a little better in 1989.

There appear to be more China Crisis compilations than you can shake a mullet at. However, *Diary – A Collection* from 1992 has a good mix of singles, acoustic versions and lesser-known tracks like 'A Golden Handshake For Every Daughter', which sounds like a cross between Care and The Go-Betweens. No 'Best Kept Secret', though.

'A ghastly mistake... [producers] Langer & Winstanley merely weigh them down with awkward, plodding rhythms and swamp them with clumsy, ill-fitting and almost completely unnecessary string and brass arrangements. This attempt to beef them up for mainstream consumption does nothing so much as destroy the very delicacy and wistfulness that makes China Crisis so appealing in the first place.' That's the *Q* review of *What Price Paradise*...perhaps someone got out of bed the wrong side.

On the other hand, the same august organ's review of 1990's *Collection* called it 'the soothing aural equivalent of slipping into a hot bath, pin-sharp production and perfectly pitched melodies applying a cold compress to fevered brows and frazzled nerve endings.'

Climie Fisher ✭✭✭
♫ **'Rise To The Occasion'** (1988, no.10)

What do you do if you're marketed as a pretty-boy duo but you're actually a pair of serious musicians with decent songs? You play the game for a couple of years, then go back to writing songs for other people. The teen-heartthrob duo with integrity, Climie Fisher got their name when they sandwiched together their surnames. (Just think – on this basis, the **Pet Shop Boys** would be Tennant Lowe, we'd know **Wham!** as Michael Ridgeley, and as for **Bourgeois Tagg**… oh.)

Rob Fisher was a former member of Naked Eyes, whose version of 'Always Something There To Remind Me' had been in the US Top 10 in 1983. Simon Climie was the hit songwriter behind the 1987 Number One 'I Knew You Were Waiting (For Me)' by **George Michael** and Aretha Franklin, as well as songs for Pat Benatar and Jeff Beck, among others. The multi-talented Mr Climie could also be heard performing synthesising duties on **Scritti Politti's** album *Cupid and Psyche*.

The duo were spoken of in the same breath as **Johnny Hates Jazz, The Blow Monkeys** and other attempts to fuse pop with a soulful, funk-lite sound in the late 80s. The best results of their endeavours are certainly the two Top 10 singles. The first, 'Rise To The Occasion', was given a 'hip-hop mix' for radio release, complete with over-familiar 'I *know* you gonna dig this' sample at the beginning and a similar bass sound to 'Pump Up The Volume', which, frankly, does the song no favours at all – the more straightforward ballad version from the album is much better. The second, of course, was the sublime 'Love Changes Everything', a big hit across the world and composed with regular co-writer Dennis Morgan – it won an Ivor Novello award for Song Of The Year.

The album *Everything* sounds cleanly produced, sporting twiddly guitars, funky basslines and the usual range of keyboard noises from lush and orchestral to squeaky-jazzy. The instrumentation has a rather too sugary sound overall – despite being offset by Climie's growling Rod Stewart-like tones – and it's the two big singles that ultimately stand out, plus the minor hit 'I Won't Bleed For You'. The band split after their second album *Coming In For The Kill* in 1989, and a solo Climie single, 'Soul Inspiration', didn't see any chart action when released in 1992.

✔ Climie was worried about the now-classic, 7-note, Celtic-sounding hook for 'Love Changes Everything' – you know, the bit where he sings that he was only seventeen when she looked at him that way. He was so convinced he'd subconsciously pinched it from somewhere that he trawled through his record collection trying to find the source. Eventually he was happy to let it stand...

♥ The immortal **Half Man Half Biscuit** pay tribute on their album *Trouble Over Bridgewater*, where the track 'The Ballad Of Climie Fisher' recounts the duo's alleged venture into the gravel business. With hilarious consequences.

▸▸ Simon Climie is still an in-demand songwriter who has provided hits for Heather Small and Louise, among others. Simon produced the Eric Clapton album *Reptile*, and is now building a studio in the US. He has a production company called Signia Music. More at his official website, **www.simonclimie.com.**

▸▸ Sadly, Rob Fisher is no longer with us – he died in 1999, at the age of 39, leaving some planned new Naked Eyes work unfinished. There is a collection of fans' e-mail tributes at: **www.pjbmusic.com/rob-fan.html**

Lloyd Cole & The Commotions ★★★

♫ 'Perfect Skin' (1984, no.26)

Dour Scottish five-piece whose lead singer apparently liked to bait English audiences about the performance of their national football team (one is tempted to think of expressions concerning projectiles and glass houses). Formed in 1983 in the famous Tennants Bar in Glasgow, they built a reputation for studenty, jangly and thoughtful guitar-pop with the albums *Rattlesnakes* and *Easy Pieces*. From the latter came their best-known single, 'Lost Weekend'.

Cole went solo in the early 90s – declaring his intentions in time-honoured fashion by sprouting facial hair – and started to produce his best work, especially the singles 'No Blue Skies' (never a hit in the UK, but huge in Europe) and 'She's A Girl And I'm A Man'.

๛ *1984-1989* contains four tracks from every album, plus some B-sides.

✔ Drummer Steven Irvine was formerly a Scottish lightweight boxing champion.

✔ Cole was so disillusioned with the business in 1985 that he gave the gold and platinum discs he received for *Easy Pieces* to his local café to use as tea-trays.

✔ There is some fun to be had at **www.emma jane.com/lloyd/magpoetry.php**, which is the Lloyd Cole Magnetic Poetry Page.

♥ Tori Amos has covered 'Rattlesnakes' on her album *Strange Little Girls*, a collection of songs all written by men and performed from a female perspective.

▶▌ Recent album *The Negatives* – also the name of Lloyd's new band – has been getting good reviews: see **www.ink19.com/issues/june2001/wetInk/musicC/lloydCole.html** for choice phrases to throw into the conversation. Alternatively you could opine that 'Lloyd Cole emerged from Glasgow in 1984 fully formed as the poet laureate of sensitive, serious cynics, awed by both the grandeur of great romance and great books, with perfect skin, pristinely glimmering melodies, and oh yes, that catch-in-your-heart voice.' Official press releases – don't you just love them?

The Colour Field ★★

♫ 'Thinking Of You' (1985, no.12)

One of the many Terry Hall projects in the 1980s – he got about a bit. This one was a bit more disappointing, in terms of success, than **The Specials** or Fun Boy Three, but it still had its moments. 'Thinking Of You' was their only hit single, but the album *Virgins and Philistines* made the top 20.

✔ 'Thinking Of You' charmingly mentions 'four-leafed clovers'. Sadly, this plural has been disallowed on *Countdown* as 'clover' is a mass noun. So, Terry, classic purveyor of quirky pop ditties with dark undertones you may be, but you wouldn't ever get to have one from the top and five from the bottom with Carol Vorderman.

▶▌ Terry has resurfaced since from time to time, although never quite hitting the charts again with the same impact. His 1994 near-hit 'Forever J' was a good one, and he did a decent version of the **Lightning Seeds** song 'Sense' (which he co-wrote).

The Communards ✭✭✭

♫ 'You Are My World' (1985, no.30)

Jimmy Somerville, the man who was once memorably described as looking like an angry baked bean, had been successful as the singer with Bronski Beat (who bravely struggled, like a headless chicken, to carry on without him). He formed the Communards in 1985 with keyboard player Richard Coles.

You might have thought Somerville, who deliberately sang in an agonised falsetto like a man with an intimate part trapped in a vice, would have trouble sounding soulful, but you'd have been wrong. Two albums, *Communards* and *Red*, showcased their sometimes-political, dance-orientated pop, and the commercial high-point was their 1986 Number One, their version of 'Don't Leave Me This Way'. You may recall that this song featured the big-voiced Sarah Jane Morris – a lady whose wide-ranging career has since covered jazz, rhythm and blues and pop stardom in Italy.

✔ Other names in the running were Body Politic and The Committee; the second at least had already been taken by another band.

✔ Richard Coles was formerly a student at the Royal College of Church Music. After The Communards split in 1988, he returned to the serenity of the classics.

✔ 'I never really made a huge financial success with The Communards. I had more of a name than I did a healthy bank account. Maybe it's because I left after a year and I didn't really give it a chance to grow. Well, none of us did. They split up a year after that. I think if I had carried on having that kind of success I would have slotted it into a nice little niche. I would have been someone like Céline Dion which, as far as a bank account is concerned, is fantastic, but I think I would have been very bored and very dissatisfied...' Sarah Jane Morris speaking in 2000.

The Cult ✯✯✯

♫ **'She Sells Sanctuary'** (1985, no.15)

You can forgive a man for wearing a dead raccoon on his head when he has been a part of one of the finest rock records of the 1980s. The band may have been Goths, but 'She Sells Sanctuary' unites rockers, indie kids and those who just like a good dance.

The Cult were Ian Astbury, Billy Duffy and Jamie Stewart, and once they dropped the words 'Southern Death' from their name, they popped up a few times in the charts of the 1980s. Top 40 hits included another one with a classic riff, 'Lil' Devil', which features in the film *Soft Top, Hard Shoulder*. On the epic 'Edie (Ciao Baby)' from 1989, you can almost hear the hair flowing in the wind-machine, the leather trousers creaking in the noonday sun and the whooshing sound as a drummer explodes without warning. It's that kind of track.

Later stuff like 'The Witch' sees them going all groovy and experimental. However, it's safe to say that the 1993 remix of 'She Sells Sanctuary', although it matched the chart peak of the original, is inferior in every way – sprawling goth-rock epics do not, in general, benefit from the addition of a Casio beat-box.

☎ 1993's *Pure Cult* compilation has everything the casual listener will need...

- The band fired their drummer Les Warner in 1988. He was offered £2,000 and a drum kit as compensation. Bit cruel, that, isn't it? Like firing a chef and giving him a Moulinex Mastermixer and a waffle-iron to see him off.

- 'Wild Flower' confused everyone by entering the charts twice in the space of two weeks, once as part of a double single.

- Astbury is often credited with being the first person to use the term 'goth' in connection with a musical movement; in 1982, during the Southern Death Cult period, he used the term in the *NME*.

- The *NME* gave the band a hard time, but guitarist Billy Duffy had this to say on the subject recently: 'We got a battering from the British music press, but the more they slagged The Cult off, the more albums we seemed to sell.'

- Although The Cult split in the mid-1990s, Duffy and Astbury got back together in 2002 with a new line-up for the comeback album *Beyond Good and Evil* and a subsequent tour. (Goths don't stay dead, you know. It's in the contract...)

Culture Club/Boy George ★★★★★
♪ 'Do You Really Want To Hurt Me' (1982, no.1)

The original gender-bender turned media icon
Many people of a certain age will remember the embarrassment of watching *Top Of The Pops* when their parents were in the room. It's quite likely that 'Is it a boy or a girl?' would

have been Mum and Dad's response to their first sighting of 21-year-old George O'Dowd with his hat, dress, make-up and braids. It seems amusing now, given that the Boy George of the Noughties is a household name and a seasoned chat-show guest as well as a respected DJ – a favourite with students as much as with fortysomething housewives. Witty, sharp and flamboyant, he's the gay man it's okay for *Daily Express* readers to like. He's even been described without irony as a 'national treasure'.

The band thankfully abandoned their early names (In Praise of Lemmings and Sex Gang Children) in favour of the alliterative Culture Club. Their first single on Virgin, 'White Boy', wasn't a success. It wasn't until the autumn of 1982 that the band took off, when 'Do You Really Want To Hurt Me' spent three weeks at Number One, despite its being written quickly as a filler for a session on Radio 1's Peter Powell show.

Of course, the tabloids were always going to have their knives out for a man in a dress, but George wasn't about to be knocked sideways by irritated hacks calling him a 'gender-bender' (he'd probably been called far worse). He knew how to manipulate the media, and the band stayed in the public eye, attracting both male and female fans. As a straight teenage boy, you could even (just about) admit to liking Culture Club without your thuggish contemporaries branding you a 'poof'.

In 1983, 'Karma Chameleon' was a million-seller and spent six weeks at Number One (the longest run since Art Garfunkel's 'Bright Eyes' in 1979) as well as topping the US charts. Not bad for a song which wasn't taken seriously by the band when George first sang it. More hits followed, including 'Victims' and 'It's a Miracle'.

However, by the time of 'The War Song', the first single from their third album, George's painful split with fellow band member and lover Jon Moss was starting to take its toll. And even though the song got to no.2, the rather risible anti-war lyrics couldn't really compete with their previous efforts.

George was convicted of possessing heroin in July 1986, and fined £250. When he appeared at an anti-apartheid concert in 1986 looking as if he'd overdone the white make-up and was in need of a few pies, it was evident that something was wrong. As news of his heroin addiction came out, it was time for another round of tabloid savaging – which he again survived. A solo Number One, 'Everything I Own', followed in 1987, plus some likeable singalong Hare Krishna-tinged pop (surely an underworked genre) under the name of Jesus Loves You in the late 80s.

Culture Club enjoyed a chart comeback in October 1998 with the pleasant and reggae-flavoured 'I Just Wanna Be Loved' – part of a Top Five mini-80s-revival in that particular week, which also saw a chart-topper from Cher and new hits from **George Michael** and **U2**.

- 'Karma Chameleon' hardly sounds dated and is the quintessential 80s single for many. It was co-written by Phil Pickett, formerly of 70s band Sailor, who also plays keyboards on the record.

- George's comment that he'd prefer a cup of tea to sex will probably haunt him. It's less well-known that, when asked on Simon Mayo's Radio 1 'God Of The Week' slot to nominate the person he'd like to make into a saint, George's somewhat controversial choice was Peter Tatchell.

- 'The ultimate rebel ends up dead. All the best people in pop, the legends, are dead. Some people say I've sold out but I haven't, I've cashed in.' Boy George speaking in *The Face* in 1986.

◀» 'I recall a headline at the height of Culture Club mania where I moaned: "Now I know how Lady Di feels." I managed to escape the spotlight. She was not so lucky.' Boy George in his *Daily Express* column, 1997.

▶▮ With his big hat, knowing smile and sharp innuendo, George, one of pop's survivors, could still be entertaining us when he's 70. And if you can't get enough of him on TV, you'll encounter a plethora of riches at the 'Devil In Sister George Homepage', to be found at **www.boy.george.net** – you lucky people. George's musical *Taboo*, based on the life of performance artist Leigh Bowery, opened to great acclaim in 2002: see **www.tabootheshow.com** for information.

The Cure ✭✭✭✭

♫ **'A Forest'** (1980, no.31)

Maudlin Goth-pop from Robert Smith and a shifting entourage of personnel, such as bassists Michael Dempsey and Simon Gallup and drummer/keyboard player Lol Tolhurst. Smith, with his wobbly lipstick, mascara and bog-brush hair, is one of those instantly recognisable 80s stars, resembling a cross between a demented Elizabeth Taylor and an extra from *Blake's Seven*.

They were formed in 1976 as Easy Cure – after toying with, and thankfully abandoning, Obelisk, Goat Band and Malice. Initially, they had something of an intellectual veneer thanks to early single 'Killing An Arab' being based on Albert Camus' classic novel *L'Etranger* (although this many not have meant much – Kate Bush wickedly confessed that she hadn't read *Wuthering Heights* when she wrote her song, after all). Whatever the truth behind the record, there was a National Front-provoked riot at one of the band's 1979 gigs.

Albums *Three Imaginary Boys*, *Seventeen Seconds* and *Faith* had a cult following, but *Pornography* broke into the Top 10 in 1982. Various scraps, break-ups and Top 20 singles later, The Cure had amassed an impressive body of work, mostly of the melodic-but-miserable kind. Along the way some classic moments were produced, such as the perennial 'Love Cats', the anthemic 'In Between Days' and the underrated and moody 'Catch'.

The Cure's process of re-invention has kept them fresh over two decades. They were always elusive; just as you thought they were going more commercial and accessible with something like 1987's poppy single 'Just Like Heaven', they'd turn around and confront you with a doomy, rainy-day, wrist-slashingly dark epic like the *Disintegration* album. If you thought **The Smiths** were miserable gits, try listening to this bugger on your own when there is no milk in the house, the girlfriend/boyfriend has done a bunk, pay-day is three weeks off and England have just been knocked out of the World Cup (unless you are Scottish). I won't be responsible for the consequences.

And then they went and did 'Friday I'm In Love' in 1992, their most cheerful and populist moment yet and a fabulous single. Was it all some kind of sick joke?

- ◑ Compilation *Staring At The Sea* collected most of the 80s singles, but the version called *Standing On A Beach* had the B-sides as well. A disappointingly sparse *Greatest Hits* was released in 2001, missing some of their greatest moments. 1990's Cure-for-the-dancefloor remix collection *Mixed Up* has its surprisingly effective moments.

- ✸ At a Los Angeles concert in 1986, a fan who had just been jilted by his girlfriend got on stage and started stabbing himself. The crowd initially thought it was part of the show. You can see where they were coming from, really.

💣 Lol Tolhurst was fired in 1988 and launched a lawsuit against the rest of the band, claiming that he'd done more than it said in his contract and that he deserved more money. The case dragged on well into the 1990s.

✔ Robert Smith disliked the 1982 single 'Let's Go To Bed' and wanted it to be released under the pseudonym 'The Recur.'

✔ A recurring series of sketches in the early 90s TV comedy series *The Mary Whitehouse Experience* had The Cure, as portrayed by Rob Newman and David Baddiel, reluctantly dragooned into performing 'happy' songs in their own inimitable doom-laden style.

Curiosity Killed The Cat ★★
⊘ Curiosity ♫ 'Down To Earth' (1987, no.3)

This cat had fewer than nine lives – five, in fact, being the total number of hit singles clocked up by the gangling Martin Benedict Volpelière-Pierrot and his boys. Ben (as we can thankfully call him for short) was unfortunately under the impression that berets were a cool pop accessory, but at least he never looked as silly as Jay Kay from Jamiroquai. Shortening their name in 1989 fooled nobody, although the 1992 hit 'Hang On In There Baby' matched the no.3 position of their first hit. They released the albums *Get Ahead* and *Keep Your Distance*.

▶▶ **www.curiosity-killedthecat.com** looks like a new official website. If you can get past the annoyingly redundant Flash effects and the finger-drummingly slow loading time, then it's worth a browse – but be ready to wince at an irritating quirk to rival the misplaced apostrophe, namely the use of inverted commas for 'emphasis'. It makes the entire site read as if it's been written by the Rob Newman character, Ray (The Man Afflicted With A Sarcastic Tone Of Voice): 'Oh, they toured with **"Alison Moyet"**, did they? I bet that was "great fun" for them.'

▶▶ Unfathomably, Curiosity have re-formed for a 21st-century tour – with, it appears, the feline suffix back in place. Honestly, you'd think there was some sort of 80s revival going on or something...

Cutting Crew ★★
♪ **'(I Just) Died In Your Arms'** (1986, no.4)

Nothing, despite the name, to do with the art of creating those memorable 80s hairstyles. The group was formed in 1985 by Canadian guitarist Kevin Scott MacMichael, from the band Fast Forward, and English vocalist Nick Van Eede of The Drivers. They were signed to Siren Records, but never really capitalised on the runaway success of their first hit, which was a Number One in America. 'I've Been In Love Before' is well-remembered too, and charted three times in the UK, twice on original release and once as a slightly remixed version a year later. Cutting Crew made their niche in the American market for a while, supporting such acts as **The Bangles** and Huey Lewis & The News. They split in 1993 after making three albums, *Broadcast* (1986), *The Scattering* (1989) and *Compus Mentus* (1992).

- ✔ Nominated for 'Best New Artist' at the 30th annual Grammy Awards in 1987.

- ▶▶ A sad note: Kevin MacMichael was recently reported to bc very ill with terminal cancer. A hugely successful tribute concert to Kevin was held in Canada in March 2002.

pause

D

dustbin lids and park railings

D Mob ✭

Oh, God. Do I have to? Right. (Deep breath.) This is it, the point at which the 80s began to self-destruct. In 1988-89, if it wasn't another vacuous soap-star stepping up to the mike, it was some bunch of chancers with a pair of decks pretending to be big and clever. To this day, this sort of thing has perpetuated the idea that pinching bits of other people's records and shouting over them is a valid musical genre worthy of critical attention. For my money, the only record of the era more annoying than this one is 'Can I Kick It' by A Tribe Called Quest, and that, thankfully, was released in 1991 so they don't qualify for inclusion here.

This belongs to another time; it's a Worst Of The 90s record a little too early, a brain-dead, repetitive hymn to the joys of Acid House. D Mob hadn't had enough either – they came back two months later, proclaiming, quite erroneously in my book, 'It Is Time To Get Funky'. What were they on? It is never 'time' to get funky. Getting funky should only be done a) spontaneously, b) drunk and c) among very good friends who will promise not to take Polaroids.

Here, boys and girls, was the future. From this moment on, some dork in a baseball cap would be taken more seriously than your favourite band. Unnaturally bright-eyed people trying to assure you that a *turntable* was a valid 'musical instrument' would succeed only in coming over as a waste of a pair of functioning kidneys. This was the insistent, annoying sound of a generation with too much time on its hands, trying to tell you that the next revolution was just around the corner, that the 80s were over, that it was time to bail out.

Acieed? Pass me the alkeea-seltzeeer.

Danny Wilson ★★

♫ **'Mary's Prayer'** (1988, no.3)

Scottish trio in trilby hats, led by singer-songwriter Gary Clark. They were named after the Frank Sinatra film *Meet Danny Wilson*, which also gave its name to their first album. So, nothing at all to do with football managers of the same name. They had two melodic and jaunty hits, the above debut and the biting 'Second Summer Of Love'. Another album, *Bebop Moptop*, followed.

Clark later became a solo artist and then turned up in his new band, King L, whose name is mildly amusing the first time you get it. But only mildly.

♥ *Mary's Prayer* is also the title of an acclaimed debut crime novel by Martyn Waites...

▶▶ Gary Clark continues to perform, produce and write songs: he's worked with Eddi Reader (ex-**Fairground Attraction**) kd lang and Julia Fordham, among others. He produced and co-wrote several tracks on the Natalie Imbruglia album *White Lilies Island* in 2001.

Terence Trent D'Arby ★★★

♫ **'If You Let Me Stay'** (1987, no.7)

The ego has landed

Living proof that, if you have a big mouth, it's always better to use it for singing than for speaking. Terence's ill-judged declarations of pop supremacy threatened to eclipse his undeniable talent, and got a few backs up as well as getting him noticed.

He was born in Manhattan in 1962, the son of a

Pentecostal evangelist, the Rev. James Darby – Terence adopted the apostrophe himself. Terry (nobody ever called him that) joined the US Army and was stationed in Frankfurt; after a spell in German band The Touch, he came to London and signed to CBS. His arrival was hyped by the music press in a way that would give him a sure-fire Number One these days – but a succession of funky Top 20 hits got him off to a great start, and he did top the charts across the Atlantic, with 'Wishing Well' in 1987. 'Sign Your Name', a smooth and old-fashioned ballad, was the biggest hit from the album *Introducing The Hardline According To Terence Trent D'Arby*, despite being its fourth single.

Along the way, though, Tel (no, they didn't call him that, either) obviously managed to persuade various people that he should be indulged, resulting in the commercial failure of the 'difficult' second album *Neither Fish Nor Flesh*. He weathered the storm, and came back with the acclaimed, eclectic 16-track *Symphony Or Damn* in 1993, on which touches of Lenny Kravitz-esque rock-out vied with mellow moments like 'Let Her Down Easy'. Tezza (well, have a guess) became blond for the 1995 album *Vibrator* (oo-er, missus) which also got some good reviews.

The comparisons between TTD and Prince now seem prescient, as he seems to have imitated the Purple One's desire for a shifting identity (and, it has to be said, for being a bit of a prat). His new album *Wildcard* is out on the Internet under the name of Sananda Maitreya; he has an official site at **www.sanandapromotion.com** which tells you all about it. Sananda (for that is now his name) is working with marketing companies to develop alternate ways of releasing different artists and styles of music to the public. Apparently.

⦿ 'You have got to keep a straight face. You have got to come across as totally serious, totally wicked, totally crucial, lethal. You saunter over, across the crowded room, and you see her looking scintillating, tantalising, delectable, delicious. You go over to her, glass firmly poised in hand, and you say, "Sweetheart, you simply must tell me your name, because last night, as I dreamed of you, I could only call you *baby*." '

Ahem, yes. Terence's wicked, crucial, lethal tips for picking up the Lay-deees. There may well have been bars in 1988 where this would have earned you a riposte other than 'Piss off, you pretentious git.' But not many.

🔊 'I'm very grateful that I was able to be squeezed by the pain into a greater realization. And with that in mind, we can just open up and be free to give the people what they deserve and not always the same reconstructed, regurgitated piece of music over and over again.' Thus spake Sananda in 2001. 'Squeezed by the pain', hmmm... well, at least it beats his famous 1987 pronouncement, 'I'm a fucking genius'.

Deacon Blue ★ ★ ★

♫ **'Dignity'** (1988, no.31)

Accomplished yet rather humourless Scottish six-piece, whose first hit in 1988 was the fruit of many labours and frustrations. Front-man Ricky Ross, a youth worker by profession, had been sending stuff to record companies since 1983. When they were finally signed by CBS, their first few singles failed to chart, despite critical acclaim for the album **Raintown**, and it was only a remixed 'Dignity' which deservedly got them underway.

Subsequent singles included 'Chocolate Girl', 'Real Gone Kid' and 'Wages Day'. Ross's growly tones are unmistakable, as are the somewhat histrionic squealings of Lorraine McIntosh in the background. 1990 became their biggest year, with sell-out shows at Wembley Arena and the Aberdeen Exhibition Centre and their cover of the Bacharach & David song 'I'll Never Fall In Love Again' becoming their biggest hit at no.2. In an injustice of **Ultravox**-versus-Joe-Dolce proportions, the record which held them off the top spot was 'Itsy Bitsy Teeny Weeny Yellow Polka Dot Bikini' by the 'wacky' (i.e. smackable) Timmy Mallet and Bombalurina.

Deacon Blue re-emerged in the 90s with a new dance edge to their sound, thanks to some production by Paul Oakenfold and Steve Osborne, although the album *Whatever You Say, Say Nothing* was more conventional than one might have expected. The band split in 1994 and Ricky Ross embarked on a solo career, but Deacon Blue have recently been recording and performing together again.

🎧 1994's *Greatest Hits* collection showcases the band's diversity and is well worth having.

⏭ In May 1999, Deacon Blue played their long-await-ed reunion gig, a charity event at the Glasgow Royal Concert Hall. Tickets sold out in less than 90 min-utes, and two more concerts followed at the Clyde Auditorium. Singles from the *Walking Back Home* comeback album failed to chart, but then you'd struggle to find them in the shops or played on the radio. Lorraine, meanwhile, has been developing a career as an actress.

Dead or Alive ✦✦✦

♫ 'That's the Way (I Like It)' (1984, no.22)

'Dead or Alive' was the name of a ghoulishly amusing quiz during Simon Mayo's tenure as the custodian of the morning show on Radio 1, in which he would invite people to win prizes by speculating on the brain-activity status of certain 'on-the-cusp' celebs.

Before that, of course, it was the name of a band led by the flamboyant Pete Burns. They formed in 1982, and the debut album *Sophisticated Boom Boom* led to dancefloor and chart success with 'You Spin Me Round (Like A Record)'. Always good to see some use of brackets at the top of the charts. Anyway, the band's UK following petered out, with only 'Lover Come Back to Me' in 1985 and 'Something In My House' in 1987 getting anywhere close to the top 10 again. They continue to be successful in Germany and Japan, as well as parts of the USA.

● Pete's, um, striking appearance recently on irreverent quiz *Never Mind The Buzzcocks* had many an 80s child doing a double-take, scarcely able to believe that the pouting, musclebound fusion of Michael Jackson, Mick Jagger and Lily Savage trading quips with Mark Lamarr was the 80s idol they remembered.

◀》 'I'm interested in the art of transformation... I've just always seen it as a form of magic. Make-up, tattoos, cosmetic surgery – any way of taking this raw material and changing it into what you want. To me, the body is like a new flat. After a few years, you redecorate, knock a wall or two down. You get bored with looking in the mirror and seeing the same old thing. I'm not going to sit here and say it's all down to exercise and brussels sprouts. I don't have any qualms about altering something. I'm not doing it to thrill anyone except myself.' Pete Burns.

Hazell Dean ★ ★

♬ 'Searchin' (I Gotta Find A Man)' (1984, no.6)

Once again, we revel in our celebration of the D-list as we welcome Hazell, the lady so memorably described by *Record Mirror* as 'The Angela Rippon of Hi-NRG' and 'the pearly, twirly Queen of disco'. She was the dancing dolly with the Diana-in-a-pudding-bowl barnet, Top Girl dress-sense (ooh, those hats!), pink-icing blusher, big chunky belts and a big chunky grin to go with them. Fanciable? Didn't really matter at the end of the day, as we always got the impression that her heterosexual male fans were few and far between.

Wholesome, polite and easily digestible, Hazell was the happy, smiling face of Eurobeat – which makes the fabricated tabloid stories about her sexual 'exploits' with peanuts all the more unlikely-sounding. And anyway – *peanuts*? Not the world's biggest aphrodisiac, surely.

◀ッ 'I have to admit I went through a stage when I thought maybe I should change what I was doing. It was awful. I actually changed my name to Jesse Miller. Don't ask me why. I had my hair cut very short and I wrote this song called "Jealous Love" which was quite a heavy rock thing. But it was just ridiculous. It only lasted about four months.' (Phew, can you imagine that? Even 'Bohemian Rhapsody' is only five-and-a-half minutes.)

▶▶| Hazell has been writing and co-producing for a new band called Krave (ooh, like the retro 80s name!), while several of her own hits have re-emerged in remixed form. She now has a successful career performing on the gay pub and club circuit.

Chris De Burgh ★★★

♪ **'The Lady In Red'** (1986, no.1)

'Oh, *who*? This is too much. This bloody book's gone too far. I've tolerated his **Bananarama** eulogy as it had a certain kitsch knowingness to it, and I've put up with the way he slags off any rap stuff he doesn't like. But if he's expecting to fob us off with some whiny crooner for menopausal women, he can expect a fight.'

Well, actually, whisper it, but – Chris De Burgh has had a bad press. Some of his early stuff is quite good... There, I've said it. My ownership of an *Unknown Pleasures* T-shirt is now a hollow triumph and nobody will ever believe that I like **Half Man Half Biscuit**.

Yes, we can't deny that in 1986 he got to the top of the charts by dancing cheek-to-cheek with the eponymous Lady, rhyming 'dance' and 'romance' in a terrible, maudlin ballad. The rest of the album *Into The Light* is quite listenable, though, and less slushy than one would expect. Dig a little deeper and you find that *The Very Best Of Chris De Burgh* – released in the mid-80s just before he peaked – still merits its title despite the additional two decades of work since. On the minus side, the saccharine Christmas single 'A Spaceman Came Travelling' is there, and the equally cloying 'In A Country Churchyard' too. However, 'Don't Pay The Ferryman' is a good rock song, and was almost a much more credible 'first hit' (it got to no.48 in 1982), 'Borderline' is a surprisingly moving slow-builder (even though he doesn't hold the big note on the chorus) and 'Waiting For The Hurricane' is brilliant and moody, with a great guitar line. There's also 'Spanish Train', an atmospheric and enjoyable morality-tale. And I defy anyone not to smile at 'Patricia The Stripper' first time round.

The early 80s albums hold some hidden gems, especially *The Getaway* and *Man On The Line*, where you will find the wry 'Moonlight And Vodka' and the up-tempo 'Sound Of A Gun', on which Tina Turner sings backing vocals.

But yes, before you fling this book away in disgust, he did let us all down by becoming another Daniel O'Donnell. And I don't think he can ever be forgiven for that.

- ✔ Chris, whose real name is Christopher John Davison, was born in Argentina in 1948 to British and Irish parents. His family settled in a castle in County Wexford when he was twelve years old.

- ✔ He's always been huge in Europe and South America, especially Norway and Brazil. In the UK it would seem he's more infamous for his extra-curricular activities (getting off with the nanny, mainly) than for his music…

- ✔ During his tour of the Lebanon, Chris hired a private army to protect him as he was afraid of being kidnapped.

- ◄» 'My dad had a dream of living in an Irish castle, even when we were in Argentina, and in 1960 he found a place without any heat or running water. We had no money, so it was tough… We had a cellar with a few good bottles of Burgundy in it, but it was easy to be the sommelier: it was basically a choice of red or white.'(From a recent interview where Chris described his early interest in wine… What? Look, it was that or a quote from a review of 'The Lady In Red'.)

Depeche Mode ★★★★★

♫ **'New Life'** (1981, no.11)

Forgive us our synths and lead us into temptation
Being dead. It's often seen as a good career move – certainly it helped Kurt Cobain, Jim Morrison and Marc Bolan to become even bigger legends. However, the panoply of pop stars who have flatlined, subsequently recovered and returned to recording and touring is, shall we say, somewhat under-populated. Step forward Dave Gahan, the clean-cut, sharp-suited and thin-tied front man of an electro-pop band who evolved into a rock animal, and very nearly became another rock casualty.

A name scrawled on many a pencil-case in the early 80s, Depeche Mode rode the early 80s wave of pretty-boy New Romantic bands. Formed in Basildon, they initially comprised the ubiquitous Vince Clarke and his schoolfriends Martin Gore and Andy Fletcher, and were briefly known as Composition of Sound. It was Gahan, recruited as singer from Southend Technical College, who suggested the name they would carry for the next two decades.

Considering the moniker came from a French fashion magazine, it was unfortunate that the Mode had a few sartorial disasters along the way, not least the notorious 'cricketing boys' photo and their flirtation with S&M gear. However, it was the music that mattered. Although Vince Clarke bailed out early on to form **Yazoo** (and later **Erasure**), replacement Alan Wilder came in on keyboards and Martin Gore took over the songwriting. The early work contains light, twee stuff like 'New Life', but did give us the classic (and staple of 80s revival nights) 'Just Can't Get Enough'. Over the course of the decade, though, the band's sound became more deep, dark and doom-laden, with tracks like 'Never Let Me Down' and 'Little 15' attaining an industrial-Gothic splendour.

As their image became more sexually ambiguous, the songwriting expanded into areas not hitherto visited much by the charts – sexual manipulation, religious fervour and perversion – and their *Top Of The Pops* performances became notable for the use of unconventional instruments like dustbin lids and park railings. You didn't get that with **Spandau Ballet**, frankly.

You always have to wonder what's going on when pop stars start sprouting facial hair (stand up **Lloyd Cole**, David Bowie et al), and as their masterpiece album *Violator* emerged, Gahan started to look distinctly more hirsute. By the time of 1993's *Songs of Faith and Devotion*, he seemed to be modelling his look on Jesus, his lifestyle on Axl Rose and his band's image on bombastic stadium-rockers. However, there were no giant inflatable pigs – except possibly in Gahan's fevered imaginings, as he became a fully-fledged heroin addict. His infamous near-death experience (thanks to an unwise drug-cocktail experiment) followed, as did Gore's drinking and Fletcher's nervous breakdown.

Amazingly, the band has survived everything fate has thrown at them and they recently celebrated twenty years in the music business with a new album, *Exciter*. At the last count, they were still with us.

☊ Two singles collections are out – covering 1981-85 and 1986-98 – and have recently been repackaged as one double album.

☊ Their perfect single, falling just outside the 80s, is 1990's 'Enjoy The Silence' (you know, the one which told us words were very unnecessary and that they could only do harm). It perfectly marries their early-80s lightness of touch with the edgy, epic feel of the *Music for the Masses* era. Also, try listening to *Violator*'s fabulously moody track 'Waiting for the

Night' with the lights out.

- By the end of the 80s, Depeche Mode were huge in America, and in March 1990, several Los Angeles fans had to be treated for minor injuries following a crush during a *Violator* promotion at Wherehouse Records.

- Other names originally suggested for the band included The Lemon Peels, The Runny Smiles and The Glow-Worms… I once heard a French DJ spoonerise them (whether intentionally or not, I don't know) as '*Despédés Moches*', the meaning of which is far too offensive to be printed here.

- There are a few tribute albums, including the strangely appropriate *No Hidden Catch (The Estonian Depeche Mode Tribute)* – yes, really – and the A&M compilation *For The Masses*, featuring versions of 17 Depeche Mode tunes covered by the likes of **The Cure**, Smashing Pumpkins and Apollo Four Forty.

- We wait with interest to see what they do next. If they get any more doomy and sparse, they'll be turning into the **Sisters of Mercy**. Official site has all the latest: **www.depechemode.com** is where it's at.

Desireless ★★

♫ **'Voyage Voyage'** (1988, no.5)

French music doesn't traditionally do all that well over here – it's probably still tainted with the image of Sacha Distel, Serge Gainsbourg and naff Eurovision ditties. That's a shame, because some Gallic talent can easily compete with home-grown singer-songwriters. Quality Francophone stars like Mylène Farmer, Jean-Jacques Goldman and Véronique Rivière have found it a tall order to have any success across the channel, probably because the traditionally insular British usually struggle even to ask for a loaf of bread in a *boulangerie*.

Quite why this record did so well, then, is a mystery. It even had a couple of stabs at the charts, peaking outside the top 50 in the autumn of 1987 before it was re-mixed. The lyrics seem to be a hymn to international unity in the form of a travelogue, over a thumping 80s-by-numbers synth beat which doesn't really do it any favours. Pleasant enough, but not truly memorable.

✔ 'Voyage Voyage' made it to Number One in Germany, but then so does all sorts of shocking rubbish. They like David Hasselhoff, you know. And folk music. And pink shirts with yellow trousers.

◀» 'At least I don't have to take my top off to get in the charts,' said Desireless, in a snipe at 'Boys Boys Boys' singer **Sabrina** (which surely had the voluptuous chanteuse quaking in her E-cups).

Dexy's Midnight Runners ★ ★ ★
♬ **'Dance Stance'** (1980, no.40)

Kevin Rowland's Birmingham band went through several changes of personnel, image and label over the years. The woolly hats and donkey jackets coincided with their EMI period and the Number One single 'Geno' (and, just to be difficult, the band dropped the song from their live set after it hit the top). The dungarees came along in 1982 for the Celtic-influenced period and the horrendously over-rated

'Come On Eileen', which should be banned if only for its unerring ability to make middle-aged aunties start dancing at weddings. A three-piece fiddle section called The Emerald Express shared the credit for this one. Then, for 1985's *Don't Stand Me Down* album, unheralded by any singles, smart suits were the order of the day. 'Because Of You' was a comeback, the theme tune to the 1986 comedy series *Brush Strokes*, but by this time it was pretty much a solo Rowland affair.

💣 Rowland seized the master tapes from producer Pete Wingfield during the recording of the debut album *Searching For The Young Soul Rebels*, in order to negotiate a better deal with EMI.

💣 We must mention their *Top Of The Pops* appearance for 'Jackie Wilson Said', for which the band performed in front of a giant blown-up photo of darts player, Jocky Wilson. It was either a hugely embarrassing mistake by the BBC or a wonderful piece of irony by the band. Maybe both.

✔ And yes, the name is a reference to the pep-pill Dexedrine, despite the band's clean-living tendencies.

Doctor & the Medics ★★

🎵 **'Spirit in the Sky'** (1986, no.1)

You may not believe it, but this was a Number One record – just as it had been for Norman Greenbaum in 1970. For Norman, it marked the beginning and the end of his chart career, but the flamboyant Doc and his attendant Medics fared a little better by getting their follow-up, 'Burn', to no.29. The Doc was Welshman and former scout-leader

Clive Jackson, and his band were sometimes described as 'comedy hippies'. (There is another sort?) Although stalwarts of the early 80s psychedelic revival and regulars at the Alice In Wonderland club in Soho, the Medics had not tasted chart action until 1986 – and with crushing inevitability, they would not do so again.

They did, though, shuffle to just outside the Top 40 with a bizarre cover of 'Waterloo', featuring none other than Roy Wood of Wizzard. Doctor and the Medics' 1987 single 'Drive He Said', their last on the IRS label, should have been a hit – it was A-listed by Radio 1 – but, as Colin has pointed out in interviews, the record company were not even sufficiently interested to make a video and so it flopped.

◁» '18 months after 'Spirit In The Sky' was Number One, I was on a building site mixing cement in the pissing rain in November for £20 a day, and I didn't have a problem with that. It was just another chapter, it was something I was doing and I was living… We were going out on tour in December and I needed cash – I needed to buy food between tours. You can't just go to the grocer's and say, "don't worry, I'm going on tour in December". You've got to give them money!' (The Doctor)

Dollar ★★

🎵 **'Shooting Star'** (1978, no.14)

Guy and doll

Shiny blond duo, fired from the not-very-hip Guys & Dolls because they, um, dared to be living together. He seemed to have forgotten how to do his shirt up, while she, depending on who had been on duty with the bleach bottle and the scissors, resembled either a *Dynasty* matriarch, a *Grange*

Hill sixth-former or Paula Yates sucking on a lemon.

Although the duo broke up as a couple in 1981, they continued to record (there's dedication for you). Upbeat dance-pop was the order of the day, from 'Mirror Mirror' to 'Give Me Back My Heart' and 'Videotheque'. They split professionally in the mid-80s to pursue solo careers – which seem to have evaded pursuit pretty fast, as the pair were soon back, charting again in 1987 with a cover of Erasure's 'O L'Amour'. And then, poised on the brink of chart supremacy once more, the JR and Sue Ellen of hi-NRG pop split up again. It must have been definite this time, because Van Day tried out a variety of nubile replacements, possibly assembled by a Thereza Bazar cloning plant in a supposedly disused plastics factory near Redditch. Thereza, unmoved by the parade of pert simulacra being groomed as her understudies, moved to Sydney and started a family. Mr Van Day then got involved with the new incarnation of **Bucks Fizz**, which you can read about elsewhere.

◀ David recently got a lot of publicity for his other 'business ventures', namely his fast-food vans on the South Coast. Here's what he had to say about that: 'I can see why somebody only read the headline, saw me serving burgers with onions and all that bullshit and thought what a shame, what a comedown... [but] I'd rather be doing this some days than working for peanuts like some groups...' Perhaps he should team up with Jason Doner-Van. (I'll get me coat.)

♥ It would be nice to think that, in recognition of Ms Bazar's new Antipodean life, there is a tribute band called The Australian Dollar, but there isn't. As far as I know.

▶▶ David recently revealed that he and Thereza do keep

in touch, and are not averse to the idea of a reunion – subject, of course, to contractual negotiations, the availability of peroxide and the seasonal demand for flame-grilled whoppers with extra cheese.

Jason Donovan ★★★

♪ **'Nothing Can Divide Us'** (1988, no.5)

Bonzer

The most famous Donovan since the one who sang 'Jennifer Juniper', and probably the most famous Jason since the one who voyaged in search of the golden fleece.

Jason first came to public attention as Scott in the soap *Neighbours*. He was the new, improved version, in fact, the old Scott disappearing and returning with a totally fresh face – not after plastic surgery but simply thanks to that old soap standby, the Stupid And Blind Family Syndrome, where an entire clan fails to recognise that a relative has been supplanted by an unconvincing (and usually better-looking) changeling. Apart from snogging **Kylie** (of course) Jason's main acting challenge as Scott was to skateboard into work, wearing a suit, without looking too much of a knob. He almost succeeded.

At the age of twenty, Jason shook his mullet to his first hit with the ubiquitous **Stock, Aitken and Waterman**. He then had a post-Christmas, post-Cliff cold turkey Number One duetting with **Kylie** on 'Especially For You'. His finest moment was to come with the video for 'Too Many Broken Hearts' in 1989, where Jason was seen striding manfully (well, okay, boyfully) across a rugged landscape, strumming the most conspicuously unplugged guitar since Andrew Ridgeley's.

After a Number One album, *Ten Good Reasons*, many thought Jason had enjoyed his moment in the sizzling sun and that he'd disappear gracefully. However, he bounced back with the lead role in a revival of *Joseph And The Amazing Technicolour Dreamcoat*, and took 'Any Dream Will Do' to the top of the UK Top 40. He was succeeded in the role, bizarrely, by Philip Schofield, but the producers sadly squandered the crowd-pulling chance to have the Pharaoh played by Gordon the Gopher.

The subsequent years saw Jason popping up more in the tabloids than in the charts. He successfully sued *The Face* for its implication that he was gay, which led some to consider him hypocritical as his image had previously played on sexual ambiguity. It was also feared the magazine might have to close as a result. Jason later made it clear that he had sued not because he thought the implication was damaging, but because he didn't want people to think he had lied about such a central aspect of his life.

His well-chronicled bouts of overwork and exhaustion, many of which seemed to take place in nightclubs and in the company of attractive young ladies, have left him looking a little more lived-in these days. Jason seems sanguine and self-deprecating about his career, though, and his recent success in the role of Frank N. Furter in *The Rocky Horror Show* demonstrates that he's willing to take the proverbial out of himself. If only that were true of so many others.

- Jason achieved a great double in 1990: he won both Best Male Solo Singer and Worst Male Solo Singer at the Smash Hits Awards. Something to be proud of.

- 'I don't care what the papers say any more. If they're still interested enough to print my picture in the paper, then they must think people are still interested in me.'

- Jason still occasionally performs his old songs, although more out of a sense of fun than a desire for a revival. He's happily settled with long-term partner Angela and their two children Jemma and Zac.

Double ★ ★

♫ **'The Captain Of Her Heart'** (1986, no.8)

Another one-hit wonder, this time from a Swiss duo. The fairly melodic song sports one of those instantly recognisable one-finger keyboard solos, but perhaps less instantly recognisable were its lead perpetrators Kurt Maloo and Felix Haug. They gave us three albums in the late 80s – *Blue*, *Double* and *Three* – but although Double toiled, they didn't trouble the charts again, despite the video for the 1987 single 'Devil's Ball' winning an award at Cannes in 1988. I'm told they were huge in Switzerland. Someone has to be.

♥ There's apparently a version of 'The Captain Of Her Heart' by Randy Crawford on her 1998 album *Every Kind Of Mood*. Perhaps someone can tell me if it's any good.

▶▶ Maloo, meanwhile, released a new version of the track, assisted by the production skills of Cretu and Jens Gad, in 1995.

Dream Academy ★ ★ ★

♫ **'Life In A Northern Town'** (1985, no.15)

Comprised the delightful-sounding Nick Laird-Clowes, Kate St. John and Gilbert Gabriel, who were dubbed 'psychedelic revivalists'. Well, with names like that, you kind of know they're not going to be New Wave Of British Heavy

Metal. The single 'Life In A Northern Town', co-produced by Pink Floyd's Dave Gilmour, has a lush, melodic, elusive quality and sounds like nothing else released at the time. It would be interesting to know exactly which Northern town they were referring to, because children drinking lemonade and Salvation army bands playing doesn't sound much like downtown Sheffield on a Saturday night to me. Not going to quibble, though, as it is a gorgeous song, apparently a eulogy for singer-songwriter Nick Drake.

- ♥ The famous 'hail ma-ma-ma' chorus was later sampled by Dario G for his surprisingly un-annoying 1997 dance hit 'Sunchyme'.

- ▶▶ Kate St. John has toured with Van Morrison and performed in the group Channel Light Vessel; her solo album *Indescribable Night* came out in 1996. Laird-Clowes performs as Trashmonk, and Gabriel recently released a single 'Reminiscence'.

- ▶▶ Send an email to **dream-academy-subscribe @yahoogroups.com** and you can spend hours running up a huge phone bill typing insults to people you have never met. Sorry, I mean you can join the Internet discussion forum.

Stephen 'Tin Tin' Duffy ★★

♪ **'Kiss Me'** (1985, no.4)

Founder member of Duran Duran who got out just before they became famous – just at the right or the wrong time, depending on your point of view. His solo single 'Kiss Me', originally released in 1983, became a catchy radio and dancefloor favourite in 1985.

Later on, objections from the estate of Hergé, creator of the Tintin cartoons, meant that he had to drop the nickname. As plain old Stephen Duffy he formed the briefly threatening-to-be-successful acoustic band The Lilac Time, but fans rate the 1995 comeback solo album *Duffy*. He also recorded *Music In Colors* in 1993 with violinist Nigel Kennedy, sang on Saint Etienne's songs 'Western Wind' and 'Fake '88', and has written songs for the Barenaked Ladies, among others. A collaboration with Nick Rhodes was anticipated in 2002.

🔊 'I feel that being on the cover of *Jackie*, being screamed at and doing *Top Of The Pops* with backing singers dressed in rubber is essential experience for a singer-songwriter. It makes a change from the garret and the habit.'

Duran Duran ★★★★★

♫ **'Planet Earth'** (1981, no.12)

If you were a girl in the 1980s, you will surely at some point have been into Duran Duran. (OK, this may not be true. Maybe you were deliberately perverse and always into Goth or Metal. Or you were simply a very quiet, shy sort who played the oboe and never listened to pop music, in which case you will now have now matured into an intriguing, sexy, willowy creature in rimless glasses who has to fight off adoring wannabe suitors with a sharp stick.) And if you were a boy, you will surely at some point have wondered why the girl you most fancied seemed far more interested in a slightly porky bloke with bleached-blond hair and a foppish name. More fool you. For Duran Duran were one of the most varied and exciting bands of the decade – and they sported three blokes called Taylor, none of whom were related. How likely is *that*?

John Taylor and Nick Rhodes, who grew up together in Birmingham, formed the band initially with the assistance of Simon Colley, a bassist and clarinettist, and **Stephen Duffy**, whose fortunes are catalogued above. Colley and Duffy didn't last very long, and nor did singer Andy Wickett; Duran Duran took off with the arrival of one Simon Le Bon, allegedly hired because he was the only one to come to the audition armed with his own songs. Good move. They signed with EMI and 'Planet Earth' was a no.12 hit, propelling them to teen-idol status. With the aid of promos directed by Russell Mulcahy (later of *Highlander* fame) the band traded on their image and used the video medium for all it was worth – especially when they dumped the futuristic image for yuppie chic.

In 1982, *Rio* took up a long residency in the album charts, and gave the world the singles 'Hungry Like The Wolf', 'Save A Prayer' and the title track. The images from this time stick with us; you could be forgiven for thinking that Duran Duran did nothing but zoom around in boats in pastel jackets and hang around on beaches with beautiful women.

Duran-mania reached a peak in the mid-80s, and the inevitable chart-topping single came with 'Is There Something I Should Know', one of the few songs to debut at the top of the charts before such performances were commonplace. 'The Reflex' hit the top as well and the James Bond theme 'A View To A Kill' was another big hit, but they were on the slide after that. Songs like 'Skin Trade' and 'Do You Believe In Shame' didn't quite capture the public imagination in the same way.

The trio of Taylors left the fold; replacement guitarist Warren Cuccurullo stepped in, and Duran Duran no doubt breathed a sigh of relief when their ballad 'Ordinary World' became a big comeback hit in 1993, as they were officially

Not Just An Eighties Band any more. Yeah, right.

🎧 The compilation *Decade* contains the 80s hits, but if you want a more comprehensive overview, go for the other one, *Greatest*. You can usually find them both in the 'CDs for £5.99' section, to be honest.

🔊 'It was bloody frightening. What a thing to happen. It didn't make sense to us... It was horrible, messy and smelly in there. Foul. I can't imagine what it would have been like to have had to spend the night in there. Pretty awful - and we were down there only 20 minutes, though we didn't have any sense of time.' Simon Le Bon talking about life on the tour bus... No, okay, about the time he cheated death when his boat capsized during the Fastnet yacht race.

🔊 Nick Rhodes: 'There's this great story I heard. It's all about this composer who wrote a piece of music for the bassoon. But it contained one note that doesn't feature on the bassoon. So instead of giving up they designed a bassoon with the new note on it! I like that story, because there was a vibrancy about the music, a feeling of breaking new ground, and nowadays that feeling is hard to come by. But we've tried to overcome that.'

❤ D.Ran D.Ran are 'the most notorious tribute on Planet Earth'. Say no more.

⏭ Ill-advised covers of 'Perfect Day' and 'White Lines (Don't Do It)' notwithstanding, they continue, with Rhodes and Le Bon the only remaining members from their heyday. In 2002, a huge bidding war got

125

under way for their new album, rumoured to be their best in years.

pause

endearing Mancunian whine

Echo and the Bunnymen ★★★★

♫ 'Crocodiles' (1981, no.37)

Not a modest man, Ian McCulloch. He proclaimed his band to be 'the best in the world', for one thing, and that kind of confidence – some might even say arrogance – took his moody, interesting, darkly-clad band through the 80s and beyond.

Another great Liverpudlian export, the Bunnymen were formed by McCulloch and Will Sergeant after the demise of McCulloch's previous incarnation in The Crucial Three with Pete Wylie and Julian Cope (later of **The Teardrop Explodes**). Some of their early stuff, not dissimilar to early **U2**, is sometimes categorised as 'post-punk', while the mid-80s saw them lumped in as 'indie' (together with everybody else who had a jangly guitar), although accusations of 'glittering psychedelic pop' have also been levelled at them.

You'll recognise the opening string riff to 'The Cutter', the doomy guitars of 'The Killing Moon' and the jangly near-poppiness of 'Bring On The Dancing Horses', all of them powered by McCulloch's echoing, reflective voice. And if you were ever a sixth-former, you'll remember mooching about in a long coat, gazing wistfully out at a snow-covered field and fingering the pages of your copy of Camus' *L'Etranger*. And wondering why you weren't getting any.

After a faithful cover version of the Doors' 'People Are Strange', McCulloch left, and despite the band producing one more album without him, it looked for a while as if the Bunnymen would live on only through retrospectives. McCulloch and Sergeant formed the spooky, rough-edged and short-lived Elektrafixion. However, the Bunnymen stormed back in 1997 with a new line-up and one of their best songs, the beautiful 'Nothing Lasts Forever', which put them back in the Top 10.

🎧 For the definitive 80s single, it's surely 'The Game' (despite it being their biggest US hit) or 'The Killing Moon', but cherish 1997's 'Nothing Lasts Forever' too. Their biggest album was *Porcupine*, which got to no.2 in the album charts.

✔ 'Echo' was the drum machine, of course. He was replaced in 1980 by Pete De Freitas, but the name remained. De Freitas was killed in a motorbike accident in 1989.

✔ Bassist Les Pattinson was once in a band called The Jeffs, all of whose members were, logically, called Jeff.

♥ **Simple Minds** did 'Bring On The Dancing Horses' for their 2001 covers album *Neon Lights*. Other artists who have covered the Bunnymen include Hole ('Do It Clean') and Pavement ('The Killing Moon').

⏭ They might not fill venues as big as they used to, but they are still going strong and other recent songs like 'Don't Let It Get You Down' are worth checking out. They recently played at the Liverpool Institute for Performing Arts, where they went down a storm. Official website **www.bunnymen.com** has the latest information. You'll find stuff about their 'collectables' at: **www.geocities.com/SunsetStrip/Towers/7979**

Edelweiss ⋆

♪ **'Bring Me Edelweiss'** (1989, no.5)

Austria. Yes, it may have given the world some beautiful scenery, Arnold Schwarzenegger and Wolfgang Amadeus Mozart. Never forget, though, its over-priced mountain resorts and the small matter of a house-painter with one bollock and delusions of grandeur by the name of Adolf Schickelgruber. And, possibly to wreak terrible revenge on the rest of Europe for never having won the Eurovision Song Contest (oh, the wounds go deep in some corners of the Tyrol), they also inflicted this pungent slice of goat's cheese on us.

Essentially a housed-up bastardisation of the 1975 ABBA classic 'S.O.S.' – with added 'amusing' cowbell and yodelling noises – it's best listened to when very, very drunk indeed. Frighteningly, lots of people bought this when it came out (just look at the chart placing). This was 1989, though – the year when **Jive Bunny** and New Kids On The Block walked among us and the collapse of Communism seemed like a welcome bit of light relief.

Eighth Wonder ★★

♫ **'I'm Not Scared'** (1988, no.7)

Yes, it's the one with Patsy Kensit – who, halfway through 'I'm Not Scared', an enjoyable piece of atmospheric synth-pop, delivers some French lyrics in a deliciously good accent. And using a subjunctive. Some thought the big mystery with Eighth Wonder was what the moody blokes who stood at the back were actually employed for. Didn't Neil and Chris from the **Pet Shop Boys** do all the instrumentation? In fact, the band was founded by Patsy's brother, guitarist Jamie Kensit, and they had some overseas success with early singles 'Stay With Me' and the funk-poppish 'Will You Remember'.

The 1988 album *Fearless* was produced by Pete Hammond – except 'I'm Not Scared', which was indeed co-produced by Neil Tennant and Chris Lowe with Phil Harding. Oh, and they were first known as Spice, so does that make Patsy the original Posh Spice?

Their second UK single 'Cross My Heart' also made the Top 20 – so, next time someone calls them 'one-hit wonders', defend Patsy's honour.

✓ **The Pet Shop Boys'** own extended version of 'I'm Not Scared' turns up on their 1988 dance album *Introspective*.

✓ One of Ms Kensit's earliest TV roles was in a wacky children's sci-fi drama called *Luna*, shown in some ITV regions.

Electronic ★★★
♫ **'Getting Away With It'** (1989/90, no.12)

And we get away with it too, as the song just sneaks in at the very scrag-end of the 80s (it first charted in December 1989). Electronic are a 'supergroup', a perenially-resurgent joint project between Bernard 'deadpan' Sumner of **New Order** and Johnny 'he plays guitar' Marr, formerly (by this stage) of **The Smiths**. The first single features the **Pet Shop Boys** (yes, them again), Neil Tennant's lighter, ironic drawl perfectly setting off Sumner's endearing Mancunian whine. A crumb of hope, a ray of light, a diamond among the morass of crap which flooded 1989, 'Getting Away With It' was a breezy, shiny, clever piece of pop which made you wonder, just wonder, if things were actually going to be all right in the 90s after all. Listen to it today and it sounds as if it was recorded yesterday.

A patchily interesting album followed after a year or two, some of which sounded like a more jangly-acoustic **New Order** (especially 'Get The Message' and 'Tighten Up').

▶▶ They've recorded on and off in the 90s, collaborating with Karl Bartos from **Kraftwerk** on *Raise the Pressure* in 1996. *Twisted Tenderness* is their most recent album.

———————————

Enya ✶✶✶

♫ **'Orinoco Flow (Sail Away)'** (1988, no.1)

New age folk with a techno twist

If ever a year was crying out for a breath of fresh air at the top of the charts, it was 1988. And finally, it came – in the lissom shape of former Clannad vocalist Eithne Ní Bhraonáin, who had re-jigged her name to Enya for the purposes of pop stardom.

Variously described as 'mood music', 'New Age' and 'trancelike', Enya's albums have sold in their millions – she's had the occasional foray into the singles charts, although her first hit still remains her biggest. A most unlikely Number One, 'Orinoco Flow' sounded deep, intriguing and soulful, a mixture of Celtic folk voices, multi-layered synth-stabs and lush orchestration. Working with producer/arranger Nicky Ryan and lyricist Roma Ryan, Enya had made a classic. The follow-up 'Evening Falls' made the Top 20.

The international success of the album *Watermark* was phenomenal – eight million copies were sold worldwide. The beautiful songstress from Gweedore, County Donegal, went on to have even more success in the 90s and beyond, although live appearances are few and far between – possibly because the ethereal, multi-tracked sound of her songs would be hard to reproduce?

● The B-side of 'Evening Falls' was a haunting Gaelic version of 'Silent Night'. It ended up being played on breakfast-time Radio 1 in December 1988 following a news item about the Lockerbie air crash.

✔ Before 1988, Enya had been best known for her soundtrack to the BBC TV programme *The Celts*, re-released in the wake of *Watermark*. She had also scored the 1985 film *The Frog Prince*.

✔ Some of her album tracks are quiet piano instrumentals – which for some inexplicable reason Enya likes to name after the twee rural stories of writer Miss Read.

✔ Enya has let slip in interviews the rather astonishing – and intriguing – fact that she doesn't actually listen to music.

▸▸ Enya has recently recorded music for the *Lord of the Rings* movie. More at: **www.enyamusic.com**, the official site.

Erasure ★★★★

♫ **'Sometimes'** (1986, no.2)

Mr Flamboyant and Mr Dour

Let's state the obvious here. Erasure are camp. They are camper than camp. They are camper than Russell Grant, Dale Winton and Julian Clary all watching Judy Garland movies together in a pink tent. Once you've learned to accept that fact and enjoy it, they are really quite fun.

So many bands from the 1980s followed the tried-and-tested formula piloted by Sparks, namely putting a dour chap behind a keyboard and sticking an outlandish gentleman up front to sing the songs. Vince Clarke (yes, him again) did have a grand plan to record an album using ten different vocalists, but when Andy Bell came along, Clarke obviously realised he was the ideal front-man.

From the outset, Erasure sounded tightly commercial. They false-started with 'Who Needs Love Like That' (although it eventually became a hit as a remix), but from then on, everything they touched turned to gold. A particularly sparkly gold fabric, in fact, which would make a lovely pair of flares. Crisp keyboard sounds and catchy melodies were very much the order of the day, with the quality and prolific nature of their output matching that of the **Pet Shop Boys**, although in a rather more jaunty manner. 'Victim Of Love' and 'A Little Respect' are strong early songs, and with 'Blue Savannah' in 1990, Erasure proved they could also do haunting (Andy Bell called it a country-and-western song, if I remember correctly).

Their commercial zenith came with their EP of ABBA covers, 'ABBA-esque', in 1992. Here, the duo staked their claim to being a serious act by dragging up as Agnetha and Anni-Frid for the 'Take A Chance On Me' video. The one they shot for 'Lay All Your Love On Me' was the best, though – mainly used in mainland Europe, it had Andy riding a *Return of the Jedi*-style turbo-bike. (All right, not strictly 80s, that bit, but it counts as retro…)

✔ Pop's other Andy Bell – the one who was in Ride and Hurricane #1 in the 1990s and is now in Oasis – is, as far as we know, no relation.

✔ Vince Clarke said for years that they'd never use guitars on an Erasure album, but he didn't seem to mind them for live performances and acoustic radio sessions.

♥ **Dollar** covered 'Oh L'Amour'. Indie-guitar band

Wheatus did a very faithful version of 'A Little Respect' in 2001. The most amusing cover, though, has to be the double A-side of 'A Little Respect' and 'Stop' by the ersatz ABBA, Bjorn Again – it's the closest we'll ever get to ABBA returning the compliment and covering Erasure.

▶▶| Erasure made a triumphant return to the top 10 after nearly a decade in January 2003 with a cover of Peter Gabriel's 'Solsbury Hill', heralding an album of cover versions entitled *Other People's Songs*.

Eurythmics ★★★★
♫ **'Sweet Dreams (Are Made Of This)'** (1982, no.2)

A man who wears shades all the time, even indoors, and a woman with a prison-issue haircut made up one of the most popular duos of all time after the split of their first band The Tourists. Annie Lennox and David A. Stewart, as he liked to be known, were initially purveyors of thumping and slightly sinister synth-pop numbers like 'Love Is A Stranger' and 'Here Comes The Rain Again'. *Touch* was a no.1 album, while their soundtrack to the film *1984* helped to raise their profile even further, despite the slight problem of not actually being used in the final cut of the film. Everyone knows 'There Must Be An Angel' as a memorable mid-80s Number One single, a soaring melody introduced by Annie's unmistakable warble.

In 1986 they discovered Rock, possibly as a result of becoming a stadium-sized band, and 'Thorn In My Side' was probably the best thing to emerge from this period. A reversion to a more technological sound came with the album *Savage*, but the chart placings were dwindling. They returned briefly to form with *We Too Are One* before splitting at the end of the decade. Annie went on to solo success with a new, sophisticated image, while Dave Stewart concentrated on being a producer and a rent-a-guitar, as well as launching his wife Siobhan Fahey's band Shakespear's Sister and their spiritual inheritors, Alisha's Attic.

- ✔ In 1984, Annie married Rahda Raman, a German who was a follower of Hare Krishna. The marriage lasted six months.

- ✔ They would have played Live Aid in 1985, but Annie had a throat problem.

- 🔊 'The public image is Annie. It is like a duo but we've always made Annie the front of Eurythmics because she is a fantastic singer – great visually with herself and everything – and I have always been like this hovering-around kind of chap, a cross between a Scotch terrier and something else, pushing buttons and twiddling knobs.' Dave Stewart talking to *Record Mirror* in 1985.

- 🔊 'Most couples get famous and then break up. But we broke up and then got famous. Our first reaction was that it was impossible – to break up and still make music together. But the experience made us stronger.' Dave Stewart in the *Los Angeles Times*, 1986.

- 🔊 There's an unusual feeling about being close to someone so gifted. When they start to play – well, there it is, you know? I didn't really talk to him very much. I was a bit in awe of him, to be honest with you. And he wasn't there for long, but just before he left he hugged me and I remember being very

thrilled by that.' Annie Lennox on... who? Dave?
No, Andy Crane of Children's BBC. Oh, all right –
Stevie Wonder (who contributes a harmonica solo to
'There Must Be An Angel').

Everything but the Girl ★★★
♬ **'Each and Everyone'** (1984, no.28)

Ben Watt and Tracey Thorn formed their duo at Hull
University in 1982 after having brief solo ventures. Several
singles on indie label Blanco Y Negro followed, but a big
breakthrough came in 1988 with their cover of 'I Don't
Want To Talk About It' and the album *Idlewild*. It didn't
seem to make the miserable pair cheer up, though. Ben subsequently battled through a life-threatening illness, and the
band got a new lease of life in 1995 with the remix of
'Missing' and the 1996 drum'n'bass-influenced album
Walking Wounded.

✔ Tracey's 1982 solo album *A Distant Shore* cost only
£120 to record and sold over 60,000 copies, a con-
siderable success for independent label Cherry Red.

✔ The name came from a shop selling bedroom furniture – 'for your bedroom needs we sell everything
but the girl'. Ah, those innocent days when PC just
meant your local bobby.

pause

f

fish'n'chips, football pages

Fairground Attraction ★ ★ ★

♪ **'Perfect'** (1988, no.1)

Folky, low-tech and skiffle-tinged pop fronted by the delightful Eddi Reader, a girl in a beret and glasses at whom, I'm sure, many men made passes. Mark E. Nevin, Simon Edwards and Roy Dodds were the other members, and together they made what was surely the unlikeliest Number One of the decade with 'Perfect'. Follow-up 'Find My Love', with its pleasant Spanish guitar, also made the Top 10, and the diverse debut album *First Of A Million Kisses* peaked at no.2. The other singles 'A Smile In A Whisper' and 'Clare', although equally melodic, didn't graze the Top 40.

Perhaps they were over-rated back then, but you have to remember that this was 1988, a year when chart records were increasingly made by computers, performed by robots and listened to by drug-addled morons in smiley T-shirts. A band which proudly displayed some real instruments, played some real songs – and did not feel the need to use the phrase 'check *dis* out' – was to be treasured.

Their one and only UK tour consisted of six sold-out shows in June-July 1989; they broke up in 1990, after which Eddi Reader launched a successful solo career.

✔ Reader and Nevin had previously worked together in a group called The Academy of Fine Popular Music.

✔ 'Perfect' won Best Single and *First Of A Million Kisses* Best Album at the Brits in 1989.

▶▶ Mark Nevin is also touring and recording: details at his site, **www.marknevin.com**

Falco ★★

♫ 'Rock Me Amadeus' (1986, no.1)

The world's second most famous Austrian paid tribute to his musical-prodigy countryman in this astonishing, absurd piece of pomp-rock in 1986.

If you have ever been to Salzburg, home of Wolfgang Amadeus, you will know how seriously they take the branding of their most famous son. (Even Liverpool doesn't do its job as efficiently, and they had four Beatles to exploit.) Mozart commercialism reaches its absurd zenith in a chocolate confection which you can buy from most Salzburg gift-shops, and which goes under the endearing name of Mozartkugeln – literally, 'Mozart's Balls'. Falco's homage, a jaunty rock-out in silly wigs, seems almost reverential by comparison.

Falco, whose real name was Johann (or Hans) Hölzel, achieved the unlikely feat of rapping in German and not sounding too much like a Dalek, for which we should be grateful. 'Rock Me Amadeus' had come as a worldwide breakthrough single after a few years' success in Austria and Germany. Follow-up single 'Vienna Calling' was also a UK hit, but then he slipped away from view despite producing further singles and albums.

Falco emigrated to the Dominican Republic in 1996. He died after his car was involved in a collision with a coach in February 1998, and the album *Out Of The Dark* was released posthumously.

◁ 'With 'Rock Me Amadeus' I had a huge hit and was without a contract. That doesn't usually happen. When a German record company offered me a five-million-Mark contract, I signed. You take five million if they're offered to you. In the end it actually harmed me more, because with 'Amadeus' I wasn't hot any more. There had already been alcohol excesses. 'Amadeus' was the beginning of the end for me.' (From his last interview, for *Bunte* in 1998. Translation by Clarissa Carim.)

The Fall ★★★
♫ **'There's A Ghost In My House'** (1987, no.30)

Why are people grouchy?
Like **The Smiths**, The Fall are one of those influential bands you have to be nice about whether you personally like them or not. Now, I imagine I can be as rude as I like about, say, **Sonia** or **Big Fun**, as most of their fans will have treated them as a passing fad and their effect on the musical zeitgeist can be said to be fleeting, at best. But I have never really seen the attraction of the shambling Mark E. Smith (the grumpiest man in rock) and his vocal tic of adding the syllable '-uh!' to the end of most lines. And so I'll have to be ready to cower from the wrath of a few thousand enraged fans ready to set fire to the book and throw buckets of cold water (or worse) over me at readings.

So, let's do something like this: 'The stuff of cults, led by the charismatic Mark E. Smith, The Fall were one of the decade's best-kept secrets. Their dearth of Top 40 singles shows that they were far too good for the charts and belies their status as one of the country's most prolific bands, who have produced album after album to the delight of their dedicated followers. They've been going since 1976 and have survived more than 30 line-up changes, so they must be doing something right. And *Hex Enduction Hour* is a great album title.'

That was all right, wasn't it?

That Top 30 hit in 1987 must have seemed like the start of a breakthrough, but they've remained an underground band, largely unplayed on the radio except by their tireless champion, the avuncular headmaster of pop, John Peel. You can usually guarantee that a Fall track or three will make his annual Festive Fifty on Radio 1. Or, as Mark E. Smith would say, 'the festive-uh! fifty-uh! on Ray-dee-oh One-uh!'

- 🎧 Smith guested on the Inspiral Carpets' 1994 hit 'I Want You', which, at no.18, got higher than any Fall track to date.

- ✔ The star ratings aren't definitive, you know. Please feel free to pencil in an extra one rather than hitting me.

- ✔ The Fall's first (and to date biggest) Top 40 hit 'There's A Ghost In My House' is a cover of a Tamla Motown song by R. Dean Taylor which was a no.3 hit in 1974.

- ✔ **www.visi.com/fall/intro.html** is a good place to find links to a discography, lyrics, and details of all of The Fall's gigs past and present. Someone obviously has a lot of time to spare. Uh.

Karel Fialka ★★

🎵 **'Hey Matthew'** (1987, no.9)

Born in Bengal of Scots-Czech parentage, and apparently 'discovered' by Tim Hart of Steeleye Span fame, he'd threatened the charts in 1980 with 'The Eyes Have It'. However, in the UK, a little ditty about his 8-year-old son Matthew's reaction to various aspects of popular culture gave Mr Fialka his best-known hit. It goes like this: Matthew does a litany of all the things he allegedly watches on TV, followed by another about what he wants to be when he grows up. Dad, meanwhile, sings in a worried, monotonous way above a 'Stop The Cavalry' beat about the effect all this TV violence will be having on him. 'It's all a game...I hope,' says Matthew at the end, obviously making it all terribly deep and meaningful. It was different, anyway, and had a catchy flute leit-motif running through it, but Karel never looked entirely comfortable.

● At **tv.cream.org/arktop.htm** there's a rare glimpse of the *Top Of The Pops* performance of 'Hey Matthew'.

✔ That list of Matthew's viewing habits in full: *Dallas, Dynasty, Terrahawks, He-Man, Tom and Jerry, The Dukes of Hazzard, Airwolf, Blue Thunder, Rambo, Road Runner, Daffy Duck, The A-Team.* And this was in the days when a mixture of cartoons and vapid American imports was not all that kids had to choose from...

✔ One of the backing vocalists on Karel's album *Human Animal* was Colin Blunstone of the 60s band The Zombies.

Fiction Factory ★★

♫ **'(Feels Like) Heaven'** (1984, no.6)

A great name – and their one hit, as well as sporting a title with fine use of brackets, certainly has that tingle factor and is instantly recognisable. Featuring one of those wistful, very 80s one-finger keyboard solos accompanied by a resonant, New Romantic-ish voice, it makes you want to go and walk along a beach at dawn in your long, serious coat, with the foam crashing on to the pebbles and the wind ruffling your collar-length hair, while thinking maudlin thoughts of your lost love. Well, if it doesn't, then it should.

The voice belonged to one Kevin Patterson from Perth (who had studied music therapy at Anniesland and Perth colleges and at the then Dundee Institute of Technology). He was ably assisted by bassist Graham McGregor, keyboard player Eddie Jordan, a drummer with the mildly amusing moniker of Mike Ogletree, and a guitarist whose name, rather wonderfully redolent of 70s disco, was Chic Medley. They did have some other pretty good songs, like the very Heaven 17-ish 'Hit the Mark' from the first album *Throw The Warped Wheel Out*, and they supported both **Paul Young** and **Orchestral Manoeuvres In The Dark**, too. They made a second album, *Another Story*, before they finally split in 1987.

✔ '(Feels Like) Heaven' was Number One in Switzerland and the song was also a big hit in Italy and Germany.

▸▸ Kevin now works in IT services at the University of Dundee. He did the *Never Mind The Buzzcocks* line-up thing a while back and was picked out by regular panellist Sean Hughes, who claimed to be a big fan...

Fine Young Cannibals ★★★★

♫ **'Johnny Come Home'** (1985, no.8)

Rock-edged anthropophagi

Lit up the latter half of the decade with some splendid singles and two albums which, together, sold around 5 million copies. Roland Gift first teamed up with two former members of The Beat, Andy Cox and David Steele (no relation to the diminutive Scottish Liberal), in 1984. They named their band after the 1960 film *All The Fine Young Cannibals* which starred Robert Wagner and Natalie Wood.

Their best stuff still stands up very well today, hardly sounding dated in comparison with some of their contemporaries. There's 'She Drives Me Crazy' with its funky bassline and jagged guitar opening, 'Good Thing' with its jazzy piano (courtesy of Jools Holland) and their pleasantly uncluttered cover of 'Suspicious Minds' with Jimmy Somerville on backing vocals. A bit of unsubtle political commentary in 'Blue' and a great re-interpretation of a Buzzcocks classic 'Ever Fallen In Love' were also thrown into the mix.

The Cannibals then memorably spent 6 years doing a bit of a Stone Roses, trying to make that elusive next album. They had the dignity to call it a day with a compilation and new FYC-by-numbers one-off single, 'The Flame', in 1996.

🎧 'She Drives Me Crazy', from second album *The Raw and the Cooked*, chugs along with a great riff and a jittery rhythm; probably the best encapsulation of their sound. 'Good Thing' was uniformly voted a 'Hit' by the panel on the brief 80s revival of *Juke Box Jury*.

✔ Cox and Steele performed on two house records in 1988 as Two Men, A Drum Machine And A Trumpet – the top 20 hit 'I'm Tired of Getting Pushed Around', and 'Heat It Up', with the Wee Papa Girl Rappers.

✔ What is it with these mid-80s artists and their former incarnations in idiotically-named punk outfits? Gift's was a Hull band called Acrylic Victims...

🔊 'It is wrong and inappropriate for us to be associated

with what amounts to a photo opportunity for Margaret Thatcher and the Conservative Party.' The band's statement on returning their two BRIT Awards for Best British Album and Best British Group, in February 1990.

◁ɯ 'People listen to every song in a different way, and you need to give them space to do that. If a film plot is over-explained, you might as well not be there as it's all done for you.' Roland Gift.

▶▶ǀ Gift has acted in films including *Scandal* and *Sammy and Rosie Get Laid*, and he relaunched his solo singing career with the single 'It's Only Money' in 2002. Cox, meanwhile, performs with his new band Crybaby.

▶▶ǀ FYC re-formed for a series of UK gigs in December 2002, kicking off at Sheffield's Leadmill.

Five Star ★★★

♬ 'All Fall Down' (1985, no.15)

We are family

They were shiny, choreographed down to the last flick, dressed to match in ultimate 80s designs and burnished with glitter. Oh, and they were Stedman, Doris, Lorraine, Deniece and Delroy. Just for the record. Encouraged – some might say unduly so – by their ambitious dad, Buster (aka Stedman senior), the perky quintet had a dozen songs in the top 20 in the latter half of the 80s, two of which, 'System Addict' and 'Rain Or Shine', were Top Three hits. The 1986 album *Silk and Steel* was huge, going triple platinum.

You might think having lots of hits and lots of money was a sure-fire route to success and happiness, but the Five

Star story is something of a salutary one. Bankruptcy loomed, and an auction of their silver discs and stage costumes in 1992 raised the princely sum of £1593. (Even worse, they were all bought by the producers of *Star Trek: Deep Space Nine*. No, not really.)

Lorraine has recently tried to resurrect Five Star with her brother Stedman and sister Deniece. Presumably no one likes to point out that there are no longer five of them. (Coming in 2018: the S Club 7 reunion featuring, um, both Tina and Bradley! Yeah!)

🎧 There is a *Greatest Hits* album (for once, a collection worthy of the name) released in 1989 with, surprisingly, only moderate success. Perhaps they were seen as being past their sell-by date.

💣 Saturday morning TV proved a chastening experience for them, as it did for **Matt Bianco**, when one young caller to *Going Live* was clearly heard to ask the group why they were 'so fucking crap'. The miscreant was cut off by the BBC switchboard, but not soon enough – embarrassing for the band, amusing for the rest of us and essential for pop history. It was almost as good when we all got a lecture from Sarah Greene afterwards. (Sarah *Greene!* Yes, I bet she's never said a naughty word in her life.)

💣 They had an odd approach to fame. Disney offered to give them their own show in 1985, but dad/manager Buster, for his own reasons, declined. Five Star also turned down an invitation to support **Wham!** at their farewell Wembley concert.

💣 However, Stedman did have a **George Michael** moment in 1990 when he was fined for public indecency in a toilet in, of all places, New Malden. Stedman, we salute you.

✔ Their 1986 tour was sponsored by a chocolate bar. Their 1987 tour was sponsored by a toothpaste company. Please draw your own conclusions.

✔ Lorraine had a book published in 1988 called *Her, Me and Reality*, and she continues to write children's stories.

✔ **www.angelfire.com/band/fivestar/tfss.html** is an online fanzine, if you're into that sort of thing. It aims to 'provide Five Star fans with a variety of articles, reviews and features spanning the career of the Pearson siblings'.

A Flock of Seagulls ★★★
♬ **'Space Age Love Song'** (1982, no.34)

Wing and a haircut

Everyone remembers A Flock Of Seagulls for their remarkable fringe sculptures of gravity-defying proportions. Well, this was in the days before people started worrying about CFCs. It should come as no surprise at all to hear that lead singer Mike Score was a professional coiffeur, although with a name like that he should perhaps have been a football pundit.

Originally called Tontrix, they signed to Jive/Arista after changing their name, and their debut single 'Telecommunication' in 1981 became an underground dance hit in the US. It's debatable if they fitted into the New Romantic slot, but their sound was at the more atmospheric end of 80s electro-pop. Surprisingly, 'I Ran', one of their best songs, only got to no.43 in the UK, but heavy

MTV rotation of the song led to transatlantic success.

▶▶ After a couple of albums failed to chart in the mid-80s and the original band dissolved, Mike Score took a new line-up out on the road in 1989. They continue to tour, with the occasional change in personnel. **www.oz.net/~davester/AFOS** is an extensive fan site with a discography, lyrics etc.

Samantha Fox ★ ★

♪ **'Touch Me (I Want Your Body)'** (1986, no.3)

TOTP or bust

Here's another shy and retiring flower. Samantha Karen Fox was born April 15, 1966, in Mile End, London, to parents Patrick and Carole, and had two childhood dreams: to become a policewoman or a singer. Voted 'Face And Shape of 1983' by that august organ the *Sunday People* (presumably amid tough competition from Limahl, Shirley Williams and Bridget 'The Midget' McCluskey), Sam ended up with an exclusive contract for topless modelling with the *Sun*. She was a favourite with builders, lorry-drivers and fervent onanists everywhere – thanks to what was usually described as her 'chirpy personality' and 'ample assets' – but when she made the crossover into the charts, cynics had their doubts.

However, her suggestive first single achieved the twin peaks of a UK Top Three hit and European stardom. Sam went down especially well in Scandinavia: just goes to show that those philosophical Nordics, while they might spend hours watching ethereal sunsets over magnificent fjords and snowcapped mountains while reading and producing profound theatrical masterpieces of existential angst, are still partial to a bird with fit jugs.

Sam's songwriters and producers did rather seem to

want to market the 'sex goddess' angle with every subsequent release. Hmmm... for some reason, the peroxide, the denim jackets and the open-fingered gloves just didn't do it for me. Sam was always going to be a fish'n'chips, football-pages kind of girl, and so she came across as something of a one-dimensional lust object. The *NME* grudgingly admitted she could sing, but compared her act to a lunchtime stripper in a crowded pub, while *The Beat* suggested that her songs were an encouragement to the violation of women. Oops.

- A shambolic performance hosting the 1989 Brit Awards left Sam and fellow host Mick Fleetwood trying to cover up some embarrassing boobs. (Although, to be fair, Sam has since given a plausible explanation of how it wasn't their fault.)

- 'Just because I've got blonde hair and big boobs, people think I'm dumb and can't do anything but smile.' (Sam stands up to her knockers.)

- Proclaimed her newfound status as a celibate born-again Christian before, in a bizarre twist, apparently announcing to the world that she was a lesbian. Oh, but recently she's been back in the business again! 1998 single 'Santa Maria' was 'funky and sexy, just like my new look', apparently. This all suggests there may be more to come, so let's, ah, keep abreast...

Frankie Goes To Hollywood ★★★★★

♫ **'Relax'** (1984, no.1)

Been there, done that, bought the T-shirt
Multi-media phenomenon making a bid for controversy at

the heart of the decade. Frankie's paean to delayed gratification became the most famous *cause célèbre* of the 1980s singles charts – surely everyone knows the story of how they famously managed to provoke the ire of the nation's moral arbiter, Mike Read. (Just to clarify, that's *not* the rather intimidating Mike Reid With An I, that cross between a barrow-boy and a thuggish PE teacher who regularly exhorted teams of cowed children to 'Runaraaaaahhnd, naaaah!' in the 1970s. This is Mike Read With An A, he of the big glasses, shaggy hair and bad poetry.)

In fact, Read was so outraged to find a record with the word 'come' in the lyrics and a suggestive 'Uhh' sound in the middle that he trashed a copy on-air. Now, I'm all for the wilful destruction of self-consciously bad art. Those Japanese gentlemen who set about Tracey Emin's bed 'exhibit' have my full approval; I only wish they'd put a match to it. And if Mr Read had taken an axe to 'The Birdie Song', or indeed fed one of his own slim volumes of excruciating doggerel into the BBC shredder live on *Saturday Superstore*, we could all have sympathised. The problem with the Frankie incident, though, was twofold: first, 'Relax' is actually a rather good pop record in its silly, bombastic, over-produced way, and secondly, it was the best publicity stunt any act could have wished for.

The band, originally called Hollycaust, had been shaped for stardom by producer Trevor Horn. With a little of their leather-and-bondage imagery toned down, they were ready for their assault on the charts – although the lavishly Bacchanalian video was initially banned as well, and only eventually got an airing late at night on *The Tube*. Combined with Mike Read's over-reaction, this was more than enough to propel the single to Number One, and to keep it in the charts for a staggering 48 weeks between November 1983 and October 1984.

Thunderous nuclear-angst anthem 'Two Tribes' and

obligatory Christmas ballad 'The Power Of Love' were the follow-ups, and both also topped the UK charts, making Frankie only the second act in history to score a hat-trick with their first three releases (following fellow Scousers Gerry and the Pacemakers). Subsequent singles obeyed the law of diminishing returns, as the band lost steam and the public lost interest.

- Frankie didn't really amass enough singles for a *Greatest Hits*, but this, like being dead, is no obstacle to record company executives. The collection *Bang!* is out there, while *Reload* features the dubious remixes from the early 90s.

- The 'New York 12-inch mix' of 'Relax' maintains the song's integrity while giving it a menacing edge – worth hearing.

- Talking of being dead, I'm sure Holly Johnson would appreciate another refutation of the rumours of his demise. His solo chart career consisted of three top 20 singles at the end of the decade ('Love Train', 'Americanos' and 'Atomic City') plus participation in the charity version of 'Ferry 'Cross The Mersey'. He was diagnosed HIV-positive in the 1990s, but he's still very much with us in the 21st century – he has exhibited his artwork at Liverpool's Bluecoat Galleries and the Tate, among others, and released the album *Soulstream* in 1999.

- A rough version of the 'Relax' video was filmed in the basement of a Liverpool pub called the Hope and Anchor. According to Holly Johnson, the landlord initially tried to stop them filming when he thought they were making a pornographic movie.

- ✔ The famous 'Frankie Says…' T-shirts were designed by journalist Paul Morley, who, to his eternal chagrin, took a one-off payment rather than a royalty.

- ♥ Beware of fakes! A 'phoney' Frankie, featuring no connection with the real band and none of the original members, has been doing the rounds in the US and has recently hit Europe. I love the idea that the dance halls and community centres of Cologne, Barcelona and Geneva are being plagued by the evil doubles of long-defunct 80s bands. International pop detectives are getting on the case right now to smoke out the Machiavellian impersonators of **Toto Coelo** and the android replicas of **Curiosity Killed The Cat**. There is a 22-episode TV series in it, I'm sure.

Freiheit ★★

♫ **'Keeping The Dream Alive'** (1989, no.14)

A rare foray from Germany into the English charts. Now, they may have brought us **Nena** and **Kraftwerk**, which is all well and good – but do remember that this is a country where a man going by the unlikely moniker of Roberto Blanco can host a prime-time, Saturday night TV show entirely devoted to folk song. It's also a place where David Hasselhoff, who would surely be arrested for crimes against rock if he were ever extradited to the UK, not only gets away with peddling his dismal musical cow-dung but is actually revered for it.

Somewhat surprisingly, then, Freiheit's only chart offering is not bad – it's a slow-building, lush ballad, whose elegantly harmonising vocals recall Queen at their best. The band, centred around singer Stefan Zauner and guitarist

Aron Strobel, are also known in Germany as Münchener Freiheit, and had several successful albums in their native land before taking the inevitable commercial plunge into the English-speaking market. You tend to know it's Christmas when you hear this on the radio.

✓ The album *Fantasie*, from which the hit came, was recorded in both German and English; the original of 'Keeping The Dream Alive' was called *'So lang' man Träume noch leben kann'*. Anybody wanting to read dodgy political symbolism into such words being sung by strapping lads with fine heads of blond hair should be advised not to be so silly. After all, Germany's most successful musical exports were Boney M, and they're hardly prime examples of Aryan genetic engineering.

Furniture ★★★

♫ **'Brilliant Mind'** (1986, no.21)

Before the stripped pine and minimalist chic of Ikea, there was the black-ash, chrome-tube urban sophistication of Habitat. However, none of this has anything to do with our latest band, who are perhaps a prime example of an act being bogged down by one overplayed track at the expense of the rest of their work. The icy, moody and catchy single may well be brilliant, but fans particularly rate the albums *The Wrong People* (1986) and *Food, Sex and Paranoia* (1990). 30,000 copies of *The Wrong People* were pressed and sold out incredibly quickly, but the record company Stiff didn't capitalise on this success.

Reportage suggests (is that vague enough?) that they were finally victims of record company politics at BMG – they were signed along with a whole host of other acts, all of which were dropped except the most successful. And that victor turned out to be Lisa Stansfield. It doesn't seem a fair trade-off, somehow.

🎧 The 1991 compilation *She Gets Out The Scrapbook,* containing tracks chosen by band members, is probably the best way of getting a Furniture fix these days.

🔊 'I liked the fact that we looked unlikely... while everything was New Romanticism and electronica, we were trying to do a kind of funky John Barry thing (which, of course, became the norm about a decade later)...' Singer/percussionist Jim Irvin.

⏭ Jim Irvin is now a journalist at *Mojo* magazine. Hamilton Lee (vocals/drums) and Tim Whelan (guitar and vocals) formed Transglobal Underground in the 1990s. Bassist Sally Still became a writer.

Fuzzbox: see **We've Got A Fuzzbox And We're Gonna Use It**

pause

G

getting a bit of a leg-up

Debbie Gibson ★★★

⊘ Deborah Gibson ♫ 'Shake Your Love' (1988, no.7)

Rah-rah-rah... the cheerleader of American pop, the Britney of the 80s. Debbie had a penchant for posing with cuddly toys, wearing stripy tops and open-kneed lace trousers, but we didn't object.

The precocious Debbie started writing songs as a child, including one when she was six called 'Make Sure You Know Your Classroom' and another aged twelve entitled 'I Come From America', which won a competition and ultimately led to her professional career being managed by Doug Breithart. She hit the UK charts seven times in six years, getting a bit of a leg-up by becoming Sandy in the West End production of *Grease* (alongside Craig McLachlan) and releasing the obvious cover of 'You're The One That I Want'.

✔ When 'Foolish Beat' hit the top of the charts in the US in 1988, Debbie was the youngest person ever to write, perform and produce a Number One single. 'Lost In Your Eyes' was also an American Number One for her a few months later, but it only scraped to no.34 here.

▶▶ After being a Broadway star, Debbie's return to pop in 1995 involved the rather surprising move of recording with an LA punk band, The Circle Jerks. She's since done more solo albums: *Think With Your Heart* and *What You Want*. These days, she prefers the more mature moniker of Deborah. Bless her.

Glenn & Chris ✱

♪ 'Diamond Lights' (1987, no.12)

Well, here's an interesting career move. If you don't actually know who this pair were, then you might have a bit of a shock – and no, they're not Difford and Tilbrook from **Squeeze**...

Up until now, you may have thought Mr G. Hoddle's most embarrassing moment was the misguidedly un-PC comment about reincarnation and disability which led to his resignation as England manager, while Mr C. Waddle's was that agonising missed penalty in the 1990 World Cup. Wrong! Years earlier (twelve and three years respectively, in fact) this pair of footballing gentlemen had appeared on *Top Of The Pops* – besuited, distressingly mulleted, almost miming in time and dancing like two dads at a wedding.

To be fair, Hoddle'n'Waddle probably did it for a laugh – both Spurs players at the time, they were about to appear in the 1987 FA Cup Final – but the worrying thing is that the song itself, a bombastic piece of power-pop, is actually not *that* awful. Still, both the perpetrators will be haunted by the shattered dreams of England fans, so they probably have worse nightmares than this.

- ✔ The drummer behind them on *Top Of The Pops* looked a bit like the England goalkeeper, David Seaman. I'm assured it wasn't him, which is a great shame.

- ✔ England footballers who also scored in the charts include Kevin Keegan with 'Head Over Heels In Love' in 1979 and Paul 'Gazza' Gascoigne with 'Fog On The Tyne (Revisited)' in 1990. David Beckham has had the dignity not to make a record so far (despite the rumours he might perform the rap on **New Order's** re-issued 'World in Motion' in 2002).

Go West ★★★

♫ 'We Close Our Eyes' (1985, no.5)

Peter Cox and Richard Drummie got together in 1974 when Richard took a liking to Peter's demo tape. Originally, they sported the frighteningly original name of Cox and Drummie, but they became Go West in time to record their first material, whose sound was described as 'Modern Motown'. It wasn't much different, in truth, from a lot of melodious, smoothly-produced mid-80s pop. The duo formed the core of the band, and used a number of backing musicians including guitarist Alan Murphy and Austrian keyboard-player Peter Wolf.

They had four UK hits in 1985, including their best-known song 'We Close Our Eyes', then made a surprise return in 1990 with 'The King Of Wishful Thinking', included on the soundtrack to *Pretty Woman*.

🎧 *Aces & Kings* was first the inevitable hits collection, but the newly-packaged *The Best Of Go West* was released in 2001.

✔ Peter's first band, which he formed at the age of 18, was called Bodie.

✔ Their song 'One Way Street' was featured on the soundtrack to *Rocky IV*, apparently because Sylvester Stallone had heard their album and liked it.

✔ Comeback single 'The King of Wishful Thinking', which got to no.18 in the UK, was a chart-topper in Canada.

⏭ Go West joined the 'Let's Go Round Again' Tour of nineteen UK venues in 2002, along with Nick

Heyward (ex-**Haircut 100**) and Ben Volpelière-Pierrot (ex-**Curiosity Killed the Cat**). Peter Cox's site is at **www.petercox.zen.co.uk** and has updates on all his latest activities.

Jaki Graham ★★
🎵 'Could It Be I'm Falling In Love' (1985, no.5, with David Grant)

Ahh, those 80s spellings. Back in our spiky decade when the forenames were as priceless as the haircuts, most school classrooms could probably boast a Rik, a Nik, a Ja(k)ki, a Vikki or a Bekki.

This particular Jaki was born in Birmingham and worked as a secretary, singing in bands in the evenings before being 'discovered'. 'Round and Round' and 'Set Me Free' were further top hits; although she never visited the UK Top 5 again, she's still recording and performing all around the world. Her recording of 'Ain't Nobody' went to the top of the Billboard dance chart in the 1990s.

I wonder if she signed her name with a little flower over the 'i'?

✔ On Kim Wilde's album *Love Moves*, Jaki provided some bakking vocals – sorry, backing vocals.

Eddy Grant ★★★
🎵 'Living on the Front Line' (1979, no.11)

Born in Guyana in 1948, Eddy Grant was the former singer with 60s band The Equals. After suffering a heart attack in 1971 he seemed to gain a new lease of life, setting up his own record label, Ice, and having hits throughout the 1980s like 'Do You Feel My Love', 'Electric Avenue', the disingenuously-titled Number One 'I Don't Wanna Dance' and the anti-apartheid protest song 'Gimme Hope Jo'Anna'. A multi-instrumentalist, Eddy performed everything on his hits, which led to problems with TV performances and the need to hire some stooges to mime on the instruments for him. Still in the business, he was back in the public eye in 2001 with some judicious remixes.

- ✔ In 2001, Brixton was featured in an English Heritage advertising campaign. One full-page advert showed Eddy Grant leaning against a wall in Brixton's Electric Avenue, accompanied by the slogan 'English Heritage – It's Mine'.

- ✔ Eddy sees a correlation between his success and the length of his hair, and so he hasn't been to a barber since the 1960s.

- 🔊 'Generally remixes are things I'm not in love with because most people don't make a very good job of my tracks. But Peter Black, who's worked on this record [the Ringbang mix of 'Electric Avenue'], has done a great job. I said to him that if he finds anything else that he likes, have a go!'

pause

H

huge hair and huge voices

Haircut 100 ★ ★ ★
♫ **'Favourite Shirts (Boy Meets Girl)'** (1981, no.4)

Barbers' adagio

Once again, we find ourselves indirectly celebrating all matters trichological, as we encounter Nick Heyward's brand of perky new-wave pop. The band came from Beckenham in Kent, that county also famous for hops, apples and Anne Widdecombe. Heyward's partners in crime were initially bassist Les Nemes and guitarist Graham Jones, from Croydon and Bridlington respectively. The line-up was subsequently bolstered by three more Haircutters: Harlem-born drummer Memphis Blair Cunningham (who later found his way into The Pretenders) saxophonist Phil Smith and percussionist Mark Fox.

The hits kept coming for a couple of years, 'Love Plus One' being the most memorable, and they got the album *Pelican West* under their belt. Unfortunately the **Kajagoogoo** syndrome struck, with lead singer Heyward wanting to pursue a solo career and the band struggling on without him when he left in 1983. Mark Fox took up the vocal duties for Paint On Paint, but it was all over bar the shouting and they soon went their separate ways.

Something for the weekend, sir?

🎧 A *Best Of* was released in 1989, and *The Greatest Hits of Nick Heyward and Haircut 100* in 1996.

✔ What was so fearful about that lake in 'Love Plus One'? We may never know.

🔊 'The way I look at it, I like the word popular as in pop music, but… credibility is… when you are enormously successful like ABBA. They are credible for me. A band that just sells 20,000 records and then disappears, or does some gig at Glastonbury and is all right one minute and then crap the next – that's not credibility to me. That's shit. Boring. And I was in that market. I'm never going to feel comfortable in that.' (Nick Heyward)

▶▶ Nick Heyward's solo career proved quite fruitful, with several albums and hits such as 'Whistle Down The Wind', 'Take That Situation' and 'Warning Sign'. The 'Let's Go Round Again' Tour of 2002 featured Nick, along with **Go West** and Ben Volpelière-Pierrot of **Curiosity Killed The Cat**.

Half Man Half Biscuit ★★★

Surrealist indie genius

Yes, OK, they've never had any top 40 hits. The very idea. But they did top the indie charts twice, and I'm not leaving them out, because for me, memories of the late 80s would be incomplete without them. If you don't find the idea of songs called 'All I Want For Christmas Is A Dukla Prague Away Kit' and 'I Hate Nerys Hughes' to be remotely amusing, then I would suggest skipping ahead to the next section, which is a good one and has **Imagination** in it.

Describing Birkenhead band Half Man Half Biscuit is a little bit like trying to explain why a joke is funny, or taking apart a butterfly to see how it works. Shambolic, surreal, idiotic, brilliant and quirky – none of these adjectives will quite do justice to singer-songwriter-guitarist Nigel Blackwell and his band. They were once described in a review as 'much more than a soggy digestive in the coffee cup of life', and seemed to be reluctant stars, turning down appearances on *The Tube* in favour of watching Tranmere Rovers.

With their tuneless guitars, wailing keyboards and deadpan vocals, HMHB painted vignettes of the eccentricities of daily life. Their songs were interlaced with childhood memories, tellingly nostalgic brand-names and an obsession with C-list celebrities. Their classic album *Back In The DHSS* contains the best version of the Trumpton theme tune you will ever hear ('Let it happen, bass player') and pastiches musical styles from **The Pogues** to punk and psychobilly. They split in 1986 but re-formed in 1990, and although the musicianship has become more polished, the sense of the absurd remains intact. One recent album was called *Trouble Over Bridgewater* – how brilliant is that?

✔ My sources tell me the HMHB track 'It's Clichéd To Be Cynical At Christmas' has been heard playing in the background in various episodes of *Hollyoaks* and *Brookside*.

Halo James ★★

♫ **'Could Have Told You So'** (1989, no.6)

So many names float on the wreckage of the 80s, those who either flashed in the pan or went down it... Anyway, this is another act who just got a foot in the door before we slammed the decade shut and deemed it sealed for posterity. The hit is perky and melodic, one of those songs which you sometimes hear on commercial radio's 'oldies' slot on a Sunday morning and which makes you stop and go 'Who the hell was *that*?'

Well, they were Christian James, Ray St. John and Neil Palmer, and they sneaked into the charts just before Christmas 1989. The band rather prophetically sang that they could have told you so, and that they could have told you dreams would come and go – they turned out to be a one-hit wonder, although previous single 'Wanted' had stalled just outside the Top 40 three months earlier and there was an album, *Witness*.

Perhaps they suffered from being marketed to rival the likes of **Big Fun** and **Brother Beyond**. It's still a top song, though.

✔ They may well have got their name from Halo Jones, a character in one of Alan Moore's *2000 AD* comic strips.

Happy Mondays ✶✶✶
♪ **'Madchester Rave On EP'** (1989, no.19)

Pills, thrills and silly haircuts
Pronounced 'Appy Moon-dayes'. Spent the 80s as the maverick Factory label's underground heroes, back when Shaun Ryder's hair was still glossy and floppy. The Mondays were formed in 1981 by Shaun and Paul Ryder and masterminded by the ubiquitous Factory boss, Anthony H. Wilson. They released their first album, the memorably-titled *Squirrel And G-Man Twenty Four Hour Party People Plastic Face Carnt Smile (White Out)*, in 1987, resulting in mixed critical reaction (see below) and numerous amusing attempts to deconstruct the title.

Their image helped – basically, they were lager louts on something stronger than lager – and they played it up for all it was worth. The fact that Shaun Ryder couldn't sing for, well, any item of confectionery you care to name, didn't seem to matter when brother Paul on bass and Gaz Whelan on drums were belting out chuggy, danceable rhythms.

And Bez – oh, how could anyone forget Bez? Officially credited on the album sleeves with providing 'vibes', Bez had the role of gyrating like a demented loon, often with a pair of maracas aloft and sometimes (but usually not) in time to the music. (A side-note: people who have read my novel *Losing Faith* – there may be a few dozen – will remember that my fictional 80s band, deVice, employed the skills of two attractive young women to perform the lyrics in sign-language on either side of the stage. When I put that detail in, I think I must have been subconsciously thinking of Bez, who was so obviously making frantic attempts to sign Ryder's gibberish for the hearing-impaired.)

1988's 'Wrote For Luck' from the album *Bummed* almost got them into the charts with a Vince Clarke remix, and this was a pointer for the future – Wilson hit on the idea of having the band work with remixers Paul Oakenfold and Steve Osborne, and behold, indie-dance crossover was born... 'Hallelujah', from the influential 'Madchester Rave On EP', gained a textured, chunky feel, stormed into the Top 20 and kicked the backside of a dismal year for music.

Then it all went baggy, of course, with the anthems everybody knows: 'Step On', 'Kinky Afro' and 'Loose Fit'. Yes, thanks in part to the Mondays, **New Order**, the Hacienda and other Factory Records baggage, popular culture went huge on Mancunian cool in the late 80s and early 90s. In practice, this probably amounted to lots of students growing unnecessarily long fringes, wearing flares and orange tops, pretending to have taken E and saying 'Top one!' and 'Sorted!' a lot, even if they were from Hertfordshire. It also meant we had to put up with Northside for a bit. But only a bit.

💣 Worst moments included an ill-advised cover of 'Staying Alive', which was never released as a single but which featured in the 1991 Malcolm McLaren Christmas TV extravaganza *The Ghosts of Oxford Street*. (The Mondays played a bunch of brigands. Is that stereotyping or what?)

- ✔ 'Shaun William Ryder' namechecks himself in full on 'Hallelujah'. To prove he can remember his name, presumably.

- ◁» The *NME*, before they fell in love with all things Mancunian, described the debut album as 'someone shouting in a Manchester accent over weak and watery foonk like nearly everything else on Factory'. *Bummed*, though, was better received in their pages, being described as a 'truly stimulating, contemporary sensory thrashing'.

- ◁» Shaun, when he was told that *Bummed* had been voted Best Album Ever Written On Ecstasy: 'Well, I'd be honoured if it was the second best album ever written on Colgate. That'd be, like y'know, cool.'

- ▶▶ Of course, it all went horribly wrong. The Mondays disappeared to the Bahamas where their producers, Chris Frantz and Tina Weymouth from Talking Heads, tried their best to get Ryder to be more interested in recording than in smoking large amounts of crack. The lacklustre album *Yes Please* was the disappointing result; Factory Records went bankrupt and the Mondays split soon after. Shaun formed Black Grape and Bez wrote his autobiography. Recently they got back together again – but it was quite gratifying, in a way, to see them stumble through Glastonbury, have a fight on the ferry on the way to an Irish festival and split again, probably for good this time...

- ▶▶ Shaun Ryder has been in Australia, apparently, recording what he calls 'a mixture of break-beat and stories put to music' under the name of Shaun

Ryder and Off World Sounds. They've been remixing some of Shaun's favourite songs and 'replacing
the vocals with some of my stories – all true, of
course!' Hmmm, can't wait…

Haysi Fantayzee ★★
♪ 'John Wayne Is Big Leggy' (1982, no.11)

80s pop stars have punk incarnations they'd rather forget,
but currently-hip DJs often bear the shame of participating
in 80s pop groups of varying quality. Norman 'Fatboy Slim'
Cook needn't be too worried at having been a member of
The Housemartins. However Jeremy Healy, latterly of
painfully cutting-edge acts Healy & Amos and Bleachin',
may want to forget this particular former life as a colourful-
ly-clothed and dreadlocked member of this bunch with
partner-in-crime Kate Garner.

Their most famous song, 'John Wayne Is Big Leggy', has
been the subject of debate over the years, but is probably
about racism and/or dubious sexual practices. Second and
last hit was the relentlessly perky 'Shiny Shiny', which
sounds like two children's TV presenters on helium singing
an apocalyptic 'Love Cats' with a pointless twiddly guitar-
solo in the middle. Debut album *Battle Hymns For Children
Singing* reached no.11 in the UK album chart.

◀» 'Hazi Fantasi [sic] are quite simply going to be
enormous. They've got looks, they've got wit, and
most importantly, they've got suss.' (*Melody Maker*
getting, ahem, a little carried away in 1982.)

◀» 'Jeremy and Kate were like Dickensian Rastas, with
the emphasis on dick.' (The ever-acerbic **Boy
George**.)

◀》 Kate Garner in 1982: 'We want to be *Dollar* – with dreadlocks!!' (Well, it's great to have ambition.)

▶▶ Kate Garner is now a renowned photographer in the rock world. **Boy George's** friend Marilyn once expressed a desire to shut her in the Tower of London 'because she's evil...'

Heart ★ ★ ★

♫ **'Alone'** (1987, no.3)

The distaff side of Rock

Seattle, before it became known for the grunge of Nirvana and Pearl Jam, was home to the enjoyable histrionics of Heart, in a time when grown men were once known to quiver at the sight of Ann and Nancy Wilson. Two glamorous sisters with huge hair and huge voices, backed by some anonymous blokes, they took off in the UK when big slow-building ballad 'Alone' got lots of airplay in mid-1987 – although 'These Dreams' had already peaked outside the Top 40 and had been, like 'Alone', a US Number One. First known as The Army, then White Heart, the band had evolved from the folk-rock they put about in the 70s into a not-unpleasant 80s melange of jagged guitars, smooth synth backing and great, stadium-filling vocals.

They faded a bit after the 80s, but 1990 shag-epic 'All I Want To Do Is Make Love To You' remains a classic homage to the one-night stand – possibly recorded with tongue hovering near to cheek?

☏ 'Alone', written by Billy Steinberg and Tom Kelly, was their biggest single and was Number One in the US for three weeks. It's great to sing along to in the car, if you're into that kind of thing and nobody is watching.

- ✔ Heart have been known to cover Led Zeppelin songs, and were even marketed as the 'female Led Zep' once... (Hmm, see last comment on **Iron Maiden**.)

- ✔ In 1975, shortly after they formed, the band relocated to Vancouver – partly so that sound engineer and manager Mike Fisher (Ann's then-boyfriend) could avoid the draft!

Heaven 17 ★★★

♫ **'Temptation'** (1983, no.2)

Back in the late 1970s, Sheffielders Ian Craig Marsh and Martyn Ware were computer operators – as they were known back then, in the days when computers were still austere, mysterious, remote and slightly sinister objects. (Like **Gary Numan**.) After joining **The Human League**, they left in 1980 and formed a production group called British Electric Foundation. One of their first projects was Heaven 17 (a group named after a fictional group in Anthony Burgess's novel *A Clockwork Orange*) for which singer Glenn Gregory was recruited.

It took a while to catch on – several releases stalled just outside the charts, including the banned '(We Don't Need This) Fascist Groove Thang'. However, the album *Penthouse and Pavement* was doing well by 1981, and in May 1983, 'Temptation' (on which Carol Kenyon also sang) became their first and biggest hit single. 'Come Live With Me' and 'Crushed by the Wheels of Industry' followed, but the band's tendency to shun the limelight meant that they had almost vanished from public view by the mid-80s.

- ✔ Martyn Ware co-produced **Terence Trent D'Arby**'s debut album in 1987.

▶▶ A remixed 'Temptation' and a re-recorded 'Fascist Groove Thang' saw a mini-revival in the early 90s. They also took part in 1993's multi-artist, multi-format 'Gimme Shelter' project; Heaven 17 appeared on the cassette version alongside the Jimmy Somerville/**Voice of the Beehive** recording. Martyn Ware has recently been working with the ubiquitous Vince Clarke; they formed a new company called Illustrious Co. Ltd. to create 3D surround-sound works in conjunction with artists and their installations.

The Housemartins ★★★★

♫ **'Happy Hour'** (1986, no.3)

Perky agit-pop from the heart of Thatcher's Britain

Interesting things about Hull:

a) The Humber bridge looks nice at sunset
b) It has an independent telephone network with white telephone boxes
c) It vies with Slough to be the most slagged-off location in the Crap Towns Index, to be found at **www.idler.co.uk**
d) The Housemartins.

Yes, a decade before Chumbawamba's Danbert Nobacon showed John Prescott the flipside of champagne socialism in a cold ice-bucket, the Housemartins were performing with hearts on sleeves and chip proudly on collective shoulder. Signed to the independent Go! Discs, the band comprised Paul Heaton, Hugh Whitaker, Norman Cook and Stan Cullimore (and later, Dave Hemmingway).

Debut single 'Flag Day' had a go at charity guilt; 'Happy Hour' combined a dancefloor stomp (and Christmas bells!) with a diatribe against yuppie bars and sexism; 'Sheep' berated us all for the flock mentality; and 'Five Get Over Excited' hid some dark lyrics in the verses behind a chirpy chorus of 'fun fun fun'. They even had a Christmas Number One in 1986 with an *a cappella* cover of the old Isley Jasper Isley song 'Caravan Of Love'. Whisper it, but the odd Tory might have bought that one.

The albums are the wonderfully-titled *London 0 Hull 4*, which asks to be listened to with the lyric sheet to hand, and *The People Who Grinned Themselves To Death*, a more mature and thoughtful work. If life's too short for more than one Housemartins CD, go for the 1988 compilation *Now That's What I Call Quite Good*. These days, their songs sound as fresh and invigorating as ever – and you'll find them still revered in Hull.

💣 On an early 1986 tour, the band had a scheme called 'Adopt-A-Housemartin', where they asked audience members to put them up for the night. Damn, why didn't **The Bangles** ever try that?

♥ The Beautiful Southmartins are, as you might guess, a tribute band to both the Housemartins and **The Beautiful South**.

⏭ Of course, these days, Norman Cook's real name is Fatboy Slim, isn't it? ... (Before that it was Freakpower, before that it was Beats International, and before he was Norman, he was Quentin, but there isn't really much room in rock'n'roll for a Quentin. Although to be fair, Normans don't have a great pedigree either.) Heaton and Hemmingway founded the more stylistically diverse Beautiful

South, while Cullimore became a children's writer (and shouldn't be confused with bellicose footballer Stan Collymore). There's an unfortunate postscript to the career of original drummer Hugh Whitaker, who was imprisoned in 1993 for arson and wounding with intent.

▶▶ Visit **http://thehousemartins.com** for more information.

Hue and Cry ★★

♪ **'Labour of Love'** (1987, no.6)

I have to declare an interest here – Hue and Cry got my back up. Now, I have nothing against Patrick and Gregory Kane for being a good-looking, if rather dour and surly, pair of Scottish gentlemen. And as for shoehorning yourself back into the charts after a four-year absence (in 1993) with a re-mix of your biggest hit – well, okay, that's business and lots of people do it. They get points, too, for a song with a fabulous intro: 'Labour of Love' with its syncopated piano and brass is instantly recognisable.

No, their cardinal sin was to attempt a cover, on their 'Violently' EP, of the classic Kate Bush song 'The Man With The Child In His Eyes'. Don't ask why, but 'Thou shalt not attempt shite cover versions of Kate Bush' is just one of the laws of pop, like 'The only way is down, baby' and 'Every new David Bowie album will be hailed as a Return To Form even though it's not a patch on the old stuff'. Hue and Cry manage to drain all the original's emotion and – the killer blow – they *change the words*. When I first heard it I wanted to burn all their records, even the reasonably good ones. The version is also on 1989's *Bitter Suite* album, so they must have been proud of it...

Okay, so there are worse crimes. Liking Jamiroquai, for example, or modelling your life on those vacuous slappers from *Sex And The City*, or being the person who first told Jamie Oliver that, yes, it is really amusing to ride a skateboard around the kitchen and proclaim everything 'pukka'. But a beautiful song is never quite the same when it has been maltreated. It's a bit like when somebody at school (who'd never done anything else to upset you) borrowed one of your favourite toys and gave it back to you broken.

✓ The Kane brothers' original band was called Unity Express.

✓ Their 1995 *Best Of* includes, for no apparent reason, alternative versions of 'Labour Of Love', 'Ordinary Angel' and 'Sweet Invisibility', as well as live versions of 'Mother Glasgow' and 'Stars Crash Down'. Oddly, an earlier compilation *Labours of Love* seems more straightforward and comprehensive, but it does include *that* cover version...

▶▶ They continued to record up to 1999, when the jazzy album *Next Move* received mixed reviews, not least thanks to an easy-listening version of Prince's 'Sign 'O' The Times'. Maybe the Kate Bush fans are not alone.

▶▶ In Oct 2001, Pat Kane stated: 'The Hue and Cry financial partnership is now in receivership... all remaining assets are being liquidated to pay off a variety of private and fiscal creditors. Gregory and I have agreed to suspend our activities in Hue and Cry for an indefinite period, so that we can concentrate on our personal revenue-generating activities (my writing and solo performing, Gregory's music production and DJing).' It's karma. Must be.

The Human League ★★★★★

♫ 'The Sound of the Crowd' (1981, no.12)

It's the Big No-Prize Human League Quiz

When you get one of these bands who practically define a decade, it's inevitable that some myths and half-truths are going to crop up – thanks to tabloid rumour-mongering, hearsay and general lying. Among the fifteen fascinating facts about The Human League mentioned below are some complete porkers, all of which exist nowhere but in my deranged imagination. I'd like you to spot them. Answers underneath.

TRUE OR FALSE?

1. Names originally tried for size included The Dead Daughters and The Future.
2. Singer Phil Oakey used to be a hospital porter.
3. The original line-up featured Adrian Wright, credited with 'stage visuals', who used to project appropriate slides and films during performances.
4. In 1980, Phil Oakey had his hair insured for £20,000.
5. Johnny Rotten, on first hearing 'Being Boiled', called the band 'trendy hippies'.
6. Phil recruited Joanne Catherall and Susanne Sulley when he spotted them working as conductresses on Sheffield's no. 52 buses.
7. 'Don't You Want Me' was the UK's biggest-selling single of 1981.
8. Joanne Catherall owned a small lucky ferret called Claude who used to have to accompany her to gigs or she would sing out of tune.
9. The band did no publicity for the 1984 album *Hysteria*, as they had assumed they were so popular they wouldn't have to.

10. The track 'Ringinglow' on their most recent album is named after a supposedly haunted area on the edge of Sheffield.
11. The Human League turned on Sheffield's Christmas lights in 2000, sharing the bill with Bob The Builder.
12. Susanne/ Suzanne/ Susan Ann Sulley (spellings do vary) is a former South Yorkshire tiddlywinks champion and had the nickname of 'Flipper'.
13. *Viz* comic used to feature a cartoon called 'The Human League In Space'.
14. The band's name came from a computer game called 'Star Force', which featured rival factions known as The Pansentient Hegemony and The Human League.
15. A tribute album called *Reproductions* was released in 2000.

How did you fare?

1. True, and recordings were made under both names. 2. True. 3. True again. Phil wanted wing-mirrors on his mike-stand so that he could see the slides. 4. False. It was £30,000. No, actually, just completely made-up. He claimed the hair was based on a horse's tail, although some believe the look comes from a then-banned film called *Freaks*. 5. True, but then Mr Rotten said all sorts of things he probably didn't mean. 6. False – they were dancing in a club, reportedly the 'Crazy Daisy'. 7. True. No contest there. 8. False. You mean you were wondering? 9. True, actually - oops. 10. True. But although I've been there several times I have yet to see evidence of spectral activity. 11. True, they did. 12. False. Come on! (But the variant spellings of her name all seem to be accepted.) 13. True. Who knows why? 14. All accounts suggest this to be true.

Somewhere out there, surely, a band called The Pansentient Hegemony is waiting to be born. 15. Yes, it's true: it features the bands Future Bible Heroes, Momus, Ladytron and Baxendale, among others.

pause

in a muddy field

Icehouse ★★

♫ 'Hey Little Girl' (1983, no.17)

Australian band, probably most famous for the above 1983 hit. I'm more fond of their 1988 dip into the charts, the song called 'Crazy', in which singer Iva Davies declares that you'd have to be crazy, baby, to love a guy like him. Essentially a showcase for the work of Davies, who first formed the band under the name Flowers in 1980.

▶▶ Icehouse continue to release albums, including 1995's *The Berlin Tapes*, on which they covered songs from David Bowie, **The Psychedelic Furs**, Talking Heads, **The Cure** and Killing Joke.

The Icicle Works ★★★★

♫ 'Love Is A Wonderful Colour' (1983, no.15)

Staggeringly-underrated guitar epics

Ian McNabb's band must have been in the right place at the wrong time, or vice-versa. A few years either side and this Liverpool three-piece could have surfed the zeitgeist and amassed at least as many chart entries as **Echo And The Bunnymen**, enough for a Greatest Hits album. Mind you, it's difficult to see how it could improve on their existing *Best Of*, a collection which does justice to the way the band encompassed a huge diversity of styles while still maintaining a strongly individual sound and identity.

That Top 20 hit in 1983 must have seemed like the start of something big – it's a great song, though still not their best. Over the course of five diverse albums on the legendary Beggars Banquet label (home also to fellow Liverpudlians **It's Immaterial** and The Mighty Wah!), the band was to build up a strong following. Between 1983 and

1988 they released such glittering pop-rock singles as 'Birds Fly (Whisper To A Scream)' with its echo-vocal and manic drum intro, the loud live favourite 'Understanding Jane', the soaring, melodic 'Who Do You Want For Your Love' and the haunting 'Little Girl Lost'. Why these are not big Top 20 hits, included as a matter of course on Best Of The 80s compilations, is a bit of a mystery. Maybe they sounded a little too bombastic and over-thoughtful for some tastes.

The best albums? 1987's *If You Want To Defeat Your Enemy, Sing His Song* is a collection of large, storming and anthemic rock songs. 1988's *Blind* is an album which grabs you by the scruff of the neck and doesn't let go, perfectly showcasing McNabb's big, rounded vocals, and encompassing an impressive number of changes of pace and mood. They signed to Epic for the disappointing follow-up *Permanent Damage* in 1990, by which time original bassist Chris Layhe and drummer Chris Sharrock had departed. If only a major label had come along in time for *Blind*, the Icicle Works could have conquered the world.

🎧 Obviously 'Love Is A Wonderful Colour' is the big hit, but if you can get hold of their *Best Of*, check out the atmospheric and stripped-down version of 'High Time', and also 'Shit Creek' for a rock-out frenzy with a false ending to beat all false endings.

✔ The band took their name from a 1959 sci-fi short story by Frederick Pohl entitled 'The Day The Icicle Works Closed'.

✔ Drummer Chris Sharrock apparently used to pay his way into gigs with sausages and cuts of meat (his dad was a butcher). We have to assume this cunning strategy wouldn't have worked with Chrissie Hynde...

✔ **http://members.shaw.ca/icicleworks** has the essential discography, pictures etc.

🔊 'A lot of the songs we do have a meaning that is personal to the band. If someone covered "Birds Fly"... well, I don't think they could because the lyrics would be meaningless to them. It's like someone trying to cover a Gary Glitter song. Even though people have done that, it always comes across as a joke, very much involved with the personality of the artist who wrote it.' (Ian McNabb in 1984.)

⏭ McNabb continues to perform as a solo artist and will throw crowd-pleasing Icicle Works songs into his set. His 1993 single 'Great Dreams Of Heaven' is fantastic. Didn't chart, though. (Sometimes the miserable British record-buying public needs a good slap...) Chris Sharrock has worked for **The Lightning Seeds**, World Party and Robbie Williams.

Billy Idol ★★★

🎵 **'Eyes Without A Face'** (1984, no.18)

Motorcycle emptiness William Albert Michael Broad – for it is he – was born in 1955. But was he punk? Was he rock? Was he... *metal?* Well, once you stop trying to take him seriously and realise that Billy Idol is essentially a fun act (who isn't afraid to send himself up in the film *The Wedding Singer*) then it all becomes a lot clearer. Previously the singer with punk rockers Chelsea and Generation X (later Gen X) Billy created an image where everything seemed manufactured for full comic effect – the studded leather gloves, the spiked peroxide hair, the motorbike and the snaaaarrrrl. 1985 was his year – 'White Wedding' and the re-issued 'Rebel Yell' became his joint biggest UK hits, although he had MTV to thank for big exposure in the States, and in 1987 'Mony Mony' gave him a US no.1. They're all great tracks for annoying the neighbours.

It's fairly well known that Harley-Davidson lover Billy had a nasty motorcycle accident in 1990, in which he almost lost a leg – just before the release of his album *Charmed Life*, which, ironically, was already named before the accident. He suffered a broken forearm, multiple fractures and muscle damage to his right leg. His cameo in the film *The Doors* was re-written to allow him to be on crutches...

Billy continued to record with commercial success until the techno-influenced *Cyberpunk* album of 1993, which was critically panned but which made him one of the first artists to communicate with his fans using the Internet. What a wacky idea, people said at the time. Typing your phone calls? It'll never catch on.

🎧 There's the inevitable *Greatest Hits*, which came out in 2001.

✔ Billy's adopted name came thanks to a school-teacher returning some work with a comment that he was 'idle' in class. He uses the name 'William Alucard' when checking into hotels.

🔊 The wisdom of Billy: 'Great sex is great, but bad sex is like a peanut butter and jelly sandwich.'

Julio Iglesias ★★
🎵 **'Begin the Beguine (Volver A Empezar)'** (1981, no.1)

Hugely successful Latin crooner who was a goalkeeper for

Real Madrid, studied law at Cambridge and once made a laddish boast of having slept with 2000 women. (Not many goalies can claim they've scored that much.) He had his big break in 1968, winning first prize at the Spanish Song Festival in Benidorm with his song 'La Vida Sigue Igual' and securing a recording contract with independent label Discos Columbia.

One would guess Señor Iglesias tends to appeal to the housewife of a certain age, and indeed he is a sort of Hispanic version of Daniel O'Donnell, or maybe of what **Chris De Burgh** became in his later, not-very-good years. Still, you can't argue with album sales of 100 million. Iglesias followed his UK Number One with three 80s duets: with Willie Nelson ('To All The Girls I've Loved Before') Diana Ross ('All Of You') and Stevie Wonder ('My Love'). He also put out cover versions of Patsy Cline's 'Crazy' and Sting's 'Fragile' in the 90s.

💣 Of course, Julio also sired swoonsome pop-idol Enrique, whose own single 'Hero' in 2002 outdid Iglesias Senior by spending 4 weeks at the top, compared with his dad's single week. The pair have now completed a unique chart feat by being the only father and son to have had separate solo UK Number One singles. Another came close: Chesney Hawkes, with 'The One and Only' in 1991, following in the footsteps of father Chip Hawkes, who hit the top as a member of the Tremeloes with 'Silence Is Golden' in 1967. Just covering all exits here!

⏭ Julio is still popular live, and now concentrates on recording mainly in Spanish.

Imagination ★★★

♪ **'Body Talk'** (1981, no.4)

Leee John – now there's a man who really understood what being on *Top Of The Pops* was all about. Never mind the song, because you're only miming anyway (except if you are **New Order**) and the very fact of being on will probably nudge you up a few chart places. No, just indulge yourself and prance about in bright gold lamé loon-pants, because you may not get invited back again. Best to make an impression now, while you've got the chance.

The flamboyant Leee (how many Es does one man need? Don't answer that) teamed up with keyboard player Ashley Ingram and drummer Errol Kennedy to create smooth, soulful records which people could also dance to and, if they so wished, get jiggy to. Nine Top 40 hits ensued, of which the biggest, 'Just An Illusion', peaked at no.2 in 1982. ('Seven Tears' by the Goombay Dance Band prevented their ascent to the ultimate peak. Oh, well.) The album *Body Talk* went double gold and stayed in the album charts for 51 weeks.

Although the chart placings had dwindled by the end of the decade, Imagination still finished the 80s in style, completing a sell-out tour in 1989 with their Christmas gig at the Hammersmith Odeon. Leee is still writing and performing today.

- **Sinitta** was one of the band's dancers, employed to entwine herself around them and smooth out the creases in their clothing in an endearingly helpful way.

Iron Maiden ★★★

♪ 'Running Free' (1980, no.34)

Perspiring to greatness

Anything I can tell you here will have been extensively documented by earnest young men in scary T-shirts who think shampoo is for poodles and poofs. There's no way, I'm assured, of giving a true flavour of a band like this unless you have seen them play live in a muddy field at something called RockPigWeekend or Greaserfest, surrounded by people whose clothing necessitated the slaughter of entire herds of cattle and whose personal hygiene constitutes a Grade One biohazard. Given the public perception of Heavy Metal (pronounced Evvy Me'uw) it seems appropriate that the most successful example of the genre in the 1980s should be named after a mediaeval torture device.

The band, driven by the influence of bassist Steve Harris, was formed in 1976 and soon amassed the trappings which define the genre: a pair of lead guitars, lots of grunting and unkempt hair, more leather than DFS & Northern Upholstery and a comic-book image full of screaming skulls and burning flesh. A lot of people are surprised, though, when you tell them that Iron Maiden were, in chart terms, a big popular success: leading lights of what became dubbed the 'New Wave Of British Heavy Metal', they had 12 Top Twenty singles in the 80s, which is more than **Tears For Fears**.

Singers came and went: Paul Di'anno, Bruce Dickinson, Blaze Bayley. Their mascot Eddie, who was probably better-looking than most of the band, was a constant. As the decade went on, the songs got dangerously close to being melodic, and the chart placings crept higher and higher. (It's worth noting that one 1988 single was called 'Can I Play With Madness'. I'm sure people would have paid good money to see that particular supergroup – Bruce Dickinson duetting with Suggs.)

They finally had a Number One single in 1991 with the endearing little ditty 'Bring Your Daughter To The Slaughter'. A chart-topper with the shelf-life of a rancid goat's cheese, it plummeted dramatically in the following weeks, but at least it had been there.

🎧 Probably one of the better examples of the genre. Their greatest moments are collected on 1996's *Best of the Beast*.

✔ The band refused to mime for their debut performance of 'Running Free' on *Top Of The Pops* in 1980.

✔ Bruce Dickinson, who left the band to pursue a solo career in 1990 but has since returned, is also a writer of Tom Sharpe-style comic novels and a champion fencer.

♥ OK, so how many Iron Maiden tribute bands does the world need? We've got Ironically Maiden, 667: The Neighbour of the Priest, Ancient Mariners (from Holland), Sanctuary (from New York), Children of the Damned (from Italy)... and that's just a few of them. And now – best of all – there is an all-female tribute called The Iron Maidens, which sounds like such a great idea that you wonder why nobody has done it before. Maybe it could start a trend. (Bonnie Jovi? Def Leppardess? Guns'n'Rosies?)

It Bites ★★

♫ **'Calling All The Heroes'** (1986, no.6)

Led by vocalist/guitarist Francis Dunnery, they were a Cumbrian blues-metal-rock band whose biggest hit was also a big pop tune. The album *Once Around the World* was acclaimed, especially for Dunnery's guitar-playing skills, which he perfected using a device called a 'Tapboard' which enabled him to play the guitar like a percussive instrument.

🎧 Their *Best Of* collection, released in 1995, showed 'a finely tuned ear for a catchy pop melody and a sharp hook' according to *Q* magazine, but 'the band's real forte, however was... lengthy, pompous but often beautifully embroidered epics.'

⏩ The band split, but re-formed as Sister Sarah and Navajo Kiss. Francis Dunnery embarked on a solo career in the 1990s: single 'American Life In The Summertime' got a lot of UK airplay but wasn't a hit.

***

It's Immaterial ★ ★ ★
🎵 **'Driving Away From Home (Jim's Tune)'** (1986, no.18)

Another of those 'But surely that was top 10?... No?' moments, this time with a synth-art-pop duo from Liverpool who deserved better success.

Vocalist John Campbell and instrumentalist Jarvis Whitehead formed the core of the band, although they were given assistance by the likes of Henry Priestman on guitar and keyboards, Julian Scott on bass and Paul Barlow on drums. Their early singles included the raucous, **Madness**-ish 'Young Man (Seeks Interesting Job)' in 1980, with its dose of early-Thatcher-era social commentary, and 'White Man's Hut' in 1983, a jaunty number with some unusual-sounding children's backing vocals and synthesised percussion very much to the fore. Their hit 'Driving Away From Home' looked as if it might be that all-important break-through, but it was the only hit single from the 1985 album

Life's Hard And Then You Die, and was to be ultimately their one and only chart success.

They returned with 1990's *Song*, perhaps a less immediately accessible album. On the basis of tracks like 'New Brighton' and the **Black**-like 'Heaven Knows', though, they deserved to hit the charts a few more times. Sadly, it wasn't to be, and we are left just with one of the ultimate 'drive-time' anthems, featured on all those compilations. And you can quote it endlessly if you plan to move out of the city, or spend your weekends visiting friends in different far-flung parts of the country.

    Alternate mixes of the hit are entitled 'Driving Away From Home (Wicked Weather For Walking)' and 'Driving Away From Home (I mean after all, it's only 'Dead Man's Curve')'. There's also a very sparse 4-track demo version which has all the essence of the song with just a few minor differences.

    The only other single to come anywhere near the charts was 'Ed's Funky Diner (Friday Night, Saturday Morning)' which peaked at no.65 in the summer of 1986. 'Space' was another single from *Life's Hard...* which should have done better, with its bassline reminiscent of **Tears For Fears**' 'Change' and its rather menacing beauty.

    Henry Priestman later joined The Christians, and also wrote an unused score for the Luc Besson film *Atlantis*.

pause

J

just like three men abusing one another violently with untuned electric guitars

The Jam ★★★★

♪ 'In The City' (1977, no.40)

Woking-based threesome with loud guitars, punchy songs and little discernible sense of humour.

Paul Weller, Bruce Foxton and Rick Buckler built up a strong live following at venues like the Marquee and the 100 Club before signing to Polydor. Half a decade of hits began, punctuated and enlivened by events such as brawls with rugby-players in Leeds, expressing mutual dislike with The Who in *Melody Maker* and expressing support for CND. Weller joined the left-wing Red Wedge movement before founding the soulful, jazzy pop band The Style Council in early 1983.

💣 In 1982, The Jam became the first act since The Beatles to perform twice on the same edition of *Top Of The Pops* when they played both sides of 'Town Called Malice/Precious'. (Other acts since to be given this honour by the programme have included Oasis and Robbie Williams.)

✔ The Jam were the first act to enter the chart at Number One three times, with 'Going Underground / Dreams of Children' in 1980 and 'Town Called Malice/Precious' and 'Beat Surrender' both in 1982. 'Start', the second of their four chart-toppers, was the only one not to debut in pole position.

✔ The Jam once had a record-breaking 13 singles simultaneously in the Top 75, all 1983 re-releases following their break-up. 'Going Underground/Dreams of Children' was placed the highest at no.21 while 'Town Called Malice/Precious' fared the worst, sneaking in at no.73 for a solitary week.

- But if you are the kind of trivia-lover who enjoys the fact that The Jam had three consecutive hits in 1977-78 with 'world' in the title, then get a life, you sad bastard.

Japan ★★★

♫ **'Quiet Life'** (1981, no.19)

Japan seem to have had this thing about names. The founder members were two brothers from Lewisham called David and Steve Batt, who bestowed upon themselves the more exotic monikers of David Sylvian and Steve Jansen. Meanwhile, their saxophonist, the exotically-named Anthony Michaelides, decided he'd prefer to be known as Mick Karn.

They famously won their deal with Ariola-Hansa in 1977 in a talent contest – the German company had just opened its London office. Their first few singles in the late 70s and early 80s made limited impact, and it was the 1981 release of 'Quiet Life' which got them noticed. The appropriately spooky ballad 'Ghosts' gained them a lot of airplay and a Top 5 hit. The band fractured thanks to various personality clashes, but unexpectedly re-formed for a while as Rain Tree Crow at the end of the decade (not listed above, as their sole nuzzle of the charts was the no.62 single 'Blackwater'). Renowned for excessive use of make-up.

- In 1982, David Sylvian teamed up with Ryuichi Sakamoto of the Yellow Magic Orchestra; as Sylvian Sakamoto, they collaborated on the theme to the film *Merry Christmas Mr Lawrence*.

- 'I think in the early years with Japan the work became an act of concealment rather than revelation or communication. I recognized that early on and the remainder of Japan's life, you could say, was spent trying to find myself or reveal more of myself in the work, to allow myself be that vulnerable, to come to the fore. I really didn't get there until I hit upon "Ghosts" and I felt that there was some kind of breakthrough. Really that is the starting point for me. It opened the door for me, and the subsequent success of that particular track gave me the courage to go on and to pursue that path of enquiry.' David Sylvian, speaking in 2001 about revisiting old songs for the compilation *Everything And Nothing*.

Jesus And Mary Chain. ✮✮✮
♫ **'Some Candy Talking'** (1986, no.13)

Natural dyed Goth
If you were walking round your local shopping centre in the late 80s and saw a pale, resentful-looking youth in leather with spiky black hair and too much eyeliner, chances are he'd have had a copy of *Darklands* in his record collection. (He'd probably have owned the rarities and B-sides collection *Barbed Wire Kisses* as well.)

East Kilbride brothers William and Jim Reid, backed up by bassist Douglas Hart and drummer Bobby Gillespie, were signed by the legendary Alan McGee of Creation in the Spring of 1984, and their first release was the storming single 'Upside Down', which topped the UK indie chart for two weeks. The band also attracted attention for such stunts as possessing speed and playing live sets of just two songs. (Maybe more acts should adopt such admirable minimalism – if you go to see The Lighthouse Family, for example, you pretty much get two songs strung out for 90 minutes anyway, and you may well find yourself longing for a dose of amphetamine sulphate just to liven things up.)

The first album *Psychocandy* was hailed by the critics, some of whom even called the band the natural heirs to punk, and it was bought by pale and shivering young men in black lipstick everywhere. In 1987 they managed, incredibly, something close to a pop song with the catchy 'April Skies', which peaked at no.8 in the Top 40. The album *Darklands* followed, though it featured only the Reid brothers (Bobby Gillespie had departed for the joys of Primal Scream). They were still doing well at the end of the decade, with the 1989 album *Automatic* making no.11.

Best-known purveyors of the 'any colour so long as it's black' school of Goth miserablism, the Mary Chain gave us some of those haunting, glittering, multi-layered 'cathedrals of sound' so beloved of *NME* hacks. They also made quite a few records which sound just like three men abusing one another violently with untuned electric guitars. It's spotting the difference which counts. Apparently the audiences at early Mary Chain concerts experienced some uncertainty as to whether the band were tuning up, experiencing technical problems with the amps or, in fact, halfway through their latest single.

Music for the well-balanced (those with a chip on both shoulders).

● In March 1985, the band were blamed for causing a riot at their North London Polytechnic gig. Their official statement on the incident said: 'The Jesus and Mary Chain are putting excitement back into rock and roll and promoters will have to bear the consequences. This is truly art as terrorism.' The *NME* carped: 'Art as terrorism or bullshit as publicity? Decide for yourself.'

◄ William Reid: 'There has never been a riot at any of

our gigs. You get the odd clown who thinks he's Rambo, doing tap dances on the mixing desk. I hate it, I despise it. We're trying to present ourselves as serious, not a Cockney Rejects Oi Oi type of group.'

◀» Jim Reid: 'They write encyclopaedias on the 80s and we're not even mentioned. We *were* the fucking 80s.' (Happy now, Jim?)

◀» Alan McGee of Creation: 'I had to sign them... they were either the best or the worst band I'd ever seen.'

Jive Bunny & The Mastermixers ★
♪ **'Swing The Mood'** (1989, no.1)

Mixer-matosis
Right, hands up if you thought Mr Blobby was irritating? I thought so. And the Birdie Song? Hmm, me too. But were they any more annoying than an animated, evil-looking white rabbit dancing about in front of lots of cut-up extracts from old swing, big-band and rock'n'roll tunes, which weren't even pretending to be anything other than straight steals (albeit re-recorded) from the original records? 'Swing The Mood' is aptly titled, as, if it came on the radio, it was liable to make your mood swing from fairly calm to bloody livid. Several more near-identical medleys followed, making you wonder what the sheer point of it all was. Surely anybody who liked the original records would rather listen to them properly, and anyone who liked upbeat late-80s pop was listening to something more worthy like **Aztec Camera** or **Fine Young Cannibals**? No...?

A nadir of the 80s, the Jive Bunny project symbolises everything that was wrong with music at the end of the decade, and will always be remembered for bringing the charts their most annoying rabbit since Chas'n'Dave. Thankfully, they were first against the wall when the indie-dance revolution came.

☀ The saddest thing of all is that they have found a quite unwarranted place in chart history by being a) only the third act ever to have three Number Ones with their first three singles (after Gerry & The Pacemakers and **Frankie Goes To Hollywood**) and b) to date, the only novelty act to have had three Number Ones. I think I need to get out more. Is Mrs Thatcher still Prime Minister? Mobile telephones, pah, they'll never catch on. Pass me that half-cooked beefburger.

✔ If you really care, John Pickles and Ian Morgan were the names of the production duo 'responsible'. Obviously, I use the word in its loosest sense.

Johnny Hates Jazz ★★
♫ **'Shattered Dreams'** (1987, no.5)

They had potential. Another bunch of clean-cut young men in smart suits doing smoothly-produced, funky-wunky guitar pop, much in the vein of **The Blow Monkeys** and **Climie Fisher**. The movie-idol looks of lead singer Clark Datchler certainly helped with the band's charisma, and their melodic pop hooks got them lots of airplay. They had a bit of a jazzy sound, ironically. Number One album *Turn Back the Clock* contained a clutch of hits.

Datchler left in '88 when fifth single 'Don't Say It's Love' didn't quite manage to do the business for them again. Phil Thornalley, famous as a producer, especially with **Prefab Sprout**, stepped up as a replacement – he had been with the band's original line-up and had written their 1986 single 'Me And My Foolish Heart'. The momentum was gone, though and JHJ visited the charts no more.

Grace Jones ★★

♫ **'Private Life'** (1980, no.17)

It's hard to decide when the fearsome Ms Jones was at her scariest. First option: rolling around with Roger Moore as the deadly assassin May Day in the James Bond film *A View To A Kill* (music by **Duran Duran**). This romp prompted the classic Bond response, when asked if he had slept well: 'A little restless at first, but I got off eventually.' Second option: the moment she chose to grab chat-show host Russell Harty's attention by thumping him with her hand-bag. These starring roles seem rather to have eclipsed her music of the 1980s, of which the best-known examples were the funky 'Pull Up To The Bumper' (only a hit when it was re-issued in 1986) and the growly-soulful 'Slave to the Rhythm'. You wouldn't want to meet her on a dark night.

- At a 1990 gig at the Brixton Academy, Grace kept an audience waiting for 4-and-a-half hours. Apparently this set a record for the venue. I hope she was worth the wait...

- ✔ Grace was a Paris fashion model in her twenties, appearing on the covers of *Vogue*, *Elle* and *Stern*.

- ✔ Her decadent, androgynous stage 'look' was master-minded by Jean-Paul Goude, her Svengali, manag-er, general consultant and boyfriend-type-person. Obviously every home should have one.

Howard Jones ★★★

♫ **'New Song'** (1983, no.3)

Sensitively boyish hero of gentle synth-pop, who was born in Southampton and grew up in Canada. Like the **Happy Mondays**, Howard employed an artist in expressive mime to accompany his lyrics. Jones's stooge, Jed Hoile, was perhaps more professional in his approach than Bez, but he could be just as mystifying.

Howard had a number of hits, including 'What Is Love', 'Like To Get To Know You Well' and 'Things Can Only Get Better' (no, not *that* one). Very popular in America, where *Dream Into Action* was a platinum album.

✔ Howard bought his first synthesiser in 1979, with the money from damages received after a road accident.

✔ On his 1984 UK tour, Howard was supported by **Strawberry Switchblade**. Which was nice.

▶▶ After the big commercial success dried up, Howard continued to record on his own label, Dtox Records. In 1998 he toured the USA with **Culture Club**, and in 1999 he did a small but well-supported UK tour.

pause

K

kicks even miserable so-and-sos on to the dancefloor

Kajagoogoo ★★

⊛ Kaja ♪ 'Too Shy' (1983, no.1)

Barnet bypass

The title of 'Silliest Haircut' is a hotly contested one, with a *Smash Hits* Awards category of its own. By the late 80s, few could mount a challenge to the Best In Show mullet of DJ Pat Sharp – but in 1983, one man stood proudly above all the rest by virtue of having three separate styles contained within one head of hair. Step forward Chris Hamill, lead singer of Kajagoogoo – alias Limahl, who'd arrived at his stage-name by simply rearranging the letters in his sur-name. (He must have been good at *Countdown*.) The rest of the band mounted a sterling challenge in the follicle depart-ment, but sadly no more anagrams. Perhaps we should pro-vide our own.

Believe it or not, they were a prog-rock band called Art Nouveau before Limahl came along. Their 80s output was purely pop, though – the first hit 'Too Shy' went to the top of the UK charts and was produced by Colin Thurston and Nick Rhodes (Din Shocker), who was of course in **Duran Duran** with Simon Le Bon (Slime On Nob). It was fol-lowed by two more Top 20 hits, 'Ooh To Be Aah' and 'Hang On Now'. However, after the album *White Feathers*, the end of 1983 brought disaster: Limahl was sacked over tonsorial differences and the bouffanted bassist Nick Beggs (B.C. Eggskin) took over vocal duties. In an attempt to distance themselves from their former front-man, the band adopted the cunning disguise of Kaja in 1984 – but it didn't work, and the split was not far away.

✔ **www.ricos-collection.de/Kajagoogoo/index.htm** has what appears to be a comprehensive discography of both Kajagoogoo and Limahl solo… it's in German, though. Look, you can't have everything.

- It was apparently Beggs who chose the ridiculous moniker, on the basis that if you could market such a silly name, you could get away with any old cobblers in the musical department. I can see the logic.

- According to Limahl: 'There will probably never be a Kajagoogoo reunion because after we met for the first time in fifteen years... we couldn't come to an agreement over the sordid but important subject of money... My e-mail exchanges with Monsieur Beggs were very heavy and I actually feel more animosity towards him/them now than I did back then.' (Handbags at dawn...)

- Limahl had a hit with a film theme, 'The Never Ending Story', and continued to record into the 90s, having some success in Germany with his album *Love Is Blind*.

Nick Kamen ★★
♪ '**Each Time You Break My Heart**' (1986, no.5)

Pants. No, not a quality assessment, but an indication of Mr Kamen's first brush with fame. The former model was the chap who, in a well-known 1986 advert for Levi's, stripped to his boxers to the sound of 'I Heard It Through The Grapevine' to wash his jeans in a launderette, inspiring an upsurge in the sale of boxer shorts. He then had three hits in the late 80s: the top five single 'Each Time You Break My Heart' (written by **Madonna**) and two of lesser status, 'Loving You Is Sweeter Than Ever' and 'Tell Me'. His 1990 comeback 'I Promised Myself' is upbeat and catchy and should have been a hit, but only reached the heights of no. 50. Well, at the end of the day a man who was 'romantically linked' (as the papers say) with both pop goddess **Madonna** and classy piece of fluff Amanda de Cadenet can't have too much to moan about.

- ✔ Durable folk-rocker Judie Tzuke sings backing vocals on 'I Promised Myself'.

- ✔ The Levi's ad resulted in an 800% increase in sales in 1986. The company kept the idea of resurrecting old songs for its adverts until the mid-1990s, when they adopted the soundtrack of more contemporary acts like Stiltskin and Babylon Zoo.

- ◀� 'He was the loveliest, grooviest person but he was completely traumatised by his experience of being ripped to shreds by the publicity machine. People wanting bits of him he didn't want to give.' Nick's former girlfriend, actress Sienna Guillory, interviewed in *Elle* (Nov 2000).

- ▶▶I Nick went back into modelling. There's no truth to the rumour that he is currently working as a lint cleaner at Kwik-Wash in Folkestone.

Katrina and the Waves ★★
♫ **'Walking On Sunshine'** (1985, no.8)

Talk about revivals. In May 1997, only two days after New Labour had swept away a decade and a half of electoral failure with a massive mandate, a seemingly long-forgotten group from the 80s did exactly the same at the Eurovision Song Contest. Katrina Leskanich and her band emerged from nostalgia-world to become the first UK winners since **Bucks Fizz** in 1981.

Formed in Cambridge – coincidentally, in 1981 – they'll forever be associated with their big 1985 summer anthem 'Walking On Sunshine', a stomping, feelgood song whose opening drumbeat kicks even miserable so-and-sos on to the dancefloor. Their 1986 follow-up 'Sun Street' was an ode to the joys of inebriation; despite a catchy piano-and-brass riff, it stalled at no.22. Then came the lost years, during which several albums came out in Germany (*Pet the Tiger*, *Edge of the Land* and *Turn Around*).

The triumphant Eurovision anthem 'Love Shine A Light' in 1997 was an uplifting Top Ten single. It wouldn't be out of place as one of those Prozac-happy modern hymns sung in churches with Ikea flooring and earringed vicars called Dave in faded jeans strumming guitars, but it's still a glorious piece of three-minute pop.

▶▶ Guitarist Kimberley Rew tried to repeat the Eurovision success, writing a 'Song For Europe' nominee in 2000. Katrina Leskanich became a presenter, hosting a late-night Radio 2 show for a while. She had a good, husky, late-night DJ voice. They should bring her back.

Nik Kershaw ★★★

♬ **'Wouldn't It Be Good'** (1984, no.4)

Nik was a pretty-boy teen idol who favoured big jackets and baggy trousers. He also almost single-handedly popularised the snood, that astonishingly impractical piece of attire which made the wearer look as if they were wearing a somewhat effete neck-brace. Mind you, he did spend three soulless years working at the Department Of Unemployment (sic) in Ipswich, so I think we can forgive the man a few sartorial excesses.

Nik is on record as saying that the lyrics of his 1985 Top Three hit 'The Riddle' (you know them, I'm sure: old men of Arran circling continually inside holes in the ground beside trees and all that kind of gibbering waffle) were rubbish because they were *meant* to be. He just recorded the lines as a guide vocal before they did the real thing, but his producers thought it was great and profound and wanted it keeping in. The rest was history, and a piece of pop serendipity.

- Mark Price, the drummer who toured with Nik, had previously found fame as the boy in the Hovis bread commercial.

- Nik wrote Chesney Hawkes' agreeable 1991 chart-topper, 'The One And Only'.

- In 1984, in a magazine feature called 'If I Ruled The World', Nik nominated John Cleese to be Prime Minister. 'We'd still be in a hell of a mess but at least it would be fun. The world gets more like *Fawlty Towers* every week!'

- It wasn't always recognised that Nik was the talented songwriter behind his hits, and recently he had a go at re-launching his career. Shaven-haired and sporting a goatee beard, he's almost unrecognisable, and not averse to the odd fun stunt like being sent out on an acoustic busking competition against Glenn Tilbrook from **Squeeze**. (Tilbrook got more money from the punters.) However, disappointing sales of his 2002 album *To Be Frank* mean that he's decided to retire... for now.

King ★★

♫ **'Love and Pride'** (1985, no.2)

Now, Paul King – here was a man who understood what being an 80s pop star was all about. Adorned with a mullet of such taste-defying proportions that it almost had to be a wig, he felt the need to lift the lapel of his dreadful baggy checked jacket and thump his chest proudly in an 'I am declaiming an anthem' sort of way. It was as if he'd suddenly defined himself as a stadium star, without having to go through all the usual dull stuff like playing the Frog and Spittle in Nether Wallop on a Monday night, or chatting with a stuffed puppet on live TV at 8.30 on a Saturday morning when the only kids likely to be awake are the swots, the insomniacs and the trainee psychopaths.

Paul was a refugee from a former ska incarnation called The Reluctant Stereotypes, and formed the band King in 1983. 'Alone Without You' and 'The Taste of Your Tears' were Top 20 hits as well.

▶▶| Paul became a well-known face as a presenter on VH-1. The website **www.loveandpride.net** may even be finished by the time you read this.

Kissing the Pink ★★

♫ **'Last Film'** (1983, no.19)

Had a name that's either a snooker reference or something very obscene, and they only had one hit. Perhaps it's remembered despite an unremarkable chart position because of a rather impressive 14 weeks on the chart. Underrated, apparently.

A multi-instrumental combo who met at the Royal College of Music, they were bigger elsewhere in Europe than in the UK. Still together somewhere, involved in production and working on something with the intriguing name of 'classical trance'...

Kon Kan ★★

♪ **'I Beg Your Pardon'** (1989, no.5)

Kon Kan were Barry Harris and Kevin Wynne, a Canadian duo whose one UK hit will have you puzzling every time it comes on the pub jukebox. A little pop oasis among the scorched earth and tumbleweeds of 1989, 'I Beg Your Pardon' hits you with an attention-grabbing, syncopated synth intro. It then segues seamlessly into a pastiche of Bernard Sumner or Dave Gahan's deadpan delivery. (I think there's a touch of Teutonic dance-popsters Camouflage's 'Love Is A Shield' as well.) Finally, it catches you off-guard by shamelessly nicking its entire chorus from the verse of Lynn Anderson's 1971 country hit 'Rose Garden'. All good fun. It ended up sounding like nothing else from the Top 40 at the time, which is always an asset.

✔ Kon Kan won the Juno Award (Canadian version of the Grammy) for 'Best Dance Recording' in 1989.

✔ The name Kon Kan is a play on 'Can Con' (Canadian Content), a rule which obliges radio stations in Canada to play 30% homegrown music.

▶▶ Barry Harris is still producing and remixing.

Kraftwerk ★★★★

♫ 'Autobahn' (1975, no.11)

We have ways of making you dance

It's probably asking a lot for a German artist to be taken seriously in this country, especially given a tabloid culture which brings out the same old, tired tropes of appropriated sun-loungers, lack of humour and numerous football-based variations on 'Hans Off' and 'Do Your Wurst'.

They sport a name which, despite decades of misinformation, is nothing to do with those popular Rhineland hobbies of batik and macramé; it is, instead, the German for 'Power Station' (which is also, rather embarrassingly, the name of one of the decade's short-lived **Duran Duran** spin-off projects).

Every band who ever put finger to synth owes a debt to Kraftwerk. Ralf Hütter and Florian Schneider-Esleben met in 1970, and in 1974 they completed the 4-piece by adding Wolfgang Flur on electronic drums. Klaus Roeder, on violin and guitar, was replaced by Karl Bartos in 1975. Following UK success with the singles 'Autobahn' and 'Trans-Europe Express', they toured here in 1977, showcasing their famous 'mannequin' look. Their signature tune 'The Model', a double A-side with 'Computer Love', only made no.36 on its first release in 1981, but dancefloor popularity and heavy airplay got it to Number One early in 1982. Fritz Hijbert replaced Wolfgang Flur in 1990.

They continue to record intermittently and remain enigmatic. And say 'Krafft-vairk', not 'craft-work'. More kudos.

✔   Karl Bartos worked with the duo **Electronic** on their 1996 album *Raise The Pressure*.

Krush ★★

♫ 'House Arrest' (1988, no.3)

And this is another 'so 80s' giveaway – spelling perfectly good words wrongly (like Kwik-Save, pik-a-stik, Jakki Brambles, etc.). Krush were a one-hit wonder who helped to pave the way, along with fellow dance acts **S'Express** and **M/A/R/R/S**, for the tidal wave of dire, repetitive house which was to clog the airwaves in the late 80s and early 90s. Obviously some sort of retribution is deserved, but on the other hand they did have a very nice, frizzy-haired redhead who delighted in the name of Ruthjoy on vocals. It is fairly melodic for a dance record; those familiar, scratchy late-80s beats lead into something akin to a proper chorus.

The band paid for the record to be promoted on pirate radio, apparently – it had picked up Radio 1 airplay by the end of 1987, and made the top 3 early in 1988. Ruthjoy attempted a solo career with the single 'Soulpower' in 1989, but it wasn't a hit.

pause

L

little beards were just around the corner

Landscape ✭ ✭ ✭

♫ 'Einstein A Go-Go' (1981, no.5)

Another contender for simultaneously the best and worst album title of the decade, competing with efforts from the **Happy Mondays** and **Bow Wow Wow**, is Landscape's 1981 opus *From the Tea-Rooms of Mars...to the Hell-Holes of Uranus*. From it came the instantly-recognisable hit 'Einstein A Go-Go' with its tootling synth sound and clipped vocals. It was a big hit in Europe and Australia.

Singer and drummer Richard Burgess started the band as a pop-jazz crossover, but as this was in 1975, he can probably be forgiven. Burgess later became a producer for **Spandau Ballet** and **Visage**.

✔ There's a useful discography at **www.algonet.se /~jonwar/landscape.html**

◀♪ Band member (and writer of the distinctive melody) John Walters on the origins of the single: 'The title comes from my own interest in Einstein's life and work... We worked very hard to make it into a proper song, with apocalyptic verses and sinister fade-out vocals... Instead of being about Einstein, the song became the story of a madman who had hidden an atomic bomb and was holding the world to ransom...The phone conversations in the intro are all genuine... I sat in Redwood Studios in Covent Garden...and dialled the White House, the Kremlin and so on, pretending to be the mad bomber!'

Cyndi Lauper ★★★

You just know, don't you, that New Yorker Cyndi is a bit wacky, a bit kooky, a bit zany, and all those other annoying words – it's the way she spells her name, combined with the helium voice and the Madonna's-little-sister look (although she is actually five years older than Madge). Her dresses came from Brides'R'Us and the Army Reject Store, and her lipstick from the shelf marked Ouch, while territorial warfare between various bottles was going on in her ribbon-festooned hair. Despite all that, she still exuded an oddly alluring charm.

In 1970, Cyndi left home to hitch-hike through Canada with her dog, Sparkle, and ended up studying art in Vermont. Her early bands included Doc West, Flyer and Blue Angel – activities with the latter led to her being declared bankrupt in 1982. Debut solo album *She's So Unusual* won a Grammy. In the UK, her best-known songs were the perky debut single (re-released in a reggaed-up version in 1994), ballads 'Time After Time' and 'True Colours', and the storming 'I Drove All Night', later covered by Roy Orbison.

☻ *12 Deadly Cyns... And Then Some* is the hits compilation.

✔ 'Time After Time', a UK no.3 hit, was kept off the top by the two **Frankie Goes To Hollywood** records, 'Relax' and 'Two Tribes'.

✔ Guess what – another one who became a born-again Christian. You could almost fill a church hall with these reformed popsters...

▶▶| Her new EP 'Shine', available through her official website at **www.cyndilauper.com**, has apparently had rave reviews from *Billboard*.

Level 42 ★★★

♪ **'Love Games'** (1981, no.38)

Bass – how low can you go?
The style of bass played by Mark King is known as 'slap', possibly because this is what some bassists want to give him when they hear it. The sound has been described by a bass-player I know as similar to that of 'twanging' a ruler on the edge of a desk, producing similar levels of pleasure for the 'twanger' and annoyance for the listener. Nevertheless, King was voted Best Bass Player in *Making Music* magazine's 1987 poll – but how many other bands can you name where the bassist is the star?

The band was formed in 1980, taking their name from '42', the answer to the Question Of Life, the Universe And Everything in Douglas Adams's cult radio series and book *The Hitch Hiker's Guide To The Galaxy*. Level 42 were originally a jazz-funk outfit, and their early singles did well on the Dance chart. You have to remember that this was in 1980, when the Dance chart was still populated by acts with some resemblance to human beings, none of whom sported the initials MC or DJ or felt the need to spell 'the' as 'tha' (or worse, 'da').

A change of gear came in the mid-80s, and their new pop-orientated direction took them to the heights of the top 10 with singles such as 'Something About You', 'Lessons In Love' and 'Running In The Family'. They continue to record and play live.

● The 1985 single 'Something About You' was accompanied by a video in which the lucky band members get to take it in turns to snog sophisticatedly shaggable thesp and coffee-empress Cherie Lunghi.

✔ Keyboardist Mike Lindup is the son of the late David Lindup, for many years John Dankworth's chief arranger, and composer of the first-ever theme tune to *Family Fortunes*. (Thanks to Louis Barfe for this info!)

✔ The trade paper *Making Music* was so devoted to Level 42's bass-slapping frontman that it was known affectionately as *Mark King Music*.

✔ In 1984, Polydor gave Mr K. the chance to record a solo album – he desperately needed the money for somewhere for himself and his family to live. They advanced him £20,000. In those days, believe it or not, that could actually buy you a house, and not just a cupboard underneath a main railway bridge and behind a boarded-up shop with a plague-warning symbol on the door.

✔ In December 1987, just after the band's most successful period in chart terms, brothers Phil and Boon Gould both left the group for health reasons. However, Phil Gould returned for the album *Forever Now* in 1994.

Lightning Seeds ★★★

♪ 'Pure' (1989, no.16)

Scouse of fun

Just a brief word, here, for Ian Broudie's little project, even though it wasn't until the 90s that they became a fully-fledged pop act. *CloudCuckooLand* was a bit of a gamekeeper-turned-poacher album, as Broudie was already a producer of some repute (**Icicle Works**, Frazier Chorus, **Echo & The Bunnymen**), and his decision to write and perform it all single-handed was perhaps something of a gamble. It comes off brilliantly, though, and it's packed full of perky, melodic songs like the 1989 hit single 'Pure', the opener 'All I Want' (later covered by **The Bangles**' Susanna Hoffs) and the lushly-arranged 'The Price'. But big success and little beards were just around the corner, with 'Life of Riley' on *Match of the Day*, 'Marvellous' on a car advert and 'Three Lions'… well, I imagine you know all about that.

🎧 'Pure' is an elegant song, structured around a 3-note sequence with lots of harmonies and a sampled **New Order** bassline. But – only no. 16? Shome mishtake shurely!

✔ After the success of 'Pure', the next two singles were 'Joy' and 'All I Want'. Both flopped, neither of them reaching the Top 100.

✔ Broudie's notes: he was born in Penny Lane, follows Liverpool FC, supported the campaign for justice for families of the Hillsborough stadium disaster and was previously in the local bands Big In Japan, Original Mirrors and Care (with Paul Simpson of **The Teardrop Explodes**). Such impeccable Merseyside credentials. I bet he watches *Brookside* too. 'Ar-ay, calm down, calm down.'

✓ Some great tunes from the Care years (83-84) have been re-issued on a compilation from Camden Originals: well worth getting, it includes the near-hit 'Flaming Sword', which Ian still sometimes does live.

_____

Living in a Box ★★

♫ **'Living In A Box'** (1987, no.5)

They were, apparently, living in a box, they were living in a cardboard box. However, one is short of any evidence to corroborate their claims of alfresco habitation. Anyway, I always thought the reason for any band naming a hit after themselves was so that journalists could show off with the word 'eponymous'.

This sartorially-elegant Sheffield trio, from the same stable of white soul-funk-pop as **The Blow Monkeys** and **Johnny Hates Jazz**, were Richard Darbyshire, Marcus Vere and Anthony Critchlow. They managed a couple more top 10 hits, the breathtakingly brainless 'Blow The House Down' (featuring a Brian May guitar solo), on which they declared that they had the power to build the highest tower, and the not-bad ballad 'Room In Your Heart'. They leave us only two albums – *Living In A Box* from 1987 and *Gatecrashing* from 1989 – as changes at record company Chrysalis caused that old favourite, artistic differences, to rear its head during the production of their third LP. The band broke up in 1990 before their third album was completed.

Richard Darbyshire escaped for the inevitable solo/ writing career as soon as was decent. He wrote songs for **Level 42** and Lisa Stansfield, among others, and his solo debut *How Many Angels* (1994) contained tracks which had been intended for Living in a Box's third album. Just goes to show, you should never throw anything away. Especially if you are living in a cardboard box.

● Richard Darbyshire was nominated for an Ivor Novello Award in 1990 for his songwriting collaboration with Albert Hammond on 'Room In Your Heart'.

✔ Darbyshire's earlier band was called The ZuZu Sharks. They wore camouflage gear and were frighteningly blond.

✔ Other bands to record an eponymous single: **Visage**, Motorhead, Goodbye Mr Mackenzie, **Talk Talk, The Colour Field**... And **Fairground Attraction's** first album had a track called 'Fairground Attraction' which wasn't a single.

The Lotus Eaters ★★
♪ **'The First Picture Of You'** (1983, no.15)

More one-hit wonders... Liverpudlian band, formed in 1982 and comprising Peter Coyle (vocals), Jeremy Kelly (guitar), Mike Dempsey (bass), and Stephen Creese (drums). Their looks were New Romantic foppish but their sound was more understated, thoughtful pop.

The hit song is notable for Coyle's breathy vocals and for producing a big-sounding chorus out of its laid-back verses. The 1984 album *No Sense Of Sin* performed well in Japan and the Philippines. 'You Don't Need Someone New' and 'It Hurts' were further singles, but they split in 1985. History does not record if they actually ate any lotuses.

● A compilation of their BBC radio sessions, *The First*

Picture Of You, is available.

✔ During their time away, guitarist Jeremy Kelly played on the album *Bringing Home The Ashes* by The Wild Swans in 1988.

▸▸ı They are back together and recording in Japan, apparently... Recently they were due to perform in the Philippines, but this gig was cancelled because of a busy recording schedule... my goodness.

pause

Marc Almond was enjoying being photographed so much that he didn't notice a small fire had started on his forehead.

© Famous

Anyone know the Norwegian for 'mullet'? A-ha, I think you're right.

The Bangles rejected early names The Large Earrings and The Chunky Studded Belts.

Bananarama: Posh Nana, Scary Nana and Sporty Nana sit out the decade, awaiting the inevitable pedal-pushers revival... (One of these women is an Eighties sex goddess. Clue: her initials might be KW.)

Big Fun: Being the poor man's Bros can be excused. Having a Michael Ball bouffant cannot.

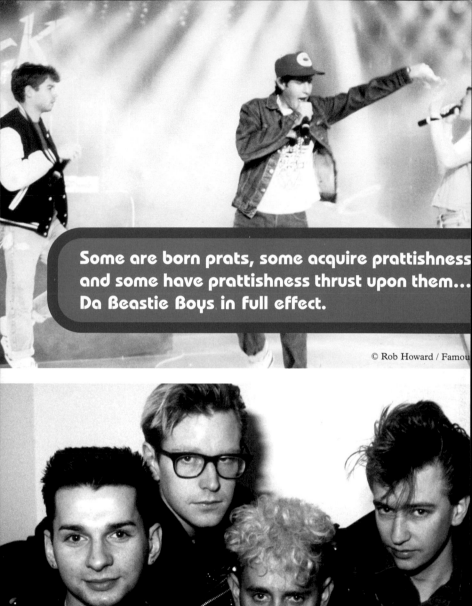

Some are born prats, some acquire prattishness and some have prattishness thrust upon them... Da Beastie Boys in full effect.

We just can't get enough of Depeche Mode. You would, wouldn't you?

Billy Idol: Mr Broad politely enquires if you, in fact, spilled his pint.

'Oh, we thought you said he had a huge collection of badgers.' Boy George avoids another controversy.

© Famous

Cyndi Lauper: a girl just wanting to have fun.

©Famous

Mirror, mirror on the wall, who sells burgers on a stall? Dollar, the artists also known as David Hot-Dog-Van Day and Thereza Bizarre.

New Romantics like Duran Duran dressed really sensibly. No, they did. This was just for a fancy dress party. Honest.

Eurythmics: We would like to point out that no animals were harmed to make Annie's coat. Several small rodents were slaughtered to create Dave's barnet, though.

© Rob Howard / Famous

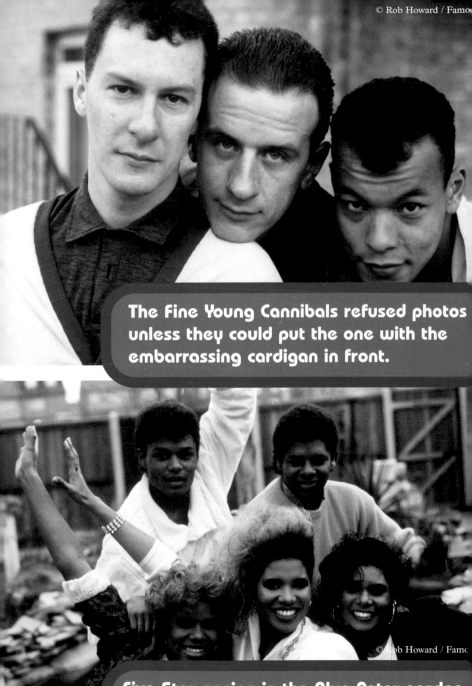

The Fine Young Cannibals refused photos unless they could put the one with the embarrassing cardigan in front.

Five Star posing in the Blue Peter garden, minutes before encountering the career-defining nemesis of a very rude child.

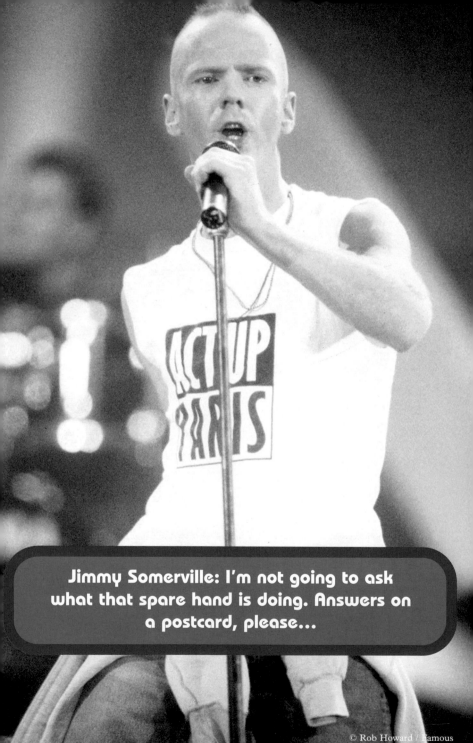

Jimmy Somerville: I'm not going to ask what that spare hand is doing. Answers on a postcard, please...

© Rob Howard / Famous

Two men, a drum machine and a rabbit. The chap with the long ears was the talented one in Jive Bunny.

Kim Wilde: If you're reading this, Kim, I have a window-box that gets full sun. Can you suggest year-round plants that are bushy and, most importantly, trailing?

Level 42: 'Say "pop-orientated jazz-funk crossover with twangy bass" one more time and we'll send Luigi and the boys around.'

'Are you wearing that jumper for a bet?'... 'At least I don't look like a drug dealer.' Tears For Fears' harmonious working relationship captured at its zenith.

Mr Hamill of Kajagoogoo
contemplating his career highlights.

© Famous

Adam Ant stands to deliver that 'rabbit in the headlights' look.

Morrissey of The Smiths contemplates the joy of specs. Sheer poetry, dear boy.

Neil Tennant actually has 'Bod' on his cap, proving the Pet Shop Boys were secret fans of children's animation.

Wham!: 'Planning on going solo? What's that all about then?' Andrew Ridgeley fails to read the writing on the wall.

© Famous

Three men and a controlled experiment in facial hair were called ZZ Top. Just don't go there.

© Famous

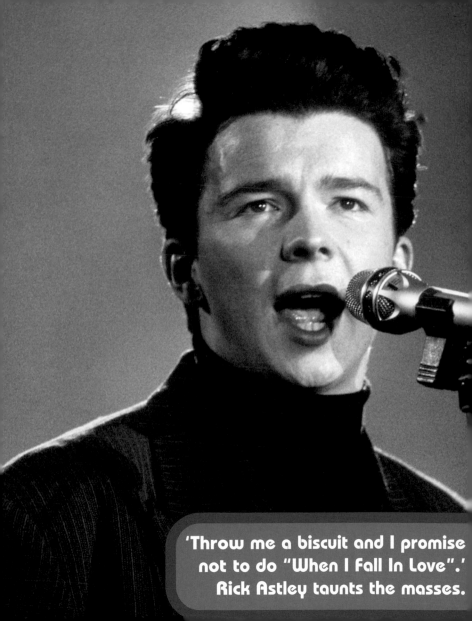

'Throw me a biscuit and I promise not to do "When I Fall In Love".' Rick Astley taunts the masses.

Sade, a woman so sophisticated that she would routinely emerge on stage from a small piece of Gucci hand-luggage.

'Ooh, and there's me mum, and me dad, and me Auntie Gladys, and...' Yazz, back when she was still convinced of the inevitability of ascent.

musical diarrhoea

Kirsty MacColl ★★★★

♫ 'There's A Guy Works Down The Chip Shop Swears He's Elvis' (1981, no.14)

From Croydon to Cuba

Daughter of folk singer Ewan MacColl, gorgeous writer and singer of equally gorgeous songs, and tragically no longer with us. Her first single 'They Don't Know' came out in 1979 (and was later a hit for **Tracey Ullman**), but she kept us waiting a decade for her first major album while putting out some interesting solo hits and collaborations.

During her earliest gigs in Irish ballrooms, Croydon-born Kirsty was so nervous that she gabbled through all the songs, then found herself with so much time to fill that she had sing them all over again. There was a time when she was better known for her backing vocals, and you couldn't even find her albums in the shops. But by December 2000, when her life was tragically cut short by a speedboat accident in Mexico, Kirsty MacColl had established herself as an artist of some repute. Not bad for the girl whose cleverly-written first hit is often misguidedly dismissed as a novelty record.

Maybe most people will remember her for two things: her acerbic and brilliant rendition of **Billy Bragg's** 'A New England', and her duet with notoriously well-oiled and Stonehenge-toothed **Pogues** singer Shane MacGowan on 'Fairytale of New York'. However, as her splendid greatest hits album *Galore* will attest, there was so much more to Kirsty than that. Her melodies were memorable, her laconic singing with its trademark multi-tracked vocals really couldn't be mistaken for anyone else and her lyrics were wry and witty.

Kirsty was as much a family person as a star, and so despite her 80s hits, it was only at the end of the decade that her first major album, *Kite,* came out. Her songs laid into Thatcherite greed, vacuous women and useless and duplicitous men – and because she was attractive in an understated way, you could like her for the music first, imagining her as the kind of girl you could have a pint or two with.

At the Freeworld website **www.kirstymaccoll.com**, you can still read about the hugely talented and much-missed Ms MacC.

🎧 The timeless 'Fairytale Of New York', kept off the no.1 slot first by **T'Pau**, then by the **Pet Shop Boys**. Some of her greatest songs were never hit singles, though: check out '15 Minutes' on *Kite*, 'He Never Mentioned Love' on *Electric Landlady* (co-written with **The Pogues'** Jem Finer), and the splendid, bittersweet 'England 2 Colombia 0' on her final, Cuban-influenced album *Tropical Brainstorm*.

✔ And now, time for the obligatory 'Embarrassing Punk Era Name' slot: Kirsty's was (frenetic drum roll)... Mandy Doubt.

✔ For the *TOTP* performance of 'Fairytale', the lyrics had to be amended: the wonderful 'you cheap lousy faggot' became 'you're weak when you're haggard'. Rather loses something, doesn't it? That pesky watershed.

🔊 'I used to worry about writer's block – after every album, basically! But I think this time it was God's way of saying, "You've got nothing to write about, so shut up!" If only more people could hear that, instead of this kind of musical diarrhoea you get with a lot of bands.'

Madness ★★★★

♪ 'The Prince' (1979, no.16)

The nickname 'Nutty Boys' never did inspire much confidence in this writer – I am usually inclined to give anything 'nutty' a wide berth, and the same goes for anything 'wacky' or 'zany'. If you remember Timmy Mallet, you will perhaps understand.

It seemed that Graham 'Suggs' McPherson and his cohorts were never out of the charts in the 1980s, and indeed they are the group to have racked up the most chart weeks in the course of the decade. Unmistakable in their suits and hats, they always seemed too big for the *Top Of The Pops* studio. Thousands of schoolboys sang 'Baggy Trousers' in the playground, and 'Our House' in 1983 was their breakthrough on to the world stage.

Time has been kind to Madness's idiosyncratic, chirpy Brit-ska-pop. People went off them in the late 80s and an attempt to re-form as a 4-piece called The Madness in 1988 didn't work out. However, they subsequently underwent a rehabilitation akin to that enjoyed by ABBA, with the added bonus that Madness are still willing to get back together and perform once in a while, most notably at the 'Madstock' festivals. Suggs managed Liverpool band The Farm for a while, before becoming the genial host of the karaoke show 'Night Fever' (which proved to be that rare beast, a popular Channel 5 programme).

You can be sure, though, that if the DJ puts 'One Step Beyond' on at a wedding disco, at least half a dozen men of similar age will be up and dancing, with their braces twanged and their knees bent. Exuberant, fun and timeless.

✔ TV screenings of the 1982 video for 'It Must Be Love' were accompanied by warnings to children not to imitate the band's actions in the promo, namely jumping into a swimming-pool holding electric guitars...

✔ In 1985, Madness performed a secret gig in a Kentish Town pub under the alias of The Wayfarers. They were trying out songs from the new album *Mad Not Mad*.

✔ The perennial Madness reunions even led to new material in 1999 – the single 'Lovestruck', very much in the style of their old stuff, was a deserving top 10 hit.

Madonna ★★★★

♫ **'Holiday'** (1984, no.6)

The hairstyles. The crucifix. The pouting. *Desperately Seeking Susan*. The Number Ones. The tempestuous marriage to Sean Penn. The children. The henna-and-tattoos re-invention. The wedding in Scotland. Blimey, you don't really need to be told about *Madonna*, do you?

Yes, you probably already know everything that's worth knowing, and more. So I'll just make one small point. On the video to 'Like A Virgin', you'll notice that Madge, while having a good time cavorting about in that gondola, almost brains herself on one of the bridges as they pass under, only just managing to duck in time. How different pop history would have been: we'd have been spared the self-indulgent onanist-fest of the *Sex* book, the early 90s Voguing craze, the fetishist indulgence of her mid-90s *Erotica* period and the perilous pointy bra. And Guy Ritchie would have remained a second-rate Brit-flick director.

♥ It's quite fun to listen to the recent release by Mad

Donna, which is essentially 'Ray Of Light' with the alternative words of the nursery rhyme 'The Wheels On The Bus'. Having small children is a good excuse to buy this. If you don't have any, borrow someone who has. You'll also find it at **www.mothergoose-rocks.com**, along with a host of other similar ventures.

Marillion ★★★★
♫ **'He Knows You Know'** (1983, no.35)

Much-adored rockers from Buckinghamshire, named after Tolkien's novel *The Silmarillion* and fronted in the 1980s by one Derek W. Dick, known to all and sundry as Fish. Just as The Porcupine Tree would in the 1990s, Marillion bravely spurned the prevailing trends of the 80s and took arty, introspective prog-rock to the masses. (Well, to those who could be bothered to listen.) The signature guitar-playing of Steve Rothery lent the band a distinctive sound, and Fish was a charismatic, eccentric front-man. Voted Best New Band by the readers of *Sounds* in 1983, Marillion broke into the single and album charts in the same year. *Script For A Jester's Tear*, another of those love-'em-or-hate-'em epic albums, featured lyrics all written by Fish and was a Top Ten album.

By 1985 and the Number One album *Misplaced Childhood*, Marillion had refined their pop sensibilities enough to produce their most commercial songs, 'Kayleigh' and 'Lavender' (generally among those most hated by the hardcore fans).

After the album *Clutching At Straws*, Marillion and Fish went their separate ways. Mr Dick ventured into a solo career where he could explore his Scottish identity and penchant for pretentious titles to his heart's content. Marillion, meanwhile, entered a second phase – less commercial but interesting in a different way, with new vocalist Steve Hogarth and the accessible albums *Season's End* and *Holidays In Eden*. Many of the die-hard fans jumped ship when they heard the first Hogarth single, the chuggingly radio-friendly rock-out, 'Hooks In You'. However, 1994's concept album *Brave* showed that they had not lost touch with their experimental roots.

🎧 1996's compilation *Best Of Both Worlds* is precisely that – half Fish-era material, half Hogarth. It's an ideal purchase if you have a passing interest in this inventive band but find yourself strangely unmoved by self-indulgent concept albums.

💣 Fish's performance of 'Lavender' on *Top Of The Pops* won't be easily forgotten – rather than miming, he held up cue-cards with key words from the lyrics in felt-tip. He had lost his voice at the time (but he wouldn't have been required to sing live on that particular occasion…)

⏭ They are still recording and performing today, and get together with their fans for annual gatherings at holiday camps, where the highlights include the songs for the set-list being chosen by a bingo machine.

M/A/R/R/S ★★★

♫ **'Pump Up The Volume'** (1987, no.1)

A God-awful strange affair

Nobody had ever heard anything quite like this when 'Pump Up The Volume' assaulted the radio. At the time, we indie-kids with our serious coats and our spiky hair thought this was the spawn of Satan. Now, it just sounds rather quaint with its Casio beat-box, its echoey samples and self-conscious loops. By the time this glittering slice of house knocked the squeaky-clean **Rick Astley** off the top spot, where he had been for 5 weeks, some people were already muttering about the death of 'proper' music. Forget air guitar: this, at a student disco in 1987, was the first record I ever saw anybody doing air *scratching* to. Any single which can inspire someone (even if it was a rather drunk 18-year-old in a daft hat) to do something so monumentally stupid has to be a genuine cultural phenomenon.

M/A/R/R/S got into trouble for sampling from **Stock, Aitken and Waterman**, but sadly, it was only in the courts and not from the taste police. The song they nicked from was SAW's no.13 hit 'Roadblock' from earlier in the same year. The efficient triumvirate won their case but, heart-warmingly, they gave all the damages to Great Ormond Street Hospital. Big 'aaaaaah'.

They weren't the first to get to Number One using samples – Paul Hardcastle had been there in 1985 – but they were arguably the most influential. In retrospect, 'Pump Up The Volume' was almost like Dylan going electric, the next stage in pop's evolution – so much since, for good or ill, has borrowed from it. And here's the problem – they opened the floodgates to the hordes of faceless techno acts whose whack-the-synth-on-and-pop-down-the-pub doodlings would plague the Top 40 in 1988 and beyond.

Various TV-friendly faces pop up now and then and claim to have cut their teeth on their first E in those 'heady' times when *rave* became a noun and *large* turned into a verb. They usually remind me of three things I want to get off my chest. First: the claim that acid house was a 'youth culture which the media didn't understand and tried to suppress'. Oh, and there was I thinking the media not only

273

understood it, but positively tried to publicise it at every opportunity. Well, silly me. Second: the whinges about 'authority' not liking lots of people gathering together in one place. I suppose that's why they're always trying so hard to discourage people from getting into football matches, stadium rock concerts, the Proms, Glastonbury and *Songs of Praise*. And third: look, it was just taking lots of drugs and waving your arms about in a muddy field for twelve hours, and all the pseudy posturing which tries to portray it as a genuine 'cultural phenomenon' conveniently glosses over the fact that most of the music was really, really crap and that people presumably had to take drugs for it to sound any good. (Okay, rant over.)

- Brothers Martyn and Steven Young stayed anonymous during the single's promotion, although they had already had some success with Colourbox. M/A/R/R/S was a merger of Colourbox, A.R.Kane, and DJs Dave Dorrell and CJ Mackintosh.

- The record was technically a double A-side with a track called 'Anitina (The First Time I See She Dance)', which must have been pretty good as it didn't get any airplay.

- And yes, they spelt it like that, complete with the slashes – but probably only people who insist on putting the asterisks in M*A*S*H would be all that bothered.

- A mildly amusing parody, 'Pump Up The Bitter' by Starturn On 45 (Pints), charted at no.12 in 1988. (The 'pork scratching' reference was probably the funniest bit...)

Martika ★★

♫ 'Toy Soldiers' (1989, no.5)

Photogenic brunette, leather jacket and fluffy bob... remember? The Cuban-American Martika hit the top of the charts in the USA with her first hit, a cautionary tale of drug abuse, which also got massive airplay on Radio 1 in the UK... 'I Feel The Earth Move' saw her in the Top Ten again, as did the Prince collaboration 'Love...Thy Will Be Done', and the raunchy 'Martika's Kitchen' was a big hit all over Europe. And she went bleached-blonde in the late 90s – startling.

🎧 There's a 'best of' collection, released 1997, called *More Than You Know*.

✔ Martika's full name is Marta Marrero: 'Martika' means 'Little Marta'. She appeared on several TV shows including the sitcoms *Silver Spoons* and *Diff'rent Strokes*.

✔ In 1990, Martika released an EP simply called *Martika* featuring versions of her songs in Spanish: 'Como Un Juguete' ('Toy Soldiers'), 'Quiero Entregarte Mi Amor' ('More Than You Know') and 'Siento La Tierra Tremblar' ('I Feel The Earth Move'). It apparently got a good reception from the Spanish-speaking community. *Muy bien.*

▸▸ **www.martika.net** is the official site. She's still recording and has released a new dance-orientated single via the Internet.

Matt Bianco ★★

♫ 'Get Out Of Your Lazy Bed' (1984, no.15)

Saturday superstars

Why are they under M and not B? Ah, well, it was a made-up name. Matt Bianco was not a person but a group – Mark Reilly, Kito Poncioni, Danny White and the woman who laughs in the face of my puny spellchecker, Basia Trzetrzelewska.

Matt Bianco were formed in 1982 from the members of Blue Rondo A La Turk. (No, don't bother looking, they're not in. Come on, I only had 80,000 words.) Their first album *Whose Side Are You On* did well in Europe, South East Asia and South Africa, but the line-up split and Reilly teamed up with keyboardist Mark Fisher. The double A-side 'Don't Blame It On That Girl/ Wap-Bam Boogie' backed a jaunty, singalong pop tune with a rather silly dance-orientated piece – both got airplay and took the single to no.11, making it their biggest hit. Like **Five Star** and **All About Eve**, though, they're possibly more memorable for their humiliation on live TV than for their musical output – see below.

✔ Icy-cool, polished Polish singer Basia went on to have a solo career with some likeable stuff in the 90s. Her album *Time and Tide* is worth a listen – it's a bit like **Swing Out Sister** in style, if you like that kind of thing. And it still is, even if you don't.

💣 Okay, in case you were one of the few people who never got to hear about this: the band were being interviewed on *Saturday Superstore*, answering the usual 'What's your favourite colour?' and 'Who do you most fancy?' type of questions. Then along came a bored teenager who didn't take too kindly to foppish, clean-cut popsters telling him to 'get out of his lazy bed' at 10 o'clock on a Saturday morning. There followed the invocation: 'Matt Bianco? Phaah, you're a bunch of *wankers*'. True TV anarchy – much funnier than some vandalistic idiot smashing up the Blue Peter garden.

▸▸ Reilly and Fisher are still working together and have a strong following in the Far East and South Africa. They had a club hit with 'River of Dreams' in 2000, and they're about to unleash a new Matt Bianco album, with tracks described as 'vibrant, up-tempo with a strong samba influence and a very relaxed, acoustic vibe.'

_____

Mel & Kim ★★
♪ **'Showing Out (Get Fresh at the Weekend)'** (1987, no.3)

They told us they were never gonna be respectable. Well, maybe not, but strutting around in Top Shop chic to a Stock (yes, them again) beat was never going to make the Appleby sisters that rebellious. Music for supermarkets? Or more precisely, music to accompany hanging round outside supermarkets in a pastel sweater and scuffed jeans on a Saturday morning? Sneering at Sarah Greene and Phillip Schofield through the window of the TV showroom, making ribald comments at passers-by from the bench next to the monstrous sculpture in the shopping arcade and snogging in public? Think so.

Their crimes against music weren't that enormous, although 'Showing Out' brings back terrifying memories of the days when huge jackets and white socks were the order of the day on programmes like *The Clothes Show*.

The single 'Respectable' has a certain kitsch charm (all

together now: 'tay, tay, tay, tay, t-t-t-t-tay, tay...'). It features a video where the pair try to look really hard by harassing a policeman; it's obviously meant to be a mean and moody psychodrama on the back streets of New York, whereas it actually looks like two girls dolled up for a night on the pull getting lost in a dingy part of South London. We could have done without the Thatcherite anthem 'F.L.M.', though (officially it was 'Fun Love and Money', although some suspect it stood for something earthier). Kim's 1991 solo hit 'Mama' is actually quite nice and tuneful.

This retro kick is obviously getting to me. I think I need to go and lie down and listen to the Dandy Warhols. Very loudly.

◀» Kim: 'We've done the hat trade a big boost. We've definitely set a trend. We've even seen shops – there's one down Walthamstow – where they've got a big sign saying "Mel and Kim hats for sale". But we don't wear them all the time.' (*Smash Hits*, 1988)

◀» Mel on the video to 'Respectable': 'It's based on a kind of *West Side Story* setting which took three days to build. We filmed it in Battersea... Just the two of us, a dog and a black guy who plays a copper who we try to pick a fight with.' (In *Number One* magazine, March 1987.)

▶▶ Sadly Mel died aged 23 in 1990, following a battle with cancer. Kim went on to have what they call 'a moderately successful solo career'.

Men at Work ★★★

♫ 'Down Under' (1983, no.1)

They came from a land down under, but singer and songwriter Colin Hay originally came from a land a little further north, as he was born in Scotland but moved to Australia as a teenager.

Their chart-topper is certainly the only 80s single we can find which mentions a Vegemite sandwich. The reference had pop-pickers puzzling back in those pre-*Neighbours* days, but now we know it's a sort of yeast extract, a bit like Marmite only not as nice.

The band were a 5-piece who'd already arrived in the US by the time they made the UK charts. The album *Business As Usual*, recorded on a modest budget ($17,000) in just a few weeks, spent 15 weeks at the top of the American album charts. Second album *Cargo* sold 3 million, but they split in 1985 citing various 'differences'.

▶▶ Colin Hay and multi-instrumentalist Greg Ham had teamed up again by the late 90s to launch a new incarnation of the Men, but without the other original members. Rumour had it that some of them weren't even on speaking terms. Perhaps one of them nicked the other's Vegemite sandwich.

George Michael ★★★★

♫ 'Careless Whisper' (1984, no.1)

When one member of a boy-band duo starts having solo hits, the other must know that the writing is on the wall. So it was for Andrew 'third wheel of a bicycle' Ridgeley of **Wham!**, whose non-participation in 'Careless Whisper' didn't affect its success one iota. In fact, George's solo debut became one of the biggest hits of the decade. It stayed in the charts for 17 weeks, with three of those at Number One (having displaced the decade's longest runner, 'Two Tribes' by **Frankie**), is still a karaoke favourite and is featured on numerous compilations called *Endearing Retro Ballads For Getting Your Significant Other In The Mood* (well, they should be). As if that wasn't enough, George topped the charts in America, too, and he followed on with two more Number Ones, 'A Different Corner' and 'I Knew You Were Waiting, Brackets, For Me, Close Brackets' (as it's known in pub quizzes), his duet with the legendary Aretha Franklin.

Throughout all this, George allowed his image to mature (the mullet trimmed back to a bouffant, the stubble a little thicker, the clothes a little more leather-based) as his fans grew up. Those giggly teenage girls who had danced to 'Bad Boys' were holding down jobs on the Boots cosmetics counter by the time George's first album hit the shops, and they had progressed from talking about sex to actually doing it. (This was back in the days when this took four years, rather than four minutes.) It was time for something a little raunchier, and 'I Want Your Sex' provided it. Yet another record banned, yet more tabloid outrage, yet more sales – it was 'Relax' all over again, but this time they couldn't even say the title of the record on the radio and we had the spectacle of Peter Powell and/or Mike Smith referring to it as 'I Want' in the *Top Of The Pops* chart countdown. After that, the less controversial no.2 'Faith' was simplicity itself – an organ intro, a simple guitar chord which anyone could copy (well, all right, perhaps Andrew Ridgeley would have had trouble) and a breathy vocal.

Mention is needed, in passing, of the strange cover of the album *Faith*, on which, extraordinarily, the now-mature artist appeared to be sniffing the armpit of his leather jacket... or possibly trying, for reasons best known to himself, to climb inside it.

He trailed the new album *Listen Without Prejudice Vol. 1* with songs showcasing a new breadth and maturity like 'Praying For Time' and 'Waiting For That Day'. It had a third of the sales of *Faith*, but George was well on his way to becoming a superstar. Awaiting him in the 1990s were the 'misunderstood' period, the record company shenanigans, the Diana-synchronicity and the frolics in public conveniences. George revelled in the irony of the latter in his song 'Outside', did his community service and seems to have avoided any associated stigma. Nothing like a criminal record to boost a flagging career – although those who have heard his cover of 'Roxanne' may beg to differ.

- His hits are collected on the double album *Ladies and Gentlemen*, which is well worth having. To celebrate it, George revisited his Greatest Haircuts.

- George was born Georgios Kyriacos Panayiotou in 1963 in Finchley, London.

- On the album *Faith*, George uses the word 'baby' 35 times in total: 4 times in the title track, 6 in 'Father Figure', 4 in 'I Want Your Sex (Part 1)', 6 in 'I Want Your Sex (Part 2)', 2 in 'Hard Day', 2 in 'Hand To Mouth', 3 in 'Look At Your Hands', and 8 in 'Monkey'. These were counted up by a George fan who, let's be honest, needs to get out even more than I do.

- George's second solo Number One, 'A Different Corner' in 1986, was the first UK chart-topper to be written, produced, arranged and performed by one person.

- He has performed at several charity concerts including the Linda McCartney tribute, the NetAid event and a concert for gay activists Stonewall.

◀» 'Bjorn Borg may have invented designer stubble, but Michael, on *Faith*, turned it into a lifestyle issue. The look was meant to suggest ruggedness and intensity. In the event, it became known as Michael's "fairy biker" look. Ridgeley, you have to feel, would not have allowed it.' From the *Sunday Times*, 7th Jan. 1996.

Mike & the Mechanics ★★★
♪ **'Silent Running (On Dangerous Ground)'** (1986, no. 21)

Cardigan rock

All the members of Genesis sensibly had Saturday jobs to dabble with whenever their three-man dad-rock industry was going through a slack phase. Phil Collins worked on his solo material (which sounded the same as Genesis by this stage), Tony Banks wrote film soundtracks (and was Minister For Sport – no, not really) and Mike Rutherford's project became a proper, fully-fledged band. Mike's sideshow was arguably more interesting at times than some of the Genesis material he had to work with. His songwriting collaborators in the Mechanics were B.A. Robertson and Chris Neil, while vocal duties were performed by former Ace and **Squeeze** vocalist Paul Carrack (a man with a penchant for headscarves and shades) and Sad Café's Paul Young (no relation, and sadly died in 2000).

Standout tracks are the 1986 single 'Silent Running (On Dangerous Ground)' and 1989's epic no.2 'The Living Years', which is about the death of Rutherford's father. I'm torn when it comes to the latter – part of me thinks it's shamefully manipulative, while part of me finds it a moving and heartfelt record. It certainly has a great feel, some poignant observations and a nicely-structured melody – and let's face it, in 1989, anything halfway decent was going to stand out.

- The Mechanics amassed enough singles for a compilation, *Hits* – well worth a listen, not just for 'The Living Years' but also for later tracks 'A Beggar On A Beach of Gold' and 'Another Cup Of Coffee', which didn't make as much chart impact. You'll like them if you prefer to get a seat in the pub, you wish you had started to play the guitar earlier and you're starting to appreciate the convenience of owning a shed. Like me.

- Radio 1's Simon Bates declared in February 1989 that if 'The Living Years' wasn't Number One on the following Sunday, he would get down on his knees and scrub the steps of Broadcasting House with a toothbrush. It wasn't, so he did. Live on air. Whether this made for brilliant radio is debatable.

- **http://home.planetinternet.be/~chrischa/Parlour.htm** is a nice tribute site.

Milli Vanilli ★

♪ **'Girl You Know It's True'** (1988, no.3)

Ventriloquism without tears
Pop duo in 'have been known not to sing on records' shock! Whatever next – rumours of the Pope's religion and the toilet habits of bears? Today's boy and girl bands, of course, are above reproach in this respect... hmm.

Perhaps the big hit single should have been called 'Girl You Know It's All A Bit Of A Storm In A Teacup, Frankly'. In case the revelation passed you by, the pop world was shaken in 1989 by the news that Milli Vanilli's front-men – the two lithe, photogenic, dreadlocked guys who pranced in the promos and generally touted themselves around as The 'Nilli – were, in fact, just models. The musical input was, and always had been, provided by some balding blokes, who were slick musicians but, well, no oil-paintings. Producer Frank Farian was behind the venture – yes, the same man who had given us Boney M in the 70s.

In the same year, it was revealed that (a) kiddies' favourite Phillip Schofield wasn't actually real either, and could only speak if he had Gordon the Gopher's paw shoved up his backside, (b) globetrotting DJ Simon Bates had not really roughed it round the world for a year but had recorded his entire world expedition from a shed in Basildon, and (c) the Queen Mother had died in 1983 and was now replaced on walkabouts by an android double.

Well, not really, of course, but it would have been a lot more interesting than this non-scandal. You have to ask yourself, really, how much less 'authentic' the whole undertaking was than the rest of the pop industry...

Oh, and the music? Dull, funky-clunky, squeaky soul-pop which sometimes backs unwittingly into melody.

💣 The pouting mimers were called Rob Pilatus and Fab Morvan. Rob first tried to commit suicide in 1991, when it all first began to go wrong. He died in 1998 at the age of 32, his death ascribed to a lethal mixture of alcohol and pills.

✔ As if all that wasn't bad enough, their biggest hit 'Girl I'm Gonna Miss You' (UK no.2, US no.1) would appear to pinch its hook from a well-known line in the, ah, not exactly obscure 'Ruby Tuesday' by a popular beat combo called The Rolling Stones...

✔ Just for the record, they had a total of three US Number Ones, and a Grammy for Best New Artist. Oh dear, how embarrassing.

✔ An interesting (if over-intellectualised) article called 'Milli Vanilli and the Scapegoating of the Inauthentic' can be read at: **http://eserver.org/bs/09/Friedman.html**

◁» The last word goes to Rob, who, interviewed in *Smash Hits* in 1989, had the following wisdom to offer: 'I dressed every time in women's clothes with the dress. Maybe this is because I was always with the nurses from the church in the childhouse [*i.e. the nuns in the orphanage he was in as a child*]. I wanted to be a prayer, you know? A priest. My adopted father took me every time to the church and I thought the priests were very glamorous and I would every time wear the woman's dress that looked like a priest...'

Kylie Minogue ★★★
⊘ **Kylie** ♪ **'I Should Be So Lucky'** (1988, no.1)

Blondes have more fun
Whether they call her the Diminutive Diva, the Pop Princess or the Galactic Goddess, it seems you can't escape Kylie in this day and age. Flashing her underwear at the Brit Awards, pirouetting in little gold dresses and being 'bootlegged' by having her latest huge hit bolted on to 'Blue Monday' – all these things and more make Kylie a media

285

darling, a fashion icon and a pop legend.

Oh, 'twas not always so. Oh, no no no. For back in the days of the twentieth century, in the year of our Lord, nineteen hundred and eighty-eight, in the Time Of The Neighbours, there was the bubble perm. And lo, there was the striped top. And behold, there was the rather unconvincing miming and stilted dancing to 'Especially For You' with fellow heart-throb **Jason Donovan**. How quickly we forget.

Kylie was one of the **Stock, Aitken and Waterman** crowd, the first of many soap stars to be rinsed down and stuck in front of a microphone in the late 1980s. Now, this wasn't always terribly advisable, was it? These days, whenever the latest chubby *Emmerdale* nymphet is squeezed into a red leather dress and wheeled into the studio to warble her way through a garage version of 'I Only Wanna Be With You', the phrase 'Remember Malandra Burrows! And tremble!' should be emblazoned in blood above the studio door.

With Kylie, though, you have to admit it seemed to work – her first single stayed at Number One for five weeks in this country, after all, and the duet with Jason narrowly missed being a Christmas chart-topper. She had the best career start of any chart act at that time, with pretty much everything she did getting into the Top Two. But there was something missing. Although Kylie *could* sing, that fact wasn't evident until later, and she was just homogenized by SAW, not given room to breathe amongst all the rest of them – 'Hand On Your Heart' could have been **Sinitta**, 'Got To Be Certain' could have been **Mel & Kim**.

It's almost physically painful to recall, now, but those early hits were... *awful*. Really God-awful, the sort of stuff which made you think that classy pop was dead and Pete Waterman was its Grim Reaper. 'Je Ne Sais Pas Pourquoi', 'Wouldn't Change A Thing', 'Never Too Late'... They are, of course, all eternally hummable and will instantly transport you back into a world where TV at breakfast was still a relative novelty, Radio 1 sported the talents of Jakki '80s spelling' Brambles, furry dice in cars were fashionable and some of the British electorate still had faith in a ginger Welsh bloke.

It was only in the 90s that Ms Minogue began to be taken seriously. She toyed with a more sexy persona on a few singles, and then her first proper 'grown-up' track 'Confide In Me' came out on the terrifyingly hip Deconstruction label. She'd straightened her hair, swapped Jason for Michael Hutchence of INXS, and before long she was singing songs written by James Dean Bradfield of the Manic Street Preachers ('Some Kind Of Bliss').

But hey, that's all to come in the 90s book, if we ever do it. For now, remember her finest moments with that cheesy grin and that terribly earnest miming. And picture that 'I Should Be So Lucky' video with her up to her neck in bubble-bath. It seems so appropriate, somehow.

✔ The Manic Street Preachers wrote their 1992 hit 'Little Baby Nothing' envisaging that Kylie would do the guest vocals. In the end, the idea was vetocd and former porn star Traci Lords took her place.

✔ Until the coming of the delectable Holly Valance in 2002, Kylie and Jason were the only *Neighbours* stars to have had UK Number One singles.

🔊 Kylie in 1989, talking about the strangest newspaper story associated with her: 'The headline was "Is Kylie An Alien?" and the story was all about how if there was an alien life form on earth then they would have certain features. And they decided to match up these features to mine. They used the topless photo of me on the front page and they were saying that these aliens would have elfin features and small breasts, and I think they said big hips, which was a bit rude because I certainly haven't got big hips.'

♥ And don't forget the French and Saunders opera version of 'I Should Be So Lucky'... especially if Kylie decides to release a 2008 anniversary remix.

Mr Mister ★★

♪ **'Broken Wings'** (1985, no. 4)

Well, Kayleigh, you thought you suffered from being born to a pair of Marillion fans in 1985. But what about your mate whose mum and dad were into Mr Mister? Yes, exactly. Bet you don't envy poor Kyrie.

The band was formed in 1982 in Phoenix, Arizona by Richard Page (bass and vocals) and Steve George (keyboards and vocals), who had established their MOR credentials as session musicians for John Parr, Chaka Khan and others. Their modest total of two UK hits in the mid-80s belies their success elsewhere – both the big songs, 'Broken Wings' and 'Kyrie', were Number Ones in the US and they were twice nominated for a Grammy for Best Pop Vocal Group, while the album *Welcome To The Real World* sold over 10 million copies worldwide.

Richard Page stuck with Mr Mister despite being offered lead vocal duties with both Toto and Chicago. However, in one of those twists of fate for which the music business seems renowned, later albums *Go On* and *Pull* didn't do so well for them, with the latter not even getting a proper release, and the band split in 1989.

🎧 'Broken Wings' is a very nice song, actually. You know those compilations with a desert highway and a cactus on the cover, and a title in metallic lettering, usually something like *Drive Carefully, Won't You?* or *Greatest Ever Soft Metal For Girls* or *Ultimate Ballads With Big Show-Off Guitar Solos?* That's where you'll find Mr Mister, alongside REO Speedwagon and **Chris Rea**.

✓ 'Kyrie Eleison' means 'God, have mercy', an invocation in the Roman Catholic Mass. Apparently the band didn't mean any great religious significance to be read into this – they just liked the emotive sound of the phrase...

◀》 'We used to call each other "Mr. This" and "Mr. That" all the time. Our record company had been starting to come up with name suggestions, and when they heard we were giving each other these nicknames, they said "Why don't you guys just call yourselves Mr. Mister?" ' (Richard Page)

▶▶ The various band members have continued to find work: Page, in particular has kept up his profile by co-writing Madonna's 1994 hit 'I'll Remember', releasing a solo debut, *Shelter Me*, in 1996, and working on Disney musicals.

Morris Minor and the Majors ★★
♪ **'Stutter Rap (No Sleep 'Til Bedtime)'** (1988, no.4)

Imitation may be the sincerest form of flattery – but taking the piss, especially out of rappers, is so much more fun. The brainchild of comedian Tony Hawks (yes, that comedian bloke who travelled round Ireland with a fridge), 'Stutter Rap' is a contender for the funniest record of the decade. The first time you hear it, anyway.

Released at the height of **Beastie Boys** mania, it brilliantly parodies the posturing of the American trio's whiteboy rap – it's all the 'shouting' which makes them so tired, snappy and irritable, apparently. It may be a one-joke record, but it's carried to its natural length and no further.

✔ Hawks was a songwriter before he became a comedian, supporting himself by playing the piano and singing in pubs and wine bars. He co-wrote three musicals, all of which got to the final of The Vivien Ellis Prize for Young Composers for the Musical Stage, has played several roles in comedy sci-fi series *Red Dwarf*, and also wrote the 'Butterkist' popcorn jingle ('Butterkist, Butterkist, ra-ra-ra').

✔ An unsuccessful second single from Morris Minor, 'Here Comes The Chorus', was a parody of **Stock, Aitken and Waterman**. Fish in a barrel, though.

▶▶ Hawks, ever one for a bet, was recently challenged by a friend to have another hit single. He teamed up with a gorgeous Romanian model to record a guitar ballad, but it flopped. He eventually had a hit in Albania with the help of Norman Wisdom.

_____

Alison Moyet ★★★

♪ **'Love Resurrection'** (1984, no.10)

Possessed of a big, bluesy voice and a tranche of melodic songs, Ms Moyet carved out a decent solo career after leaving **Yazoo**. Albums *Alf* and *Raindancing* were big commercial hits. While her 90s albums *Hoodoo* and *Essex* didn't have the same success, they saw her unafraid to experiment musically, and to change her look as well. The 'Alf' moniker may have deliberately downplayed her femininity, but she imbued her performances with a sensual charm. Her versatility shines through as she gives equal force to strong pop-rock like 'Is This Love', late-night mellow covers of 'Love Letters' and 'That Ole Devil Called Love', and up-tempo stuff like 'Whispering Your Name'.

- ☻ A shame 'Ordinary Girl' wasn't a hit (it got to no.43 in 1987). It's on the *Singles* collection, but doesn't qualify for inclusion on *The Essential Alison Moyet*.

- ♥ Her most famous impersonator is probably Jacqui Cann, who won *Stars In Their Eyes* in 1993 by 'doing' Alison.

- ▶▶ The official site **www.alisonmoyet.com** is very much about the Alison of Now, rather than Then. Watch out for the irritating Flash graphics, especially if strobe lighting gives you a headache. Alison recently appeared on stage in *Chicago* and popped up on Lesley Garrett's TV show.

- ▶▶ 2002 album *Hometime* has gained much critical favour. Alison stuck to her guns to record it – apparently the A&R men at her previous record company had been trying to steer her towards boy-band songwriters, with the instruction that 'Beggars can't be choosers'. Alison, bless her, informed them, 'This beggar's choosy.'

Musical Youth ✩✩

♬ **'Pass the Dutchie'** (1982, no. 1)

In 1982, the concept of child pop stars wasn't one which

inspired confidence. Recent juvenile offenders in the charts, after all, had included Little Jimmy Osmond and the **St Winifred's School Choir**. Then along came the Youth from Birmingham with their reggae-flavoured pop, and the rest was history.

The group was formed in the 1970s by brothers Junior and Patrick Waite, helped by their father Freddie, who had been in the Jamaican band The Techniques. Brothers Michael and Kelvin Grant also joined, and Dennis Seaton became the lead singer. When they appeared on *Top Of The Pops*, all aged between 13 and 15, they looked as if they could scarcely believe it. Their chart-topper achieved some notoriety as – and you may know this story – the original song by the Mighty Diamonds referred to the passing to the left-hand side of a 'kutchie', slang for a popular home-made device for ingesting herbal substances. It was always going to be, shall we say, unlikely that a band would promote the niceties of drug etiquette on *Blue Peter*, and so the alternative lyric referring to a 'dutchie' was smuggled in. The only thing a 'dutchie' could be, apparently, was a sort of casserole dish, and so overnight the song became a culinary metaphor. (Just imagine how other chemically-enhanced lyrics could have been adapted by the cunning use of food euphemisms: the Shamen could have sung 'Peas are good, peas are good! Egg and peas are good!', for example, or Afroman might have regaled us with 'Because I Like Pie'.)

Often thought to be one-hit wonders, Musical Youth also sneaked into the Top 20 with 'Youth of Today' and 'Never Gonna Give You Up' (not the **Rick Astley** song but a different one). They split in 1985, but will always be remembered for transforming a cheeky drug anthem into a wholesome tale of boy scouts sharing a hearty stew around the campfire.

✔   The group also appeared as backing vocalists on

Donna Summer's 1983 single, 'Unconditional Love.'

▶▶ Dennis Seaton did well for himself by putting all his royalties in trust. He recently fronted a band called 'XMY' (ex-Musical Youth). Patrick Waite died in 1993, and the brothers Grant continue to work in the music industry.

pause

**narrative rather than
enigmatic allusiveness**

Nena ★★★

♪ '99 Red Balloons' (1984, no.1)

Nena Kerner was the front-girl for the band Nena, if that's not too confusing. Famous for her raffish, hirsute-armpit look, she got plenty of attention when the UK version of their German hit '99 Luftballons' made it to the top of the charts over here. The song, about Cold War paranoia, was released internationally after its German success; it has survived well, and its upbeat exuberance makes it a favourite for compilations and retro nights.

✔ A 'Luftballon' is just the word for a balloon, whatever its colour; the translators took a few liberties to make it scan better.

✔ The others? Carlo Karges (guitar) Uwe Fahrenkrog-Petersen (keyboards) Jürgen Dehmel (bass) and Rolf Brendel (drums).

✔ Their first TV appearance was on the German programme *Musikladen* in 1982.

✔ Not to be confused with: other Teutonic rock-chick Nina Hagen, news correspondent Nena Nanna, or, indeed, **Neneh Cherry**.

▶▶ If you know any German, **www.nena.com** (*'die Offizielle Nena-Homepage'*) is well worth a look. Although the band broke up in 1987, Nena the solo artist continues to be a big star in Germany as a musician and TV presenter. She performs material written with a number of different collaborators, including music for children. (She has four *Kinder* of her own.) And it looks as if she's worn well.

New Order ★★★★★

♪ 'Ceremony' (1981, no.34)

From post-punk to Ibiza

Cards on the table again: foursome New Order are, if I have to have such a thing, my favourite band of the 1980s – at least, when I'm in the mood for glacial minimalism, alarmingly opaque lyrics and a frequently frustrating lack of erudition.

They surged from the ashes of **Joy Division**, with the artist formerly known as Bernard Dicken and Bernard Albrecht now reborn as Barney Sumner, a guitarist and singer who admitted he had trouble doing the two activities simultaneously. Peter Hook continued to crouch scarily over his bass like a Neolithic man skinning a small mammal, while Stephen Morris, who banged the drums, added programming the drum-machine to his repertoire. Morris's girlfriend Gillian Gilbert was brought in on keyboards, her qualification for the role being an endearing inability to tell the black notes from the white ones. Perhaps the spirit of punk still lingered in the streets of Manchester.

Some **Joy Division** material, especially the menacing 12" mix of 'She's Lost Control', had hinted at what was to come. Early New Order hits 'Ceremony' (which was an old Joy Division song anyway) and 'Everything's Gone Green' (is that title a reference to schizophrenics' 'green-outs'?) still struggled to shake off the ghost of Ian Curtis, but Sumner soon developed his own vocal style.

Pale, worryingly smart and unsmiling, they gave their own chilly take on the sparse electronic landscapes of the early 80s in the albums *Movement* (1981) and *Power, Corruption & Lies* (1983). Then came the single of all singles: 'Blue Monday', charting twice in 1983, didn't feature on a studio album, although its roots can clearly be heard in the track '586' from *Power Corruption & Lies*. Crisp, uncluttered and hugely influential, 'Blue Monday' is driven by its structure rather than its very simple melody. It was, and remains, the biggest-selling vinyl 12" of all time, and its profits helped to fund the Hacienda club.

The brief but intensely varied *Low-Life* (1985) was the first album to feature the band's photos on the sleeve, and gave us some of their best songs, including 'Subculture' and the epic ghost story rock-out 'Love Vigilantes'. After the well-received *Brotherhood* (1986), the band looked to their past to cement their future – the 1987 double album *Substance* was a collection of all their 12" singles together with their B-sides. Now, at last, those who had come late to New Order in the 1980s could discover where they had been – but it wasn't always pretty, as some of those B-sides are strange beasts. There are tedious dub versions of hits ('Kiss of Death' from 'The Perfect Kiss') and dull switch-the-drum-machine-on instrumentals ('The Beach' from 'Blue Monday', fun for rookie DJs, boring for a normal listener) but also some hidden gems (*crime passionel* vignette '1963', one of their very best songs and finally released as a single in its own right in 1995). All this esoteric stuff created a brand of fan who'd never set foot in a club, the New Order anoraks (24-hour parka people?).

A pert, tinny 'Blue Monday' remix, boxing its elegant sprawl into four minutes, rewarded them with a Top 3 hit in the spring of 1988. They ended the decade by sunning themselves in Ibiza, and as Barney admitted on the album which emerged, you didn't get a tan like that for nothing. The first single was an odd choice, a jaw-dropping moment of revelation for the post-punks who'd hung on since the Curtis days – the moment when New Order's total embracing of dance culture was unleashed upon the world. 'Fine Time' was packed so full of breaks and amusing vocoder antics and blinky-bloinky stuff and twiddly bits (you'll notice I'm getting really technical here, so keep up), that it sounded for a few glorious minutes as if New Order had finally gone mad, flipping out on too much sun and Ecstasy. The Balearic-bronzed album *Technique* remains one of their best, with holiday romance story 'Mr Disco' and the crunchy-guitar-driven 'Run' just two of the high points. And, capping the decade, their soccer anthem 'World in Motion' from 1990 is the second greatest football song ever (after Ian Broudie's 'Three Lions').

- If you don't get a little shiver hearing the original 'Blue Monday' in a club, then you probably don't like the 80s. As well as the radio-friendly '88 remix, there is – if you are feeling really brave – the Hardfloor Mix of 1995, which is a pretty powerful reworking. Could it have been inspired by the success of the dance record 'How Does It Feel' by Electroset, which samples that particular line from 'Blue Monday'?

- I like 'Temptation' myself, and it was re-done for the promotion of the 2002 Commonwealth Games. If you want your New Order songs with a vestige of narrative rather than enigmatic allusiveness, go for 'Love Vigilantes' or the splendid, timeless hymn to lost innocence, 'True Faith'. And 'Ruined In A Day' is a moving elegy for Factory records.

- Their *Best Of* is a fair compilation of their creative peaks, but *Substance*, if you can still get hold of it, is a sequence of fascinating snapshots of an evolving band. I've almost worn out the tape copy I bought in 1987 – can anyone get me the CD cheap? (Well, it was worth a shot.)

- Many a *Top Of The Pops* has been enlivened by Barney's off-key singing, Hooky's primeval bass antics, Gillian's monodigit keyboard skills and Stephen's manic 'it's me, honest, not the machine' drumming.

- On *Brotherhood*'s final track 'Every Second Counts', Barney has a 'laughing Elvis' moment: presumably realising the silliness of the lyrics, he has a fit of the giggles in the opening verse, which he then only just manages to contain for the rest of the song.

- The original 'Blue Monday' single was packaged to look like a computer floppy-disk.

- New Order song titles can seem elusive because they often mean bugger-all, having been chosen from a shortlist of random words written up on a board by the band. Depending on how you feel about them, this is either a) the postmodern, media-savvy deconstruction of vapid commercial demands, or b) lazy.

- One of the best covers is a sparse, acoustic version of 'Bizarre Love Triangle' by Frente which appeared on the *Melody Maker*'s *Best of 1994* compilation. There's also a French version of 'Blue Monday' called 'Lundi Bleu', by The Times.

- Barney's **Electronic** was the most successful sideshow, with Peter Hook's Revenge failing to make much more of an impact than the other two's, er, The Other Two. After the famous and public demise of the Factory label, they came back for one 90s album, *Republic*, on London Records, after which Hook formed Monaco. The 2001 comeback *Get Ready*, a hard-edged return to rock, was the album they said they'd never make. 'World In Motion' was re-released in 2002 to tie in with the World Cup.

Olivia Newton-John ★★

♫ **'If Not For You'** (1971, no. 7)

This blonde bombshell's early career need not preoccupy us much here, as most people of a certain age will have become aware of her during the late-70s *Grease* craze. As primary-school kids, we loved the songs and weren't yet cynical enough to realise that, if the best the post-punk 70s could offer was a 50s revival, we were in trouble. However, her transformation from demure cheerleader to slinky, cat-suited temptress is an undeniable high-point of a film which isn't really my bag. If you're a fan of that movie genre where people act woodenly for five minutes before breaking with visible relief into a 'spontaneous', choreographed dance routine in a school playground, you're welcome to it.

'Xanadu' took her to the top of the charts again with the Electric Light Orchestra, even though the fantasy musical it came from was savaged by the critics. Just over a year later, the video for her Top 10 hit 'Physical' memorably featured Ms N-J in various soft-focus poses in a pastel leotard and a sweat-band, working out in a gym. Because that's what the song's about, you see. It's a paean to the delights of aerobics, thigh-trimmers and half an hour on the rowing-machine just to keep the cellulite at bay. What, you thought it was about shagging? How rude.

Although Olivia's chart career never again reached such heights in the 1980s, she kept herself in the public eye with other activities like hosting a reception for the American Olympic team in 1984, marrying dancer Matt Lattanzi, giving birth to daughter Chloe and becoming a Goodwill Ambassador for the UN. She even had her own long-term stalker – which, let's face it, is much better for your street-cred than any schmaltzy musical.

Nicole ★★

♫ 'A Little Peace' (1982, no.1)

You can count the number of UK hits actually sung in German on the fingers of one hand and still have enough left for an obscene gesture – although three German acts topped the UK charts in the 1980s (plus one misleadingly-named band who were American but sported the name of a German city). This winsome Fräulein from Neunkirchen in the Saarland was one of them. Armed only with a guitar and her disarming naïveté, she stormed Eurovision in April 1982 with '*Ein Bißchen Frieden*' and consolidated this with a UK no.1 in May. It goes without saying that the English version 'A Little Peace' was the one to be a hit over here.

The Eurovision Song Contest was 27 years old – ten years older than Nicole – when she became its first German winner. The 1982 competition was hosted by Jan Leeming in Harrogate (thanks to **Bucks Fizz's** win the previous year) and will always be remembered for Nicole's lap-of-honour performance in a succession of languages. Nicole, who performed last, was the runaway winner with her perky hymn to world peace; she came a clear 61 points ahead of the Israeli runner-up, Avi Toledano, and 9 of the 17 other countries taking part gave Germany the top score of 12 points. Up-tempo British duo Bardo, who had been tipped to repeat the UK's success, had to make do with 7th place.

Anyway, it's a pleasant enough song – the sort of thing you start out thinking you should hate, then find yourself humming on the bus.

Oh – **Kraftwerk** and **Nena,** to answer your question. And **Berlin,** to answer the other.

✔ There have been at least four other recording artists called Nicole, including a Chilean star and an American R'n'B diva who narrowly missed the

UK charts in 1985.

✓ 'A Little Peace' is the ninth biggest Eurovision hit in the history of the UK Top 40, and the best-selling one not to have been originally recorded in English. Pay attention at ze back, zere vill be a short test at ze end.

▶▶ **www.geocities.com/TelevisionCity/1812/where now. htm** features Nicole, who's still a big star in Germany, along with some other past Eurovision winners. I'm sure you'll agree it's unmissable.

1927 ★★

This Aussie group had no UK hits, but deserve an honourable mention for trying: the hauntingly catchy 'That's When I Think Of You' just missed our Top 40 in 1989.

A shame they couldn't have been bigger: in their native land, the album ...*Ish!* was a Number One, even though the band – comprising Gary Frost (guitar), Eric Weideman (vocals), Bill Frost (bass) and James Barton (drums) – had initially been rejected by record companies all over Australia. Just goes to show you have to keep trying. The band broke up in 1993 after three albums.

✓ 'That's When I Think Of You' won the 1988 Australian Record Industry Association (ARIA) award for Best Debut Single.

Nu Shooz ★ ★

♫ **'I Can't Wait'** (1986, no.2)

More orthographically-challenged performers, this time a couple from Portland, Oregon in the USA. John Smith sported a frizzy look under a beret, while Valerie Day favoured a broad-brimmed hat and blonde highlights. Remember them? Probably not. Their albums were *Can't Turn It Off* (1982), *Poolside* (1986) and *Told U So* (1987). You can read a lot more about the history of Nu Shooz and associated bands at (deep breath here): **www.clubfree style.com/onstage/history_of_freestyle/freestyle-dance-music.htm**

♥ Oh, the joy of 'UK garage'. Yes, 'I Can't Wait' was exhumed and given the Noughties treatment by leather-clad sirens Ladies First in 2002.

Gary Numan ★ ★ ★ ★

♫ **'Are "Friends" Electric?'** (1979, no.1, with Tubeway Army)

Eccentric superstar whose industrial synth sounds first caught the ear in 1979 with Tubeway Army. Gary decided to record under his own name from then on, and topped the charts again with 'Cars' in the same year. Tall and striking, leather-clad with teeth like a heliograph, he was always good at his own publicity – despite the fact that he would never again have a Top Ten single after 1982, he kept himself in the public eye throughout the 80s, and 'Cars' cracked the American Top Ten (his one and only US hit).

The boiler-suited, robotic image of his backing musicians recalled **Kraftwerk**. Numan fans, who call themselves 'Numanoids', like to copy Gary's dress sense (such as it is) and make-up, and will devotedly travel the world to see him. Or even marry him.

- In 1982, Gary appeared at Uxbridge Magistrates' Court, charged with carrying an offensive weapon (a baseball bat). The charges were dropped.

- Real name Gary Webb, he was the son of Tony, a British Airways bus driver. His dad became his manager and Mum, Beryl, looks after the correspondence with fans.

- His obligatory 1976 punk outfit had the disappointingly sensible name of The Lasers.

- Gary holds a pilot's licence, which he obtained in 1980; he then flew around the world in a single-engine Cessna in 1981, and was forced to make a premature end to the journey in India.

- 'I just want to be proud of the music I make and that pride does not come only from chart success. It's true that I want to be successful but there are ways of being successful that don't involve the singles chart and being interviewed on children's TV in between the latest boy-band and Britney.'

pause

odd fixation with a French martyr

Billy Ocean ★★★

♫ **'Love Really Hurts Without You'** (1976, no.2)

Girls, if a man tried to chat you up by telling you get outta his dreams and get into his car, you'd tell him where to go – wouldn't you? Still, this purveyor of corny chat-up lines to rival those of **Terence Trent D'Arby** had an impressive run of hits from the late 70s through to 1988, including the gnomic 1986 single 'When the Going Gets Tough, the Tough Get Going', which one just can't resist saying was a chart-topper on both sides of the… ah, yes, moving on to avoid the obvious joke. He was Trinidadian by birth and an Eastender by adoption, and his mother knew him by the somewhat less watery moniker of Leslie Charles.

Famous also for the impressive piece of niche marketing which saw 'African Queen' released in Africa, 'European Queen' in Europe and 'Caribbean Queen' in the US (and also over here, in the end).

✔ Sources disagree as to whether he was born in 1950 or 1952, which is mildly interesting.

✔ 'Caribbean Queen' won Billy a Grammy in 1985 for 'Best Male Vocal Performance in R&B'.

▶▶ Today, Billy is a Rastafarian who enjoys gardening. Really.

Hazel O'Connor ★★

♫ **'Eighth Day'** (1980, no.5)

Hazel was from the unglamorous Coventry, and before becoming a pop star she worked as a dancer, English teacher and nude model (although, we think, not all at the same time). Got noticed when she starred in the 1980 punk movie *Breaking Glass*, whose strapline was 'The experience is shattering!' and which is memorably described in *Halliwell's Film Guide* as a 'garish, freakish musical with unattractive characters'.

Hazel's first LP was recorded with the group Megahype, including her brother Neil on guitar. She's probably most famous for 'Will You', an epic ballad of late-night beverage drinking and anguished indecision, featuring a sax solo rather longer than mortal man was born to endure. The most reassuring thing is that she's not related – as far as we know – to either Sinead or Des.

● Hazel was involved in a 14-year legal battle to claim royalties for her songs, which left her financially and emotionally drained. The 'men in suits' from her former record company are now satirised in her live show as two glove-puppets called 'Mr Pelvis and Mr Damage of Shaft Records'. When she tells the audience that these gentlemen are now bankrupt, there are usually wild whoops of joy.

▶▶ Her show *Beyond Breaking Glass* was performed at the 1998 Edinburgh Festival and subsequently toured. She has recently released a new album, *Ignite*, but has no plans to tour to support it.

Orange Juice ★★★

♪ **'Rip It Up'** (1983, no.8)

It's that 'before he was really famous' moment from young Edwyn Collins, whose distinctive voice tells us to rip it up and start again. Famous for helping Alan Horne to found Postcard Records, which became a home to **Aztec**

Camera and The Go-Betweens, then deserting them for Polydor. Orange Juice also brought us the drumming of Zeke Manyika, who went on to be an acclaimed artist in his own right. Unfortunately for the band, having an illegal Zimbabwean immigrant as their drummer made it rather difficult to tour internationally...

The band disintegrated with members moving on to other projects. Mr Collins, of course, recorded the international smash hit 'A Girl Like You', which took the world's playlists by storm in 1995. He still continues to record as a solo artist, and **www.edwyncollins.com** has all the info on his latest releases.

- ✓ Silly punk name: the band were known as Nu-Sonics when they formed in 1976. (Probably one of the more sensible ones we have encountered...)

- ✓ At **www.twee.net/labels/postcard.html** you can read the Postcard story.

- ◀» 'That's the premise Orange Juice started out on. It wasn't for glory or riches or honour. It was freedom. Even though it was only pop music.' Edwyn Collins.

- ◀» 'I'm just not having it. I'm not having another fucking Mod revival... A revival of a revival. What are we going to have next? The New Romantic of New Romantic of New Romantic? No thank you!' Edwyn getting overwrought back in 1995.

- ◀» Collins once caused a stir in an interview by describing the Sex Pistols as 'just a crap heavy metal band'. Well, someone had to...but I think the Pistols were in on the joke, or at least John Lydon was.

Orchestral Manoeuvres in the Dark ★★★★

⊘ OMD ♫ 'Messages' (1980, no.13)

Futurist keyboards and haunting nostalgia

Founder members Paul Humphreys and Andy McCluskey initially wanted their name to make it clear to audiences that they weren't a punk band. A good job, then, that they didn't go with the name of their first group – it's unlikely anyone would have bought idiosyncratic and melodic synth-pop by Hitlerz Underpantz.

After McCluskey's stints in The Id and Dalek I Love You, the **Kraftwerk**-influenced OMD played their first gigs at the very hip Liverpool venue, Eric's, in 1978. Along with **The Human League**, they were pioneers of the then-unfashionable art of performing to a backing track, which in those days was provided by a tape recorder called Winston. (That's the third such instance I've found of bands naming a piece of studio hardware – see if you can spot the other two. Go on, it's not hard.)

Jump to a decade later: OMD are at the Milton Keynes Bowl, supporting **Simple Minds** on the back of a mini-revival in both bands' fortunes. Suddenly, the power cuts out, their instruments grind to a halt, and McCluskey laughs his head off because he has to see the ironic side of it – after all, they were playing a song called 'Electricity'. I have the whole incident on tape – er, of course, I mean I have a photographic memory.

What on earth happened in between? Well, they were one of Tony Wilson's first signings for Factory, and that song 'Electricity' was their first single, an underground success which led to a contract with Virgin. McCluskey and Humphreys released six albums in five years, sometimes visiting the singles charts along the way. A drummer, Malcolm Holmes, got drawn into the mix, along with a brace of bassists, first David Hughes then Martin Cooper; then, for the 1984 album *Crush*, the two founder members were complemented by two newcomers, Graham and Neil Weir.

Their most memorable singles had the haunting, elusive quality of all the best pop. They combined futuristic instrumentation with endearingly retro technological references: to electricity, to radio messages, to the Hiroshima bomb. 'Enola Gay', its upbeat melody counterpointing the sombre subject matter, has an incredibly simple yet catchy chord sequence, while the atmospheric 'Souvenir' became their biggest hit. Their most memorable chart performances, though, must be the twin singles detailing McCluskey's odd fixation with a French martyr: 'Joan Of Arc', with its wintry video, and 'Maid Of Orleans', which initially assaults the ears with its off-key whine before giving way to a melodic, modulating waltz. The ballad 'Talking Loud And Clear' unfolds in pleasant fashion, as its slow-building keyboard and gentle drums are overlaid with a summery oboe. 1986's quirky but epic-sounding 'Forever Live And Die' is also worth a mention, as it was to be the last of their big hits of the 80s.

The album *Sugar Tax*, with OMD now solely under the guidance of McCluskey, brought a brief 90s revival and bounced the up-tempo single 'Sailing On The Seven Seas' into the charts, equalling their previous biggest success at no.3. However, OMD were pure pop music by then – still very good, but commercial and no longer experimental.

- There are two decent compilations: 1988's *The Best Of OMD* collects all the 80s hits except 'Genetic Engineering'. 1998's *The OMD Singles* gathers in some 90s singles too, but in the unlikely event that your all-time favourite OMD hit is 'Secret', you should be warned that it isn't on there.

- A collection of *The OMD Remixes* was released at the same time. Is there room in your life? I'd imagine there's only so much OMD you need, and only so much CD-space under 'O'.

✓ 'If You Leave' featured on the soundtrack to the film *Pretty in Pink*, hence its status as their biggest US hit.

🔊 Andy McCluskey: 'We just picked the most ridiculous name we could think of and then we were stuck with it for twenty years!' (Yes, but I bet you'd have felt even sillier if you'd stuck with Hitlerz Underpantz.)

🔊 'We thought we were making obscure, experimental music. Without realising it, we'd honed it down to the three-and-a-half-minute electronic pop song.' (McCluskey sums the band up in 1998.)

⏭ Andy officially ended OMD in 1996. He continued to write songs for a band with a Liverpudlian connection – namely the perky girl trio Atomic Kitten, who topped the charts with 'Whole Again', giving Andy the UK Number One he never had with his own group. And that answers the **Bangles** question, as the Kittens also took their 'Eternal Flame' to the top. (I know this because I still occasionally watch *Top Of The Pops*, but only to marvel at the anodyne karaoke acts who pass for pop stars today. You will probably find me saying that you can't hear the words, that we had proper tunes in my day, and what are they wearing? And is *that* a boy or a girl?) In August 2002, Andy and the Kittens went their separate ways following a dispute over royalties.

pause

penchant for bleached denim

Vanessa Paradis ★★

♫ 'Joe Le Taxi' (1988, no.3)

Cunning linguist

The English are disgracefully lazy when it comes to learning languages, but when the teenage Vanessa pouted her way through a Top 3 hit concerning a taxi and traffic jams, many a schoolboy perked up and became more interested in his French oral.

Vanessa was born in the Paris suburb of St. Maur on 22 December, 1972. She first performed in public at the age of seven, when her uncle, a record producer, entered her in the amateur talent show *L'Ecole des Fans*. She recorded two albums in France, *M&J* and the wonderfully-untranslatable *Variations sur le même t'aime*, before Lenny Kravitz was let loose on her and she started to record in English (a cover of 'Be My Baby' in 1992 was her other UK hit). A long-term liaison with Johnny 'lucky bastard' Depp ensued too. Possibly the very embodiment of what the words 'pert' and 'nubile' were invented for, she continues to be successful – and even committed Europhobes are keen to have a bit of instruction in her Gallic tongue.

✔ In 1991 Vanessa signed a contract with Chanel to be the face of their perfume Coco, photographed by Jean-Paul Goude. In the adverts she appeared dressed as a caged bird, swinging on a trapeze and watched by a white cat. We like.

Mica Paris ★★

♫ 'My One Temptation' (1988, no.7)

Her first name pronounced 'Mee-sha', the young soul diva started in church and joined the Spirit of Watts gospel choir. She was a session singer for Shakatak at the age of 16 and then recorded with Hollywood Beyond. She had solo hits in the 1980s as well as collaborations with saxophonist Courtney Pine and fellow velvety warbler Will Downing. Another notable success was in 1995 with a version of **U2's** 'One', which, although passable, occasionally crosses a line into the dangerous Mariah Carey territory of never singing one note where warbling an entire octave will do.

She's been in and out of the charts over the last fourteen years and has recently become a Radio 2 presenter, a fate which seems to have been accepted gracefully by a number of former pop stars… is there some secret agenda they're not telling us about?

✔ Mica's real name is Michelle Wallen. Apparently at the age of 16 she knew too many girls called Michelle, so she had to change it – first to 'Micha' and then 'Mica'. The 'Paris' part came from finding the name on an engraved brooch which she bought in Covent Garden.

◀» 'I was always the one that had to do live stuff, like six in the morning, and all the others got away with miming. I used to get so hurt by that. It was hard, seeing my records go out the charts and seeing less talented artists dominate and make my record go down. It can be very demoralising and it can be very painful, but you just have to get on with it. I thought "OK, it's **Bros's** time and **Kylie's** time now, maybe it'll be my time one day!"…' Mica on pop's injustices.

▶▶ New album *Black Angel* has recently been gaining some good reviews. So perhaps it is her time now.

The Passions ★★

♫ **'I'm In Love With A German Film Star'** (1981, no.25)

This languid, atmospheric, synth-rock single deserves to be one of the best-remembered one-hit wonders of the decade. An *NME* Single of the Week at the time, it featured the voice of Barbara Louise Gogan, whose ethereal tones still sound haunting after all this time. Some spacey guitar work from Clive Timperley stalks around on a long intro (the vocal comes in at 59 seconds precisely).

The Passions released their one and only hit in 1981, a time when being in love with a German film star still sounded exotic and romantic and probably conjured up images of people in coats with turned-up collars hurrying through rainy streets to secret assignations. In these more cynical days, you might be more likely to think of a badly-dubbed bloke with a Rudi Völler moustache and mullet combo, simulating foreplay with a bottle-blonde whose peak reproductive years lie somewhere on the other side of the fall of the Berlin Wall. You have to wonder.

✔ If you want to see the original single artwork, it's archived, along with others, at **www.stylorouge.co.uk/1981.htm**

✔ An album, *Thirty Thousand Feet Over China*, crept into the Top 100 following the success of the single. It was their second album, the first being *Michael and Miranda*.

♥ The song was covered by indie band Linoleum in 2000, to general critical acclaim.

▶▶ Barbara has since lived in America, France and Russia. She was one of several artists to record on

Hector Zazou's musical anthology of Arthur Rimbaud poems called *Sahara Blue*, while her 1997 album *Made On Earth* is released by Crammed Discs and is also a collaboration with Zazou.

___

Owen Paul ★★
♫ **'My Favourite Waste of Time'** (1986, no.3)

You may remember that Glaswegian Owen McGee, aka Owen Paul, sported a mullet in the style of Michael Praed's Robin of Sherwood. He was once taken on as an apprentice for Celtic football club, but an encounter with the sound of the Sex Pistols convinced him that he wanted to pursue a career in music. An appearance on BBC2's *The Oxford Roadshow* proved to be his big break. His first single was called 'Pleased To Meet You' and made little impact. 'My Favourite Waste of Time' became his first and only Top 40 hit; however, a technical hitch marred one of his biggest TV appearances as, in **All About Eve** style, he and the band stood there not miming as the song played. Still, no.3 is not to be sneezed at. A big fall-out with his record company led to Owen leaving the music business.

◁ Marshall Crenshaw, who wrote the hit song, says that the oddest version he's heard is one recorded in Taiwan and sung in Cantonese: 'I just howl every time I hear it!' Crenshaw says. 'It's kind of 80s electropop. I got an English translation of the Cantonese lyrics which is really funny. It says "That's the way to kill my time, don't wear a suit and tie, it only makes you look sombre." Just really funny convoluted lyrics. I also like the Owen Paul version because I made a lot of money off it.'

◁» Owen on the circumstances of the split: 'They wanted me to make records I didn't like. I didn't care
how much money it would have made me – I could-
n't go on TV and have people say, "You must be
really proud of this record", when I knew I wasn't…
Everybody thought I was insane [to walk out] but to
me it was obvious. I couldn't express myself in that
environment. If I had been attracted by fame it
would have been different… [But] if I couldn't
make the music I wanted and be happy within
myself, I wasn't going to do it.'

▶▶ He has recently returned to music in happier circumstances, recording under his full name of Owen
Paul McGee.

Pebbles ★★

♬ **'Girlfriend'** (1988, no.8)

American songstress, real name Perri McKissack. A one-
hit wonder in this country but had three top 5 hits in her
native land: 'Girlfriend' (the UK hit), 'Mercedes Boy' and
'Giving You The Benefit'. Fashion-wise, she exhibited a
penchant for bleached denim, belt-chains, leg-warmers
and an sort of ankh symbol around her neck. Wouldn't
have stuck out much in 1988, then. Pebbles gets the extra
pointy thing for the credibility of 'Girlfriend' being covered
– in a non-ironic way, as far as I can tell – on the **Beautiful
South's** first album.

✓ No silly punk name, but a silly funk name! Pebbles
used to be in a band called Con Funk Shun in the
early 80s. Hooray.

> ▸▸ In the 90s, she became the manager of the very successful girl trio TLC, whose best-known hit is probably 'Waterfalls'.

Pepsi & Shirlie ★★

♫ **'Heartache'** (1987, no.2)

Pepsi Demacque and Shirlie Holliman, to give them their full names, were former backing singers with **Wham!** who just missed the top slot with 'Heartache' in 1987. 'Goodbye Stranger' was the follow-up hit, also Top Ten. Think inoffensive bubblegum pop, think striped tops, think puffball skirts.

Shirlie (the bottle-blonde one) married Martin Kemp from **Spandau Ballet** and Pepsi went back to the stage, most notably in the 1993 revival of *Hair*. They turned up together most recently presenting a **George Michael** retrospective on VH-1. They need not preoccupy us more, except for this one rather surprising little musical update:

> ▸▸ In March 2000, Pepsi & Shirlie's backing vocals featured on Geri Halliwell's Number One single 'Bag It Up'.

Pet Shop Boys ★★★★★

♫ **'West End Girls'** (1986, no.1)

Being Interesting
Obviously they've emerged as a huge pop phenomenon and one of the best British songwriting duos in the last two decades. However, it was the late 80s which gave the Pet Shop Boys their biggest success in chart terms, their four Number One singles all falling within a period of just over two years.

Former *Smash Hits* editor Neil Tennant and his collaborator Chris Lowe famously met in a King's Road hi-fi shop. Their first single 'West End Girls', originally recorded with producer Bobby Orlando in 1983, became a success when remixed by Stephen Hague; with its dour semi-rap verse, languidly catchy chorus and louche atmosphere, the song was a huge Number One on both sides of the Atlantic and still regarded by many as their best single. The next two hits, the mournful 'Love Comes Quickly' and the ironic yuppie-anthem 'Opportunities (Let's Make Lots Of Money)' both stalled outside the Top Ten, but 'Suburbia', with its jaunty, very 80s narrative of suburban edginess, bored housewives and police sirens (remixed from the version on the album *Please*) put them back in the game. Three more chart-toppers followed: the epic 'It's A Sin' (dealing with Catholic guilt), a storming cover of 'Always On My Mind' (recorded to sound 'as unlike Elvis as possible') and 'Heart', the boys at their most straightforwardly poppy in a song originally written with **Madonna** in mind.

Although Tennant's lyrics swirled with gay undercurrents, the duo always maintained that one's sexuality shouldn't define one's work – true enough, as their wit, irony and spot-on feel for a driving pop melody were always their prime characteristics.

The Pet Shop Boys settled into a pattern of releasing one 'proper' album alongside an accompanying album of dance remixes: *Please* was attended by *Disco*, *Actually* by *Introspective* and, later on, special editions of the masterful *Very* would be packaged with the remix album *Relentless*. Their videos saw them in increasingly bizarre scenarios such as posing with numerous babies (1989's 'It's Alright') and bouncing around Virtual Reality landscapes in pointy hats and 3-D glasses ('Can You Forgive Her' in 1993). Possibly their funniest promo is 1996's 'Single', a Euro-satire with Tennant barely keeping a straight face as a businessman and Lowe as an impassive policeman, surrounded by an army of marching airline stewardesses.

Recently they have managed the feat of sounding like the Village People one minute (on 'New York City Boy') and Oasis the next (on 'I Get Along') without ever losing their idiosyncratic sound. Their hair may have thinned, but their humour and inventiveness certainly haven't. British pop music of the last 20 years would have been very different and much duller without them.

Pet Shop Boys: Essential.

☊ *Discography* collects 18 singles, from 'West End Girls' up to and including 1991's 'Was It Worth It'. We are surely due a sequel, as there have been another 16 hits since.

💣 2002 album *Release* was touted as a turning-point with the duo embracing the guitar, but they'd had guitars on their records since Johnny Marr contributed to 1991's *Behaviour*, and Tennant's acoustic rendition of 'Rent' and 'Suburbia' had been live favourites. As Tennant deadpans on the 1994 *Live In Rio* video: 'We've never been asked to perform on *MTV Unplugged*... but if we did, it might sound something like this.'

✔ 'Jealousy', written in 1982, became a hit nine years later. Tennant and Lowe had planned to record it with Ennio Morricone in 1987, but his other commitments made this impossible and it finally turned up on the *Behaviour* album.

✔ At the fan site **www.petshopboys.net**, you'll find out about the fanzine 'Literally', among many other things. The official site is **www.petshopboys.co.uk**, and is also very informative.

◀» Neil: 'I'm sure if the Beatles had formed in 1983, they would've been a duo. John and Paul would be using synths and drum machines instead of George and Ringo.'

◀» 'There are two very distinct ways that people consume pop music, if you like. Your laddish music you react to like, "Isn't it great, they're just like us". And then there's what I call aspirational music which is "Oh, I wish I was like that". I'm not suggesting people should be like me or Chris but I think to a certain extent our music is aspirational. People like the fact that there are references to other stuff in it, that you can dance to it and it's cultural as well.' (Neil in the *NME*, 1991)

♥ Some daring covers over the years: Carter The Unstoppable Sex Machine have done a wonderful version of 'Rent', in which 'Broadway' becomes 'Fulham Broadway'. (I've always thought it would be great if the Pet Shop Boys returned the compliment by covering a Carter USM song: possibly 'The Only Living Boy In New Cross' ?) Singer-songwriter Merrill Bainbridge performs a laid-back, acoustic but essentially faithful rendition of 'Being Boring' on the B-side of her 1996 single 'Mouth'. And in 1993, boy-band East 17 did their own take on 'West End Girls' which is, let's say, not quite in the same league as the original.

PhD ★★

♫ 'I Won't Let You Down' (1982, no.3)

Can't think of many 80s bands who have taken their name from university qualifications (unless you count Graduate, precursors to **Tears For Fears**)... This is the one, in case you've forgotten it, on which the singer promises that he won't let you down, won't let you down again. What may not immediately be apparent is that this singer was Glasgow-born Jim Diamond, who was to have a chart-topping solo single with 'I Should Have Known Better' two years later. His collaborators here were keyboard player Tony Hymas and drummer Simon Phillips (both of the Jeff Beck Band). Nice enough, but didn't light up the world. More of a diploma, really.

The Pogues ★★★★

♫ 'Poguetry In Motion EP' (1986, no.29)

Luck of the Irish

Terrific, loud, punky, inventive folk-rock group from Ireland (well, sort of). When the definitive story of the Pogues comes to be written, pop historians will recall their fine ear for melody, their acerbically political lyrics, their many nostalgic and tender moments and their inspired reworkings of folk melody within a rock framework. Oh, and they might mention that they liked a drink.

For their first five studio albums, The Pogues were led by the legendary, gap-toothed Shane MacGowan – stories abound of his stumbling on stage, forgetting lyrics and spilling beer on the audience, but the fans didn't seem to mind too much, as MacGowan and songwriting partner Jem Finer were responsible for many of the Pogues' finest moments. Their first album, *Red Roses For Me*, balances original compositions with raw interpretations of traditional songs, and has a great exuberance to it. 1985's *Rum, Sodomy and the Lash* features more diversity – bassist Cait O'Riordan (now Elvis Costello's wife) has the chance to shine as a vocalist on 'I'm A Man You Don't Meet Every Day', there's a lean, world-weary version of Ewan MacColl's 'Dirty Old Town' from MacGowan, and near-hit 'Sally MacLennane' combines high-speed punkiness and folky melody to very likeable effect. The new influences were making themselves felt, not least the production of Costello and the input from new member, guitarist Phil Chevron.

1987 brought widespread recognition for Stiff Records' best-kept secret, when they exploded on to the *Top Of The Pops* stage performing their first Top Ten hit with folk band the Dubliners, the rollicking and witty 'The Irish Rover'. When the Pogues next visited the charts at Christmas, audiences were wrong-footed if they expected more of the same, for The Pogues had teamed up with the wonderful **Kirsty MacColl** on their finest moment, the timeless, untouchably brilliant 'Fairytale Of New York'.

The Pogues (the name is a shortened version of 'Pogue Mahone', which, charmingly, is the Gaelic for 'kiss my arse') seemed to become more diverse with every offering, as if determined to show that their influences were more than just Irish. Their masterpiece album, 1988's *If I Should Fall From Grace With God*, features Eastern chord sequences in 'Turkish Song Of The Damned' without losing the unmistakable Pogues style. There's zingy brass and festive Spanish spirit on 'Fiesta' (a minor hit single) as well as a melodic medley of folk songs, the reflective 'The Broad Majestic Shannon' and possibly the best song ever about Irish immigrants in America, 'Thousands Are Sailing'.

The next album *Peace And Love* saw more new members in the band, even more variety in the songwriting, and an increasing shift away from the rambling MacGowan – although his contributions as a songwriter are still great. Finer's hauntingly beautiful 'Lorelei', though, is the album's standout track. *Hell's Ditch*, on which further Hispanic influences came through, was, perhaps inevitably, the band's last stand with MacGowan.

- ✓ The band named the track 'Planxty Noel Hill' after a music journalist who had been less than complimentary about them.

- ✓ Shane MacGowan sings on the 1997 multi-artist version of Lou Reed's 'Perfect Day'. All he sings is 'It's such fun', and yet he manages to infuse those three syllables with the distinctive Shane sound.

- ✓ How could we let Shane go without mentioning that essential Silly Punk Name moment? His band were called The Nipple Erectors, later shortened to The Nips. (Perhaps they should have got together with Colin Vearncombe's band The Epileptic Tits...)

- ▶▶ Despite suffering a lot of well-documented problems with alcohol and drugs, Shane MacGowan later formed his own band, The Popes, who had some success.

- ▶▶ The Pogues had two albums in the 90s after MacGowan was asked to leave: *Waiting For Herb* and the almost-eponymous *Pogue Mahone*. Both were well-reviewed, but sank without much of a trace. However, 1993's excellent single 'Tuesday Morning', on which tin-whistle player Spider Stacy performed the vocal duties, deserves a mention.

The Police ★★★★

♪ 'Roxanne' (1979, no.12)

Law and disorder

Believe it or not, there was life before Sting started poking his social conscience into everything, writing impenetrably intellectual sleeve-notes and walking around dressed like a South American Indian. It's only when you hear all their hits side by side that you realise The Police were a great singles band.

Sting (Gordon Sumner) and Stewart Copeland met when former Curved Air drummer Copeland saw Sting's jazz-rock band performing – he didn't care much for the music but liked the singer. They dabbled with a punk sound and a Corsican guitarist called Henri Padovani, but really took off with the arrival of guitarist Andy Summers. A sound which became described as 'white reggae' developed over the course of several singles, but they soon evolved beyond this and were putting out perfect 3-minute pop singles. They'll sound as familiar as anything from the 80s: 'Walking On The Moon' with its distinctive lolloping bassline, 'Don't Stand So Close To Me', a reminder of Sting's former vocation as a teacher (play the 1980 original, though, not the bafflingly emasculated 1986 re-recording) and ultimate stalker-paranoia anthem 'Every Breath You Take', now misleadingly used to sell insurance or something equally inane. When they recorded *Regatta De Blanc* in 1979, they were broke and needed to do Wrigley's chewing-gum adverts to survive, but by the time of *Ghost In The Machine* in 1981, mega-stardom had arrived and they could afford George Martin's AIR studios in Montserrat.

It has to be said that the band held together despite what one could euphemistically call 'friction' between the members – fist-fights between Sting and Copeland were not unheard-of. Allegedly, Copeland had some very uncomplimentary words – mostly four letters and all about Sting – written across his drums, and enjoyed hitting them in a therapeutic kind of way. Perhaps it's best that it all ended when it did, leaving us with the perfect number of hits for a compilation and a selection of fine albums.

- The 1992 *Greatest Hits* probably has the best to offer – more comprehensive than 1986 selection *The Singles*.

- In December 1979, The Police played two London venues on the same night – the Hammersmith Palais and the Odeon – and were escorted between the two gigs in an army personnel carrier, with 40 police (the other sort) on standby.

- If you were a Police fan in 1980, you doubtless felt it was the height of sophistication to be able to say *Zenyatta Mondatta* without sounding silly. You probably also knew it to be the Sanskrit for 'top of the world'.

- 'Whenever we had our hands round each other's throats, Andy would hold this reel of two-inch tape over our heads and chant "I am nothing" until we stopped. To this day, it still settles me when I think "I am nothing"…' Stewart Copeland, interviewed for *Revolver* in 2000.

- 'People thrashing out three chords didn't really interest us musically. Reggae was accepted in punk circles and musically more sophisticated, and we could play it, so we veered off in that direction. I mean let's be honest here, "So Lonely" was unabashedly culled from "No Woman No Cry" by Bob Marley. Same chorus. What we invented was this thing of going back and forth between thrash punk and reggae. That was the little niche we created for ourselves.' Sting, interviewed for *Revolver* in 2000.

♥ Shawn Colvin does credit to 'Every Little Thing...' on her *Cover Girl* album, despite the risk of doing a gender-change on the lyrics (see **Hue and Cry**). And Feeder's beefed-up take on 'Can't Stand Losing You' from 2001 is joyous, mean and magnificent. Two other Police covers, though, are worth noting because they are both so awful. **George Michael** disgraces 'Roxanne' by turning it into a jazz number on his ill-advised covers album *Songs From The Last Century*. But this pales into insignificance beside the monstrous Puff Daddy/ Faith Evans 'version' of 'Every Breath You Take', re-titled 'I'll Be Missing You'. It doesn't so much re-work the song as subject it to a drive-by shooting and leave it dead in a ditch – if there has been a more horrible cover version of anything, ever, then I want to know. And the ignorant hordes sent it to Number One for six weeks. It just makes you want to cry.

▶▶ Let's presume Sting's later career is no mystery to you, dear reader. Copeland has been busy writing TV and film scores, while Summers has concentrated on exhibiting his photography.

Prefab Sprout ★★★
♫ **'When Love Breaks Down'** (1985, no.25)

Perennial under-achievers of the decade, Prefab Sprout were cruelly denied the profile and chart action they deserved – and when things did start to perk up a bit in 1988, along came **Deacon Blue** doing much the same thing, and snatched it all away. Led by singer-songwriter Paddy McAloon, they formed in Durham in 1982 and signed to the indie label Kitchenware.

From *Langley Park To Memphis* is probably their best-known album, and it gave them the quirky Top Ten hit 'The King Of Rock'n'Roll'. Even then, the band were unwilling to tour – and Paddy, in fact, was still living at his parents' home in Consett at the age of 30.

Something of a perfectionist, Paddy can be working on up to five albums at a time and will only release one if it feels right. Hence the gap between 1990's *Jordan: The Comeback* and 1997's *Andromeda Heights*.

✔ Early album *Steve McQueen* was adored by the critics, but had to change its name to *Two Wheels Good* in the US after complaints from McQueen's family.

✔ The versatile Paddy McAloon wrote the theme tune to the hit ITV series *Where The Heart Is* and songs for Jimmy Nail's debut album ('Cowboy Dreams' turns up again on the 2001 Prefab Sprout album, *The Gunman And Other Stories*).

✔ Among the other projects Paddy has 'filed away', apparently, are *Behind The Veil* – a musical based on the life of Michael Jackson – and an album of gospel-style songs called *The Atomic Hymn Book*.

The Pretenders ★★★★
♪ **'Stop Your Sobbing'** (1979, no.34)

Ohio-born Chrissie Hynde has now passed her fiftieth birthday, an appropriate age for a rock legend. Hanging out with punks led Malcolm McLaren to line her up for a punk band called Masters Of The Backside; having escaped that fate, she formed the Pretenders in 1979.

Other members came and went, but the charismatic Chrissie remained constant. Her sultry, husky, sneering voice was ideal for the punk-edged songs, but it could also do justice to tender moments like 1986's 'Hymn To Her'. Finding time amid all the stardom to be an environmental campaigner, animal rights activist, partner of Ray Davies and wife of Jim Kerr, Chrissie became one of the 80s' essential icons.

🎧 Get *Greatest Hits* rather than *The Singles*: it's got more tracks on (including the superb comeback material from the 90s like 'I'll Stand By You') and has a much nicer cover. *The Isle Of View* is an interesting acoustic take on the band.

💣 You may recall Chrissie's appearance on US sitcom *Friends*, when she was taught by Phoebe to sing the immortal 'Smelly Cat'.

✔ Some of those Pretenders pretenders who came and went over the years: bassist Pete Farndon (fired in 1981), guitarist James Honeyman-Scott (died of a cocaine-induced heart attack just two days after Farndon left), drummer Martin Chambers (left in 1986) and even ex-**Smiths** guitarist Johnny Marr for a brief time.

The Primitives ★★★

♪ 'Crash' (1988, no.5)

Blonde, ambition and a jangly guitar
Band from Coventry who played melodic, immaculately-produced songs, too good just to be labelled 'indie'. Formed in 1985, the group was driven by guitarist-songwriter Paul Court and the photogenic peroxide-blonde Tracy Tracy (who replaced original singer Kieron). Early singles 'Thru The Flowers', 'Really Stupid' and 'Stop Killing Me' are awash with exuberance and great crunchy guitars and are given a fragile, pure quality by Tracy's voice.

With a major label (RCA) behind them, the Primitives launched their 35-minute debut album *Lovely* in 1988, trailing it with the chugging single 'Crash', whose unmistakable, spangly opening riff still gets indie boys and girls everywhere on the dancefloor. The later albums *Pure* and *Galore* saw them sounding more polished but perhaps losing that little edge and spark they had, although 'Earth Thing' and 'You Are The Way' were still enjoyable tracks to turn up loud.

Other girly-guitar bands are available. **Transvision Vamp** were their feistier and more commercial counterparts, while the poor man's Primitives were The Darling Buds.

🎧 New versions of the early hits appeared on *Lovely*, but the compilation of early stuff called *Lazy 86-88* is worth checking out to see what they used to sound like. The track 'Lazy' itself, on which Paul Court sings, is a bit **Jesus and Mary Chain**-ish. He claimed to have got the drawl in his voice through lack of practice.

💣 Tracy became a raffish brunette for the second album, and her new, doe-eyed look, complete with a neckful of trinkets, got her on the cover of *Melody Maker*. One of their best ever covers, in my unbiased opinion.

- Drummer Pete Tweedie was allegedly kicked out of the band for being cruel to Tracy's cats, and was replaced by Tig Williams.

- Chart promotional stunts: initial copies of the 12-inch of 'Crash' featured a free poster, and 2000 Crash chocolate bars were also in circulation... Also, 8,000 copies of the 7-inch of 'Way Behind Me' came with a free bubble bath sachet. This got them into trouble with chart compilers Gallup, who wouldn't allow these copies to count towards the chart placing. I promise you, I don't make this stuff up.

- Claws out in the *NME*'s review of *Galore*: 'The Primitives are flogging the space where a dead horse should be.' (Oooh, get *her*.)

- Paul Court got honest about *Lazy 86-88* in an interview with the *Melody Maker*: 'Well, the first four songs are crap for starters!... We managed to get half an hour studio time to remix the four tracks, but the woman who was mixing them was pretty pissed off that she only had half an hour. We thought we could do it in that short space of time in those days, though...'

- When the Primitives broke up, Paul formed the band Starpower, which later became Hedy. Tracy contributed some vocals to the second Starpower single, 'Drifter'.

The Proclaimers ★★★

♫ 'Letter From America' (1987, no.3)

Conspicuously bespectacled, defiantly Scottish and quietly Christian, twins Craig and Charlie Reid were late contenders for the Christmas Number One slot in 1987. They didn't make it, but the song remains a classic, combining a big, soaring, sing-along chorus with Scottish place-name-checks in the verses. Refreshingly, they chose not to refine their voices into the usual mid-Atlantic whine, instead giving full rein to their Caledonian vowels.

The first album *This Is The Story* was a minor masterpiece of stripped-down melodies, most of the tracks being acoustic versions only, although the more full-blooded single mix of 'Letter From America' was included. The second single 'Make My Heart Fly', even though it was beefed up with bagpipes, flopped. However, a 1988 comeback brought the stompalong 'I'm Gonna Be (500 Miles)' from their rockier second album *Sunshine On Leith*, and their 1990 cover of 'King Of The Road' became their second and last UK Top 10 hit (to date).

✔ The Proclaimers broke the American market after 'I'm Gonna Be (500 Miles)' was used in the 1993 film *Benny & Joon*, and 1995's third album *Hit The Highway* perhaps reflected this transatlantic success more in its style.

✔ Still active, they returned with *Persevere* in 2001, an album which saw something of a return to Scottish source material. Don't write them off yet.

Propaganda ★★

Wacky Teutonic funsters fronted by the enigmatic Claudia Brücken, who were almost good enough to make me wish I hadn't been so rude about German music elsewhere. We have that man Trevor Horn to thank again, producer extraordinaire who was also responsible for bringing us The Buggles and **Frankie Goes to Hollywood**. Seminal album *A Secret Wish* is typical of 80s (over-)production values. It spawned the single 'Duel', with its turbo-driven flipside, 'Jewel', a rougher, more industrial-sounding version of the same song featuring some very odd noises indeed, some of which sound like cattle being prodded. The haunting 'Dream Within A Dream' opens the album and is reprised at the end. One to listen to alone with the lights off.

Late in the decade, after Claudia had already gone off to form Act, percussionist Michael Mertens resurrected the defunct band with a new vocalist, American Betsi Miller, plus some former members of **Simple Minds**. However, the wheel has since come full circle, and Mertens was back together as recently as 2000 with Claudia and the other vocalist from the original line-up, Susanne Freytag.

✔ German site **www.propaganda.de** has an irritating layout, but it's worth visiting if only for the retro computer-screen lettering, nostalgic for anyone who ever touched an early Apple. Rather better is the fan site **www.p-fan.de**, but mind the odd translations.

✔ Claudia's ex-husband, and co-owner of the band's label ZTT, was Paul Morley – yes, him again.

✔ Claudia recorded a solo album in 1990: the singles

'Absolut(e)' and 'Kiss Like Ether' peaked outside the Top 40.

🔊   Original keyboard player Andreas Thein: 'There was never any question of our signing a deal with a German label. They're far too rigid and inflexible. We are original and we don't want to compromise.'

―――――――――

The Psychedelic Furs ★ ★

♫ **'Heaven'** (1984, no.29)

Neither especially psychedelic nor, indeed, particularly furry, and technically a two-hit wonder.

Formed in 1977 by the Bowie-esque Richard Butler and his brother Tim (vocals and bass respectively) they released their eponymous debut album in 1980 and, with various comings and goings of personnel, recorded throughout the 1980s until *World Outside* in 1991. Richard Butler's LoveSpitLove had some success in the mid-90s, but recently he was back at the head of a re-formed Furs, performing small gigs across America.

✔   Their most famous song 'Pretty In Pink' didn't make the charts first time round in 1981, but it went to no.18 five years later (re-recorded) on the back of the eponymous film.

pause

quite difficult, actually

And here it is: confession time. I did want to have some-one (anyone!) from the 80s to represent every letter of the alphabet. I just didn't realise that this one was going to be, well, quite difficult, actually. It might lend its name to one of the most serious music magazines of the last two decades, but when it comes to bands, Q is a quintessen-tial non-starter. Very few people have chosen the under-populated record shelves of the seventeenth letter in which to display their musical wares. You'd think it would make sense to do so, given the heavy competition in, say, S and T.

So, please sympathise here. To have included Suzi Quatro would have violated my self-imposed rules: her famous chart-topper 'Can the Can', after all, was as far back as 1973 and 'Mama's Boy' was the only one of her eleven hit singles to fall in the 1980s. And The Questions, Quick and Quiet Riot simply didn't make enough of an impact on my consciousness, despite each having a single in the Top 50 in the early 80s. Sorry.

To feature Queen wouldn't be fair – they first hit the big time in the mid-70s and arguably only had great singles from less-than-great albums in the 80s before reaching the heights again with epic album *Innuendo* in 1991. They have had their fair share of criticism, not all of it justified; when it comes to Freddie and the boys, many journos over the years have glanced briefly at the stick and proceeded to grasp the wrong end with an amusingly misplaced firmness. There's no point berating the fabulous foursome for their bombast, rock posing and theatricality – these are all attrib-utes which they have gleefully embraced and parodied. These days, bereft of Freddie, they are a shadow of their former selves; bassist John Deacon has sensibly washed his hands of the band's attempts to stagger on into the new mil-lennium with the likes of Will Young on guest vocals. He, like the rest of us, must have decided it was too painful to watch. (Now, if only they'd had Robbie Williams at the Jubilee gig...)

Quartz were a dance-pop outfit whose rather good version of 'It's Too Late' introduced the world to the sultry tones of Ms Dina Carroll – but, rather appropriately given the title of the song, that didn't happen until February 1991.

And so it's left to two long-haired rock bands to carry the torch of the letter Q. First, the Quireboys just sneak into the back end of the decade with '7 O'Clock'. And then we have Queensryche, one of those scary combos who insist on printing their name in big, angry, fiery letters on their album covers just to show how hard they are, and who sometimes put a spurious umlaut over their letter Y. People who take their Metal very seriously will go into rhapsodies (of the non-bohemian variety) over this band's seminal 1988 concept album *Operation: Mindcrime*, and so I will merely acknowledge it here, even though I have tried and failed to appreciate it on several occasions. I think I finally realised in about 1995 that I was never going to get it and taped over it with something else (probably Blur). And now I have got all the enraged metalheads up and down the country jumping up and down and gnashing their teeth, but they probably gave up after I was so rude about them earlier.

I really want to make life easier for whichever young whippersnapper ends up compiling *The Encyclopaedia Of Classic 21st-Century Pop*. I therefore feel it my duty to suggest to any youthful people out there who are thinking of forming a band that they should consider the following attention-grabbing monikers: Quad, Quango, The Quartermasters, Queer, Quench, Quick and the Dead, Quicklime, Quicksilver, Quietus, Quint Major, Quiver, The Quixotics and QWERTYUIOP. I won't charge copyright on any of the above.

It's time to acknowledge the paucity of the Q, and move on to a more profitable letter.

pause

rock had the last laugh

Chris Rea ★★★

♫ **'Fool (If You Think It's Over)'** (1978, no.30)

It seems to be compulsory to refer to the Geordie singer-songwriter as 'gravel-voiced', so we'll get that out of the way to begin with – as well as the old joke about him teaming up with Mark Knopfler of Dire Straits to form a band called... Chris Straits. (Think about it.) He's a purveyor of bluesy pop-rock who never quite made it as huge as he could have, but whose output has been remarkably consistent.

Chris Rea was a former labourer and ice-cream sales-man who became lead singer with Middlesbrough group Magdalene, replacing David Coverdale (later of Whitesnake). The band turned into The Beautiful Losers and were *Melody Maker's* Best Newcomers of 1975, but when this award led nowhere, Chris struggled to establish himself as a solo artist. Popular in Europe, Chris had only intermittent chart success in Britain throughout the 80s, his most memorable songs being the gentle and summery 'On The Beach' from 1986 (remixed in 1988) and the lively 'Let's Dance', his first British Top 20 single in 1987.

What really put him on the map, though, was the spec-tacular 1989 single 'The Road To Hell (Part 2)', a gloomy-but-catchy epic inspired by the nightmare of driving on the M25. It was to be his first – and, to date, only – UK Top Ten single. The album *The Road To Hell* is generally thought to be his best work, although an ill-advised re-working of the album more than a decade later didn't go down too well.

🎧 Compilation *New Light Through Old Windows* brings together most of the 80s stuff. The 90s turned out to be a better decade for Chris as his career took off again: 'Auberge' and 'Looking For The Summer' from 1991 are worth a listen, as is 'Julia' from 1993.

- ✔ Chris has an acting role in the 1997 Michael Winner film *Parting Shots* – he plays a dying photographer who sets out to kill all his old enemies. (I've not seen it, but I'm told it's rubbish.) He also wrote the soundtrack for the 1993 British road-movie *Soft Top, Hard Shoulder* starring Peter Capaldi. (I *have* seen this, and it's pretty good.)

- 🔊 'I felt sorry for my father... I'd become a man, I'd joined the family ice-cream business and then one day I heard a record and said, "I'm leaving the business and becoming a slide guitarist." He didn't know what a slide guitarist was, and to him it just sounded dreadful. He must have thought I'd lost my marbles.'

- ♥ Some interesting cover-version choices: 'Fool If You Think It's Over' (with the brackets cunningly dropped) was also a hit for Elkie Brooks in 1982. The guitar riff from 'On The Beach' was sampled for a dance version by York in 2000. And Michael Ball, the balladeer for ladies of a certain age from whom no song is safe, has done something to 'Driving Home For Christmas' which I'm not really sure I want to hear.

Red Box ★★
♪ **'Lean On Me (Ah-Li-Ayo)'** (1985, no.3)

Lively pop with world-music influences and twiddly bits of flute and sax... You may remember that they were a duo, but what seems less well-known is that Simon Toulson-Clarke and Julian Close emerged from the ashes of a larger Red Box who had formed in 1982, a vocals/guitar-bass-keyboards-saxophone-drums fivesome.

They signed to WEA and had two hits, the catchy no. 3 'Lean On Me (Ah-Li-Ayo)' and 'For America', which was a Top Ten record the following year. Both helped their album *The Circle and the Square* to do quite well. A 1990 single, 'Train', preceded a new album called *Motive*, which didn't earn critical acclaim or produce more hit singles.

✔ The original five members of Red Box were: Simon Toulson-Clarke (vocals/guitar), Julian Close (saxophone), Rob Legge (bass), Paddy Talbot (keyboards) and Martin Nickson (drums).

The Reynolds Girls ★

♪ **'I'd Rather Jack'** (1989, no.8)

Supergroup-dissing crimpers

All Linda and Aisling Reynolds wanted to do was have a good time, then someone went and took their house away. Good thing too, as this duo of hairdressers with their 'comedy' air-guitar routines were possibly the most terrifying sight to appear on TV in 1989. They aspired to the dizzy heights of **Mel & Kim**, and would rather jack than Fleetwood Mac, apparently. As we'd suspected all along, Pete Waterman believed that plastic pop was the future and that guitar music was dead.

Thankfully, rock had the last laugh. The duo flopped when they broke away from Waterman and co, and the British indie-guitar revival (led by Suede, The Auteurs and Radiohead) was only three years away. Bad luck, girls. I wonder if, now that they're in their thirties, they listen to Radio 2 like the rest of us?

🔊 'Nobody will get rid of The Reynolds Girls that easily.' Aisling in *Number One* magazine, 1989, failing the audition for Mystic Meg.

▶▶ The girls have given up 'jacking' and now own an unfeasibly large collection of Fleetwood Mac CDs... Look, I'm just guessing, all right?

Lionel Richie ★★★

♫ **'Endless Love'** (with Diana Ross, 1981, no.7)

Soulful Alabama-born merchant of ballads and up-tempo danceable pop, and owner of a quite remarkable moustache-perm combo which wouldn't have shamed a Dutch footballer. Lionel was formerly front-man of the Commodores, whose blissful metaphor of 'Easy Like Sunday Morning' obviously comes from more innocent days before the delights of 24-hour garden centres.

As a songwriter, he is perhaps best-known for 'We Are The World', the USA's answer to the **Band Aid** single, which he co-wrote with Michael Jackson. As a performer, though, it's 'Hello' that springs to mind – it's a thoroughly maudlin ballad, and in the video Lionel lays himself right open for ridicule by addressing the lines to a blind woman who's making a sculpture of Lionel. Well, it looks a bit like him. The equally mournful 'Say You, Say Me' saw him back in the Top Ten, and he was around again in the 90s with 'My Destiny'.

💣 In 1985, Lionel achieved the record of having nine US Number Ones in nine years.

🔊 'I give credit to my co-writer because all I did was write down what He told me to write down... From about eleven to about seven in the morning is a very wonderful time because ... God ain't worried with too many other folks... I know He is very busy during the day, so I wait for late night, and it works for me.' This is Lionel's tip for booking co-writing sessions with the Almighty, although 'Richie/God' doesn't feature anywhere as a credit on his album sleeve notes.

Stan Ridgway ★★★

♫ **'Camouflage'** (1986, no.4)

A brief mention for one of the most original one-hit wonders of the decade. Former Wall Of Voodoo member Stan had a country-sounding hit with 'Camouflage', a Vietnam ghost-story of a soldier's near-death experience and his mysterious assistance by a spectral marine called Camouflage. Was it an allegory? It left people baffled, but still strangely haunted by its unusual lyrics and insidious melody, perfectly delivered by Ridgway's laconic drawl. And it's one of the least irksome cultural contributions which the Yanks' obsession with Vietnam has brought us. Quirky and likeable.

✔ Singer-songwriter Stan has recorded several successful albums, including *The Big Heat, Mosquitos* and *Holidays In Dirt*.

◀» 'I grew up listening to Johnny Cash and Merle Haggard. And I love that sound – that lonesome individual with a guitar and a mic. Telling a horrific tale over a simple, beautiful melody. There are a lot of horrible things in folk songs and country music. People get cut up and lovers kill each other. It's all a mask and metaphor for things the subconscious doesn't want to deal with. But it's also entertaining; that's the beauty of it.'

Roxette ★ ★ ★

Enjoyably straightforward Nordic rock-pop duo. They manage to get in here despite only just starting their career in '89, as their entire look, sound and *raison d'être* seems to come from somewhere around 1984. This is no bad thing. Vocalist Marie Fredriksson pinched Annie Lennox's look, spiced up with a touch of **Billy Idol's** hair and some trousers made out of black bin-liners. As for guitarist Per Gessle, well, he favoured the 'electric shock' hairdo for at least five years after it had ceased even to be funny. However, their cartoonish demeanour aside, Roxette gave us some pretty memorable tunes.

After 'Dressed For Success' came out as their second single, pop guru and pundit Jonathan King infamously wrote them off as one-hit wonders. I think it's fair to say Roxette had the last laugh there. For a while, it looked as if the bespectacled one was going to be right – the song peaked at no.48 and the next single, the strong power-ballad 'Listen To Your Heart', fared even worse. However, the huge success of 'It Must Have Been Love' (on the soundtrack of *Pretty Woman*) was just around the corner, and the duo never looked back. Except, of course, when seeking inspiration for key changes, trousers and haircuts.

♀ The singles are all pretty much OK, but tucked away near the back of their album *Joyride* you'll find the outstanding track 'Things Will Never Be The Same', which is well worth hearing. Honest. Their hits package is called *Don't Bore Us... Get To The Chorus!* This tells you everything you need to know, frankly.

✔ **http://runto.roxette.org** is interesting if you have

time. The fans' personal stories are quite touching... and written in English which, although quirky at times, still puts most British people to shame when it comes to non-native proficiency. **www.roxette.co.uk** is the British fan club, a site packed with interesting nuggets.

Run-DMC ★★★

♫ **'Walk This Way'** (1986, no.8)

Oh, dear, I'm going to get into trouble here. Both detractors and fans would probably agree on the phrase 'hugely influential rap band' to describe Run-DMC. The question is whether this constitutes a compliment, or something to be thoroughly ashamed of. As founder members Run (yes, really) and DMC (again, yes, really) and Jam Master J (oops, couldn't squeeze him into the band's name) are all pushing 40, they must be seen, like it or not, as elder statesmen of the empire of rap.

Looking at their 80s publicity now, it's hard not to see a cartoon band, as everything which has since become a hip-hop cliché is present and correct. Silly hats with designer logos? Yup. Shiny jackets bearing the daft names of baseball teams whose relevance to anyone outside God's Own America is debatable? Yup. Fetishistic worshipping of trainers –over-priced *plimsolls*, for God's sake? Oh, yes. Excessive amounts of gold jewellery, including watches on *both* wrists (presumably in case they forget if they are left- or right-handed) and medallions resembling lavatory chains? Ah yeah, mo'fuckaz, as they would probably say. Excuse me if that isn't quite the correct expression, but I didn't take O-Level Rap.

It's fair to say, though, that their enduring contribution to the history of pop is the introduction of guitar noises into an arena usually shy of proper instruments. 'Walk This Way', a collaboration with rockers Aerosmith, came about as a result of a suggestion from producer Rick Rubin. It remains a classic, the decade's most successful fusion of rock and rap aesthetics, with that instantly-recognisable 'dt-dt-dt duddily-dah, de duddle-dah du-dah!' guitar intro. Jason Nevins' 1998 remix of 'It's Like That' was their other greatest moment, a chart-topper for six weeks at the end of a decade which appeared to have consigned Run-DMC to history. Whatever happens, they will always be seen as prime movers in one of the most self-absorbed and essentially witless musical genres.

✔ Jam Master J of Run DMC, real name Jason Mizell, died in October 2002 after being shot. He was 37.

💣 If you want a really good laugh, track down *Q* magazine's 1997 interview with the inheritors of Run DMC's crown, the Wu-Tang Clan. With its painful phonetic spelling and deadpan faux-reverence, it's one of the most unintentionally funny things they have ever printed.

pause

s

squeaky pop-by-numbers

S'Express ★ ★ ★

🕭 S'Xpress ♫ 'Theme From S'Express' (1988, no.1)

Pioneering dance magpie

I've always wanted to go up to DJ Mark Moore and say,
'Sir, your record is, in parts, both good and original.
Unfortunately the parts which are good are not original,
and the parts which are original are not good.' A guaranteed
dancefloor-filler both then and now, the original S'Express
single, which heavily samples Rose Royce, is a triumph of
slick, energetic production over actual quality. It has
achieved a certain timelessness in retrospect, even though it
sounds as dated as the hits by fellow crossover acts **Krush**
and **M/A/R/R/S** the year before. The single reputedly cost
just £250 to make.

Moore's list of collaborators is, with the benefit of hindsight, somewhat star-studded: 'Theme From S'Express' was
co-produced by Pascal Gabriel, who would later work with
many acts including the Inspiral Carpets and **New Order**.
Also featured on the first album *Original Soundtrack* was a
little-known singer called Billie Ray Martin, who was to
have a huge European hit with 'Your Loving Arms' in 1995.
Moore also worked with producer William Orbit, later
famous for **Madonna's** *Ray Of Light* album and his own
dancefloor re-working of Barber's 'Adagio'. And, last but
not least, the second S'Express album *Intercourse* featured
Sonique, now a hugely successful DJ and singer who topped
the charts in her own right in 2000 with 'It Feels So Good'.

Okay, so the three stars are, like those for **M/A/R/R/S**,
more for being influential on subsequent acts than anything
else. Is that bad? No, that's good.

💣 Mark Moore on *TOTP* with one of those irritating
    guitar-shaped synthesisers slung round his neck,
    which he wasn't even pretending to play. Subtle

comment on the pressure to mime, or just musical inability? Place your bets.

▶▶| Moore is a remixer, producer and record company boss. Splish, Stylofiction, Placenta and Bone are the names of his three genuine labels, plus one which I made up when I was bored. If you're really bothered about which is the impostor, e-mail me.

Sabrina ★

♪ **'Boys (Summertime Love)'** (1988, no.3)

Yes, I'm afraid it's time to get this one off our chest. This is pneumatic Italian songstress Sabrina Salerno, born in Genoa in 1968. A former Miss Liguria and a TV presenter in Italy, she made the move into pop after Italian music-producer Claudio Cecchetto groomed her look and sound. Her debut single 'Sexy Girl' was released in Italy at the beginning of 1987.

Then came her huge summer club-pop crossover song in 1988 – and that's about the size of it, really. A minor hit, 'All Of Me', followed on the back of this one, and then that was all for the UK charts; she released another couple of dozen singles, none of them a hit over here. Her management team got her to record an album quickly, filling it up with cover versions of Prince's 'Kiss', Patti LaBelle's 'Lady Marmalade', The Knack's 'My Sharona' and Rod Stewart's 'Da Ya Think I'm Sexy'. It did well in Italy, France and Korea. But then, as we know, these Johnny Foreigners will buy any old crap.

◀»   'I am, how you say, a womanly woman. I have certain charms and I like to wear clothes that display them. I will not hide myself. People know when

Sabrina is around.' Sabrina warning us all to be very afraid in a *Record Mirror* interview from 1988.

▸▸ Sabrina is still a big star in Italy. She has acted in several films including the 1998 Italian musical comedy *Jolly Blu* and the TV series *Tutti gli uomini sono uguali*.

Sade ★★

♪ **'Your Love Is King'** (1984, no.6)

It's 1985. You have just acquired a fabulous piece of real estate by selling arms to the Third World, Maggie looks comfortable for a few more years now that those nasty miners have been put in their place, and you decide to invite the neighbours round for a cocktail party to show off your new leather sofas, chrome stools and – in pride of place – your Compact Disc Player. What else do you put on but Sade? Yes, okay, possibly Dire Straits, but you are trying to appear ultra-sophisticated here. And Nigerian-born Helen Folasade Adu (technically, the singer and songwriter for the group which took her name) provided an easy kind of faux-sophistication, the sort you could buy from the Virgin Megastore. If she was a drink, she'd be something with Kahlua in it. A book? Probably some sort of a blockbuster with the title in gold block letters.

Let's be fair here for a moment. (No, let's.) Sade's music itself is pleasant if you are in the mood for it, and her silky-smooth voice is quite splendid, perfect for the material she sings. It's just that there is ultimately nothing particularly challenging or even unusual about it; perhaps a dash of silliness would have helped. Still, it's hard to argue with a succession of Top 40 singles, even if none of them ever came close to matching the chart peak of her debut.

- The famous first album *Diamond Life* won her a Grammy for Best New Artist in 1984, as well as spending 80 weeks in the *Billboard* album charts.

St. Winifred's School Choir ✶
♬ **'There's No-One Quite Like Grandma'** (1980, no.1)

Led by a gap-toothed girl in a hideous pink dress, this bunch had actually featured on a Number One two years before – as backing singers for Brian and Michael's 'Matchstalk Men And Matchstalk Cats And Dogs' in 1979.

Interestingly, it is the second Number One to refer to an aged relative, following Clive Dunn's 'Grandad' which hit the top in 1971 (unless you want to make a case for David Soul and 'Silver Lady' ?). Anyway, the deluded children are assured for ever of their place in rock history by knocking John Lennon off the top when he wasn't yet cold in his grave, so points for unintentional iconoclasm.

In these enlightened days, we are used to the charts being clogged with short people with Smarties on their riders. The 90s brought perky teenagers like Billie, Hanson and Britney, and now we have the more disturbing phenomenon of the S Club Juniors (doesn't anyone else shudder and think '*MiniPops*' ?), not to mention Samantha Mumba's smackable little brother. Now that the airwaves seem rife with popstrels who need to get the encores done before it's time for their milk, biscuits and bedtime story, it shouldn't be too long before we hear the first single released by a foetus.

- In a poll of all-time most annoying records conducted by the Dotmusic website, this song came in 7th place. In first place was 'The Birdie Song' by The Tweets.

>> One of the choir was Sally Lindsay, who became an actress and went on to star in *Coronation Street*.

Salt 'N'Pepa ★★

♬ **'Push It/Tramp'** (1988, no.2)

Rather puzzlingly, I've seen them described as 'the most successful female rappers to date'. Does this mean they have the edge over their hipstress and hopstress colleagues when it comes to taking da guyz out for da coffee? And what constitutes a successful date anyway?

The condiments in question were 19-year-old Cheryl James (she was Salt) and Sandra Denton (she was Pepa); they also sported another, invisible member – their DJ, Spinderella. Among her skills were those of 'cuttin' it up one tahm', apparently.

Their re-issued anthem 'Push It' filled dancefloors in the summer of '88. The follow-up 'Shake Your Thang' didn't do as well, despite the helpful footnote 'It's Your Thing' in the title (presumably provided just in case anybody still thought a Thang was something from the first series of *Star Trek*). The other huge single 'Let's Talk About Sex' came in 1991, and features an amusing discussion about whether the song will get radio airplay. It's fun, but not exactly Shakespeare. As you will have guessed.

Scarlet Fantastic ★★

♬ **'No Memory'** (1987, no.24)

Boy-girl band, and not to be confused with underrated 90s girl duo Scarlet. This pair were Rick P Jones and Maggie De Monde, whose good-to-drive-to hit single should have got a lot higher than it did. Maggie actually had a bit of previous form, as the vocalist on the 1984 hit 'Soul Train' by Swans Way (no apostrophe, *sic*). Their second single 'Plug Me In (To The Central Love Line)' stalled at no.67. Such is life.

- ✔ Someone liked them enough to emblazon their name in graffiti above a flyover in Reading, where it stayed for about five years. (Now *that's* trivia…)

- ⏭ Maggie De Monde and husband Leif now own the underground music club El Dorado in Notting Hill: see **www.mynottinghill.co.uk/nottinghilltv/faces-maggie&leif.htm**

Scritti Politti ★ ★ ★
♫ **'Wood Beez (Pray Like Aretha Franklin)'** (1984, no.10)

No disrespect to his parents intended, but there is something annoying about the name Green Gartside. Anyway, leaving that aside, the girly-voiced Green formed his band in 1977 with Nial Jinks and Tom Morley. Green recovered from a heart complaint in 1980 and spent the year convalescing and writing new songs. 'The Sweetest Girl' was the first song to get widespread public attention, when it appeared on one of those free *NME* cassettes (you know, the ones you think look really good until you get them home and find out that all the tracks by well-known bands are dodgy demos, horrible live versions and songs that were dropped from their albums for being crap, while the best thing on it is inevitably something by someone you've never heard of).

Green had drawn in new members David Gamson and Fred Maher by the time of their first hit. 'Absolute' and 'The Word Girl' followed. After a couple of years contributing songs for **Madonna**, Chaka Khan and Al Jarreau,

Scritti Politti hit again in 1988 with the melodic 'Oh Patti (Don't Feel Sorry For Loverboy)'. At the end of the decade, Green retreated to Wales to tinker with new technology, and somehow managed to team up with everybody's favourite modest, self-effacing, feminist, right-on activist ragga star, Shabba Ranks, for 'She's A Woman' in 1991.

✔ In a career marked by lengthy absences, Green has impressed quite a few fawning journalists over the years, managing to seem well-read by chucking in the odd reference to French philosophers. Some of them would even like to see him as the British answer to Prince.

♥ **Madness**' version of 'The Sweetest Girl' was a hit in 1986, even though the original did not make the Top 40.

Sigue Sigue Sputnik ★★★

♪ **'Love Missile F1-11'** (1986, no.3)

Never mind the Pistols, here's the bollocks
One can only assume it was meant to be a joke. How do you describe their look – neo-Goth-techno-punks? The bastard offspring of Sid Vicious, Bowie and **Toto Coelo**? If you were going to walk around in 1986 with a cockatoo mohican and a fishnet over your face, then you had to be very confident indeed of the quality of your music – or your hype. And Sigue Sigue Sputnik had hype in spades. They have a certain fascination as the embodiment of the 80s ethos of style over content, where image leads and talent can follow if it likes. In fact, as founder member Tony James has attested, the group's origins lay in one simple concept: was it possible to sit down and devise a group as an 'idea'?

James, formerly in Generation X with **Billy Idol**, formed Sigue Sigue Sputnik with the fantastically-coiffured Martin Degville, Neal X, Chris Cavanagh and Ray Mayhew. The band's name was allegedly that of a Russian street gang, and was spotted by Boomtown Rats manager Fachtna O'Kelly in a copy of the *Herald Tribune*.

They were marketed as postmodern, ironic, a band immersed in 80s media. Their first album *Flaunt It* on EMI used the gimmick of selling advertising space between the tracks. (You just can't imagine their more po-faced contemporaries doing that, can you? Sting slipping the Nescafé Gold Blend couple into side one of *The Dream of the Blue Turtles*? Dire Straits fading *Brothers In Arms* into a quick plug for Shake'n'Vac?) Their songs didn't venture into vastly original chord changes or melodies, but managed to sound more interesting than they actually were by means of superfluous technology. And that's just as well, really, given that they all had the kind of haircuts that make you want to say, 'Excuse me, sir, but would you mind stepping out of 1976?'

They must have done something right to get a Top Three hit, but the album didn't sell well. After 1988's follow-up *Dress For Excess* – which featured the slogan 'This time it's music' – the band split... but surprisingly, it wasn't yet over.

🕯 The band were often in cahoots with the *Sun's* Garry Bushell to provide outrageous media copy. Their headline-grabbing activities drove rival paper the *Mirror* to invent even more shocking ones, like allegations of racist jokes and half-empty venues. The *Mirror* even offered the band a front-page story if they could run a (made-up) scoop about Degville being 'crucified' on a cross of burning TV screens – on Good Friday. The *Sun's* response was to offer the band the lead story if they would break the Wapping workers' strike by riding into the compound with

Samantha Fox on the back of a Chieftain tank...

✓ TV presenter Magenta DeVine was an influence – yes, *that* Magenta, she of the irritating voice, tailor's-dummy hair and surgically-attached sunglasses – and some of the band's first songs were written in her house. Neal X was recruited through a *Melody Maker* advert, while Magenta found Martin Degville dancing in a Kensington shop called YaYa. God knows how she spotted him, though, wearing those shades.

✓ The third album was apparently to be called *This Is Terrorvision*, pre-dating the 90s rock band of that name...

✓ It has been suggested that **U2**'s media-manipulating activities on their *Zoo TV* tour owed more than a little to the Sputniks' 1986 Albert Hall performance.

◁» 'Often, in England especially, the crime *is* success. As soon as you make it, the people who last week told you [that] you were great and new and exciting tell you [that] you never were, that they always hated you, and won't play your records or write about you – and worse, [they] will destroy everything you ever stood for.' (Tony James)

▶▶ Tony James joined the **Sisters of Mercy** for a bit in 1991. However, there have been signs of recent activity, with James resurrecting the band and promoting their new album *Piratespace* through the Internet – a gig at London's Borderline in 2000 was the launch of the 'new' Sigue Sigue Sputnik.

Simple Minds ★★★★

♪ **'Promised You A Miracle'** (1982, no.13)

Bombastic stadium-conquerors fronted by Jim Kerr, who were famous for not being **U2**, at least until their 1989 chart-topper 'Belfast Child' threw aside any pretence and proved that imitation was the sincerest form of flattery. (It helped that it came at a time when U2 had, temporarily, stopped making decent records.)

The band had its origins in the wonderfully-named Johnny and the Self-Abusers, a seven-piece with three guitarists, some of whose members formed Simple Minds after the inevitable split. Early days in Glasgow and some time on the indie label Zoom led to Simple Minds being signed by Arista, then Virgin. One thunderous epic after another followed, some of which were pretty good: 'Waterfront', 'All The Things She Said' and 'Don't You (Forget About Me)' spring to mind, the latter inspiring a rather embarrassingly girly dance where fingers are wiggled to simulate the effect of the rainfall referred to in the lyrics.

Sometimes a little too humourless for their own good, they nevertheless produced an impressive canon of work.

- When the band played at Nelson Mandela's 70th birthday party in 1988, they were described by a Scottish MP (who shall remain nameless here) as 'left-wing scum'.

- 'Belfast Child' is based on the traditional melody 'She Moved Through The Fair'. It clocks in at just over six-and-a-half minutes, which made it the second longest Number One single after 'Hey Jude' (and without endless, tedious repetition of 'na-na-na-na' to bulk it out).

Sinitta ★ ★

♫ 'So Macho/Cruising' (1986, no.2)

The path from children's TV to the pop charts is littered with casualties; few tread it without coming a cropper. So far, we have been spared Christopher Biggins' industrial techno album and the nu-metal crossover period of Andi Peters, although if the lovely Philippa Forrester ever made a trip-hop record, I'd probably buy it. Sinitta, however, smoothed the route from ITV kids' game show presenter to pop bimbo by showing off her legs in a very short skirt and singing some perky little ditties penned by *that* trio (you know the ones).

Born Sinitta Renay Malone in 1966, she was the daughter of singer Miquel Brown and looked a bit like a younger, dirtier Floella Benjamin. Her songs, if you can call them that, centred around every girl's desire for a musclebound oik with a flash car. (I wouldn't like to call her shallow, but if she was your local pool you'd be scraping your knees on the bottom.) Highlights of her career include the video to 'Cross My Broken Heart', in which Sinitta discovers her boyfriend is cheating on her. Failing spectacularly to realise that this is probably because he's sick of going out with someone who wears curtain-rail earrings, lime-green tights and lilac leotards, Sinny goes off on one. She storms into a cinema and covers him in popcorn and Coke, all the while glancing surreptitiously off-camera to where someone is, presumably, holding up the lyrics. It's almost Expressionist.

Her string of hits in the 1980s came to an end with the inane 'Love On A Mountain Top' – without our quoting from it directly, some measure of this ditty's lyrical genius can be gained from the fact that the love in question is, apparently, being drunk from a *fountain*. You get the idea.

We shudder to recall it, but there was a somewhat insane attempt to redo **Blondie**'s 'The Tide Is High' in 1990, plus

'Hitchin' A Ride' (possibly a song about a dull town in Hertfordshire). 'Shame Shame Shame' in 1992 was her last chomp at the chart cherry.

Still – six-year pop career, eh? Kids today would sell their grannies to Simon Cowell for such longevity.

✓ Her name is rhymed with 'meet yer' and 'St Peter' in the 1992 **Half Man Half Biscuit** song 'Mars Ultras, You'll Never Make The Station'. I'd like to think it was an affectionate tribute, but on balance I'd say they were taking the piss, wouldn't you?

◀» 'I still got a bit upset when we went to Japan because I felt that Pete [Waterman] didn't think of me the same as he thought of **Kylie**. I know **Kylie's** been more successful than me, but I was one of the orig-inal people with him and I thought 'how come you're not getting behind *me* and pushing *me*?'. I thought my loyalty wasn't paying off and all the other new acts were coming before me and it'd be "oh, good old Sinitta is always there!". But I'm a bit too fiery and adventurous to be reliable like that. It's the wrong profession to expect someone to be "reli-able".' (Interviewed in *Number One* in 1989)

▶▶ Currently relaunching her career, the undeniably easy-on-the-eye Sinitta has become a born-again Christian. See also **Sam Fox**. What is it with these 80s popstrels and their God-squaddery? Some kind of desire to atone for past musical sins?

Siouxsie and the Banshees ★★★

♪ 'Hong Kong Garden' (1978, no.7)

Innovative weirdos from the punk and post-punk era. Siouxsie Sioux's first brush with infamy came during the infamous Sex Pistols interview with Bill Grundy – she was there in the background, with regulation eyeliner and bin-liner in place.

Siouxsie, born Susan Dallion, formed the band with Steve Severin, John McKay and Kenny Morris, and a bit of John Peel support got them noticed in the late 70s. Later recruits included Budgie (formerly of The Slits) and John McGeogh on guitar. Broody, bleak, but still hauntingly melodious, the Banshees' music transcended its punk origins and got them through a couple of decades. The early 80s albums *Kaleidoscope* and *Juju* helped to define their sound and cemented their influential position, while 1988's *Peepshow* saw them coming back with a vibrant, sophisticated look and sound.

- Amazingly, only two of their singles ever made the Top 10 – the debut and 1983's 'Dear Prudence' – but the singles compilations *Once Upon A Time* and *Twice Upon A Time* are a solid testament to an eclectic, sporadically brilliant band.

- Siouxsie spent much of their 1985 UK tour with her leg in plaster, following an incident where she dislocated a knee on stage at the Hammersmith Odeon.

- Among the charity concerts the Banshees have played are gigs for MENCAP, the Disabled Children's International Games and the Italian Communist Party.

✔ An early line-up had Sid Vicious on drums, and performed a legendary 20-minute version of The Lord's Prayer. Steve Severin was known at the time as Steve Havoc, and Marco Pirroni, later of **Adam & the Ants**, was also involved.

◀» 'We did a *Top Of The Pops* appearance for this ['Fireworks', 1982], and they had this horrible flashing neon sign going "SIOUXSIE! SIOUXSIE!" and then they were going to have fireworks... We said, "No! No! No!" – so they got the hump. They really do take it personally if you object to anything they do. The video we did was cut short 'cos the guy who was in charge of pyrotechnics blew his face off!' Siouxsie reflects on explosive moments.

▶▶ 'As the "music industry" prepares to relive the heady days of "punk", when, confusing the opportunists with the protagonists, it proceeded to sign anything with a safety-pin that could spit, Siouxsie and the Banshees would like to say Thank You And Goodbye.' From the press release announcing the band's split in 1996. Siouxsie and Steve Severin returned to their side-project, The Creatures.

Sisters of Mercy ★★★

♪ **'This Corrosion'** (1987, no.7)

Goth opera

There are a few useful reminders throughout this book that the 80s were not all dodgy barnets, panda mascara and poncing about in frilled shirts. There was Indie, there was the New Wave Of British Heavy Metal, and there was Goff. Sorry, Goth. One of the best manifestations of the latter came from Leeds in the shape of Andrew Eldritch (the name his mum knows him by, I am sure) and the other assorted personnel who made up the Sisters over the years: guitarist/ bassist Gary Marx, a drum machine called Doktor Avalanche, Wayne Hussey from **Dead Or Alive** and The Mission, Tim Bricheno from **All About Eve** and Tony James from **Sigue Sigue Sputnik**. Bestriding the comings and goings like a colossus was the ragged Eldritch, not someone you can ever imagine sunning himself in Tenerife, frankly. He was all cheekbones, paleness and permanent shades, and looked as if he could do with a few good Yorkshire steak-and-kidney pies in him.

'Temple Of Love' gave them their biggest hit when it was re-released in 1992, the original pale and skinny sound beefed up by magnificent backing vocalist Ofra Haza. Since the third album *Vision Thing* it's all been a bit quiet.

🎧 The eight-minute Jim Steinman epic 'This Corrosion' is perhaps their best-known song, and you can dance to it as well (I know, because I have). But if you can get hold of the collection of early stuff, *Some Girls Wander By Mistake*, it's worth a listen, especially to hear how they sometimes sounded like **The Cure**.

✔ Eldritch's mini-album *Gift* was released under the name of The Sisterhood. It was allegedly rushed out to deny Hussey and Marx the rights to the name and also to obtain the remaining advance from the record company – the 'two five zero zero zero' in the background to the first track is thought to be a cynical reference to the cash that Herr Eldritch was in the process of pocketing, but we couldn't possibly comment on that.

✔   Eldritch's lyrics play with language, especially the tensions between German and English: there's a line in 'Mother Russia' (on *Floodland*) which only rhymes because he pronounces 'the DDR' in the German way ('day-day-airr'). *Gift* is therefore double-edged – 'Gift', you see, is German for 'poison'. So do be careful when filling in the customs labels on your Christmas presents for those friends in Baden-Baden...

The Smiths ★★★★

♫ **'This Charming Man'** (1983, no.25)

The Mancunian Candidates

When, in a recent *NME* poll, The Smiths were voted the most influential act of the last 50 years – with The Beatles in second place – a few shock-waves reverberated around the music-fan community. One puzzled correspondent to the *Guardian* wrote: 'The news that The Smiths are regarded as the most influential band in the history of rock music has thrown me into utter confusion. I wholly agree, but have nothing in my record collection that suits my celebratory mood.' And that, in a nutshell, sums up the public perception of The Smiths – a bunch of miserable, black-clad gits from Manchester (where it is always raining).

The truth is that Stephen Patrick Morrissey, Johnny Marr, Andy Rourke and Mike Joyce weren't miserable – at least, not until the court case where Joyce sued Morrissey and Marr for 25% of the band's earnings. They were wry, and dour, and their lyrics weren't exactly cheerful, but they were never as depressing as people try to make out. And they certainly didn't wear black all the time (another popular myth).

Morrissey, of course, was adopted as an icon by every specs-wearing nerd who couldn't get a girlfriend. The only man who could be taken seriously with a hearing-aid as a fashion accessory and a bunch of gladioli in his back pocket, he was the indie darling of the bedroom outcast who had experienced the pain of being sixteen and unloved. Now, at last, the sensitive souls – every sixth-former who loved to gaze wistfully into the middle distance under a large quiff and to write poetry about the girls they fancied who, unaccountably, didn't fancy them back – had their hero.

Of course, The Smiths' true hero was co-writer and guitarist Johnny Marr, the man who could sound like someone playing two guitars at once. 'The Boy With The Thorn In His Side' and 'Big Mouth Strikes Again' showcase Marr's talents particularly well. On occasion, however, there actually were two guitars, as so-called 'fifth Smith' Craig Gannon lent support on tour (the live album *Rank* has a big and chunky rock sound, which led one critic to remark that they sounded surprisingly red-blooded for a vegetarian band). It's just a shame that Morrissey's somewhat overrated, whiny voice often sounds a little too much like someone trying to yodel through a colander, and doesn't do justice either to his own witty lyrics or to the intricate guitar melodies being expertly picked out by Marr.

Creative tensions between Morrissey and Marr came to a head, and The Smiths disintegrated as a band shortly before the final studio album *Strangeways Here We Come* in 1987. Their work has been endlessly repackaged and re-issued ever since.

Oh, and I think it's time to break it gently to people that Morrissey wasn't *really* a sexually frustrated celibate, any more than **Adam Ant** was a highwayman or **Kraftwerk** were robots. And Johnny Morris wasn't really a zoo-keeper. And the tooth fairy, well, that was your mum. Sorry.

🎧 The mid-career retrospective 'Hatful of Hollow' captures many of their best moments.

✔ There's a good *Guardian Weekend* article about The Smiths, archived at: **http://shopping.guardian. co.uk /music/story/0,1587,653917,00.html** (and if you can be bothered typing all that in, you must be keen). It's fannish, heartfelt and more than a little pretentious, so don't say I didn't warn you. But it does have the distinct advantage of not being written by Julie Burchill.

♥ Perhaps surprisingly, nobody has yet had a UK hit by covering a Smiths single (unless you count Sandie Shaw's co-performance on 'Hand In Glove'). However, as you'd expect, they have spawned bucketloads of covers, and these pointers to the better-known ones only scratch the surface. So, deep breath: 'Heaven Knows I'm Miserable Now' has been recorded by Act (Claudia Brücken's band after **Propaganda**) ... The version of 'How Soon Is Now?' by Love Spit Love (the new band from **Psychedelic Furs** frontman Richard Butler) is on the soundtrack to the film *The Craft* (yes, the one with the fit witches) and you may also know it as the theme song for TV show *Charmed* (yes, the other one with the fit witches)... 'Panic' has been a B-side for Carter the Unstoppable Sex Machine, and those other unstoppable sex machines the Nolan Sisters have done a version too... In 1996, French magazine *Les Inrockuptibles* voted *The Queen Is Dead* the best album of the 80s and, to celebrate this, they released an album of covers called *The Smiths Is Dead* featuring covers of all the tracks by current UK acts. These included 'The Queen Is Dead' from The Boo Radleys, 'Never Had No One Ever' from **Billy Bragg**, 'Big Mouth Strikes Again' from Placebo and 'There Is A Light That Never

Goes Out' from The Divine Comedy... Sometime Smiths backing vocalist **Kirsty MacColl's** version of 'You Just Haven't Earned It Yet Baby' can be found on her *Kite* album... And finally, not a cover but a steal – Soho's single 'Hippy Chick' from 1991 does its own funky thing with the bassline of 'How Soon Is Now', included here just to annoy all the Smiths purists who can't even think about this without wincing. Is that enough to be going on with?

♥ 'Shakespeare's Sister' inspired another band's name, of course, while 'Girlfriend In A Coma' gave its moniker to the novel by Douglas Coupland and 'Big Mouth Strikes Again' to a collection of Tony Parsons' journalism.

▶▶ Given the current state of play between the band members, it's unlikely that they'll be re-forming for the 'Here And Now' Tour 2006... although stranger things have happened. Morrissey's solo career flourished but now seems to have stumbled to a halt, while Marr played with The The, among others, and became part of **Electronic**. He has been touring with his new band, Johnny Marr's Healers.

Soft Cell ★ ★ ★ ★

♪ **'Tainted Love'** (1981, no.1)

Time again for that good old combination of the surly one in the background and the exhibitionist at the front, only this time with a touch of melancholia, depression, leather and sado-masochism. Marc Almond and David Ball, who met at Leeds Polytechnic, first unveiled their trash-tinged glamour to the world with the single 'Memorabilia' – still available on the compilation of the same name if you can find it.

Their breakthrough, though, was 'Tainted Love', the cover of a Northern Soul classic, a Number One which was destined to stay in the charts for a whole year. They went on to revisit the charts with haunting melodies like 'Torch', 'Bedsitter' and 'Say Hello, Wave Goodbye'. Marc's vocals are more redolent of theatre than pop – you can hear him reaching for the back rows on some notes as he really puts his all into it, perfectly complementing the crisp and mini-malist instrumental arrangements.

- ✔ Various causes have been attributed to their break-up, but it seems likely that drugs – in particular, an early discovery of Ecstasy – may have had something to do with it... Whatever, it seems that a taint of naughty scandal will forever be associated with their name. There's that infamous urban myth about Marc Almond and a stomach-pumping incident which seemed to get round every secondary school in the early 80s – let's just say he has always denied it, and move on. It's dogged him for long enough.

- ♥ David Gray had a hit with a cover of 'Say Hello, Wave Goodbye' in 2001, and it's also on his *White Ladder* album. But then you probably knew that.

- ♥ A memorable *Not the Nine O'Clock News* sketch had Rowan Atkinson as Almond, lip-synching his inter-view responses to a hidden tape-recorder which then starts playing at the wrong speed. Very much of its time, and funny – the first couple of times you see it...

- ▶▶ Almond went solo with some interesting results, most notably on his 1992 album *Tenement Symphony*, which is worth checking out. Ball (how very singular) became half of techno duo The Grid, whose biggest success was with 'Swamp Thing' in 1994.

Beloius Some ★★

♫ **'Imagination'** (1986, no.17)

Oddly, the works of Mr Some rather passed me by the first time round; I was aware of him, but only vicariously through rude comments in magazines. So, I have had to rely on the kindness of others to inform me that his real name was actually Neville Keighley. Undeniably, he was very blond and somewhat chubby – the publicity stills suggest a prototype Gary Barlow. His only other hit was the cunningly-titled 'Some People', which also gave his 1986 album its name. However, his song 'Round Round' appeared on the Pretty In Pink soundtrack, which gave him a little more exposure.

- ✔ Nev was the bottom-of-the-bill support act for Queen at their 1986 Knebworth concert (their last-ever performance as the original foursome). Other acts on the bill were Status Quo and Big Country.

- ✔ 'Imagination' did well in Europe – it reached no.7 in Italy on its first release in 1985, only charting in the UK with a 1986 re-issue.

- ▶▶ He returned briefly from obscurity for a 1993 album, *Living Your Life*, which apparently sees him celebrating his roots (so the peroxide had worn off, then) by embracing the wacky world of techno. Or, as they would have said in 1993, 'Techno, techno, techno, techno'.

Sonia ★★

♪ 'You'll Never Stop Me Loving You' (1989, no.1)

Still spoken of in hushed tones around Liverpool, this daz-zlingly original young singer-songwriter exerts a powerful influence on today's cutting-edge acts. The dangerously subversive lyrics and multi-layered instrumentation of her beautifully-crafted songs reverberate through the end of the decade like –

Oh, God, I can't keep this up. Look, it was *Sonia*. You know the rest. Scouse bird, nice arse, red hair, big smile, squeaky pop-by-numbers. First hit was OK in a jolly dancealong sort of way, the rest rather mediocre. Didn't win Eurovision in '93, and I think it's safe to say she was never in a punk band with a silly name. (Although if you grew up in Liverpool in the 80s and you know any different...)

She is nice, apparently. Which makes me feel sorry for being rude.

◀» Sonia on why she likes her camp followers: 'When I first had a few hits I did a couple of straight venues and I didn't like it at all. You get a lot of bitchy girls and lads leering at you ... There's just craziness and mayhem in many straight clubs. So the only gigs I will ever do now are gay ones. I haven't done a straight gig for six years; you never know if you're going to get a bottle thrown at you. I've never had one bit of trouble with a gay crowd. When I step on stage I feel a sense of love as if they care about me, they would never hurt me in a million years. All they want to do is smile.'

▶▶ Sonia returned to stage shows, including 1997's 'What A Feeling!', which also starred Luke Goss (from **Bros**) and **Sinitta**. They'd only have needed

Rick Astley and they could have had a surreal, post-show bridge party entirely for the purpose of post-80s trauma therapy.

_____

Spandau Ballet ★★★★
♫ 'To Cut A Long Story Short' (1980, no.5)

Necessity being the mother of re-invention, these laddish types experimented with quite a number of image-changes over the years. They never looked comfortable in the New Romantic gear of ponchos, berets, kilts and frilled shirts, but it was the music that counted.

Spandau Ballet were the brothers Gary and Martin Kemp on guitar and bass respectively, vocalist Tony Hadley, drummer John Keeble and guitarist/saxophonist Steve Norman. After early gigs in exotic locations like HMS Belfast and the Scala Cinema, they were persuaded by manager Steve Dagger (an old schoolfriend of Gary's) to set up their own label, Reformation, licensed to Chrysalis. The first pulsating single plunged into the Top 5 and got them instantly noticed. 'Chant No.1 (I Don't Need This Pressure On)' was a no.3, although things tailed off a bit until Trevor Horn gave 1982's 'Instinction' his magic touch. 'True' was the big chart-topper in 1983, given an additional lease of life by being used as the BBC's Olympic theme a year later. 'Gold' was a worthy follow-up, even if its chart medal was silver. However, legal wrangles with Chrysalis temporarily called a halt to proceedings in the middle of the decade.

After the well-remembered 'Through The Barricades', they seemed to lose their way a bit, a disastrous re-invention as leather-clad biker types for non-hit 'Raw' being the low point. 'Be Free With Your Love', also a flop, saw an unintentionally amusing performance on the BBC's *Wogan*, with the title prompting the genial host himself to add 'but don't send me your medical bills'.

- ✔ Gary Kemp was given his first tape-recorder in 1969 by the Bishop of Stepney, who was visiting his primary school for prize day.

- ✔ Tony Hadley was a former star of photo-stories in the teen magazine *My Guy*.

- ▶▶ The nostalgia circuit has been kind to them – the Kemp brothers have not participated, but the others have performed as the clumsily-named (and hence writ-avoiding) 'Hadley-Keeble-Norman ex-Spandau Ballet'.

The Specials ✇ The Special AKA ★★★

♫ **'Gangsters'** (1979, no.6)

Had their roots in the punk/reggae fusion band The Coventry Automatics, formed by Jerry Dammers, Lynval Golding and Sir Horace Gentleman (known to his mum as Horace Panter). After Terry Hall joined in 1978, they became The Coventry Specials, then The Special AKA. Jerry Dammers set up the 2-Tone label under Chrysalis, with an agreement to produce at least six singles a year; the Specials became leading lights of the movement which took the label's name. There was never a more perfectly-timed Number One than the haunting, catchy, insidious and brilliant 'Ghost Town', its feel and lyrics capturing perfectly the background of social unrest in mid-1981.

- 💣 In 1980, after audience trouble forced them to stop a performance, Jerry Dammers and Terry Hall were charged with incitement to violence and fined £1000.

- The debut single 'Gangsters' was recorded on a shoestring budget. Because they couldn't afford a B-side, they used instrumental track 'The Selecter', credited to a band of the same name who were only formed after the single was released (and went on to have a hit that same year with 'On My Radio').

Spitting Image ★★

♫ **'The Chicken Song'** (1986, no.1)

Amazing, the things which could get to Number One in our decadent decade. Who would have predicted such success for an imitation holiday song with deliberately annoying lyrics, performed by a band of mindless latex puppets? But never mind **Big Fun** for now. This nonsense hit, a parody of 'Agadoo' and its ilk, stayed at the top for three weeks before **Doctor & The Medics** stepped in to save us all.

The TV programme which spawned this often featured a parody song over the end credits, but they were rarely good enough to be heard more than once. You won't find much incisive political satire in 'The Chicken Song', frankly. But you might learn to speak Arapahoe.

Squeeze ★★★

♫ **'Take Me I'm Yours'** (1978, no.19)

The Squeeze story is one of vacillating fortunes but a triumph of talent over adversity. The original 1975 line-up was Chris Difford (guitar/vocals), Paul Gunn (drums), Jools Holland (keyboards/vocals), Harry Kakoulli (bass) and Glenn Tilbrook (guitar/vocals), but it went through quite a few changes over the years, including such luminaries as Paul Carrack (later of **Mike and the Mechanics**) and even

Boston-born singer-songwriter Aimee Mann for one tour in the mid-90s. However, traditional singer-songwriters Difford and Tilbrook have always formed the core of the band, and have been hailed at various times over the years as the saviours of British pop, the new Lennon and McCartney, or simply a classic songwriting duo.

With their endearing songs like 'Up The Junction', 'Tempted', 'Labelled With Love' and 'Take Me I'm Yours', Squeeze always sounded terribly quirky and British; it took them until 1987 to gain recognition in the US.

Albums *Squeeze, Argybargy, Cool For Cats* and *East Side Story* were all well-reviewed, but by 1982's *Sweets From A Stranger* the cracks were starting to show and the band split. However, Difford and Tilbrook stayed together, working on songs for other people and their musical *Labelled With Love*, and in 1985 they decided to resurrect Squeeze in a new incarnation. A high-point of this new phase was 'Hourglass', a catchy new hit on both sides of the Atlantic.

Things went wrong again when1989's *Frank* album didn't do so well, and Squeeze were dropped by their label; however, a new deal in the 90s brought another resurrection and some of their best songs, like 'Some Fantastic Place' and 'Third Rail'.

- At Chris Difford's suggestion, the name was taken from a Velvet Underground album. They were going to be 'Cum', but common sense prevailed when they realised they'd never get on *Top Of The Pops* with a name like that. However, they did perform as Captain Trundlow's Sky Company (or Skyco for short) for a while.

- In America, they initially had to change their name to UK Squeeze, to avoid confusion with an American band called Tight Squeeze. Similar fate has befallen other successful British bands: Suede, for instance, are known in the US as London Suede.

🔊 'I went to see... *Summer Holiday* when I was five... And the basic plot was about [Cliff Richard] and his band, the Shadows, driving around Europe, leaping out and playing on beaches, and everyone being terribly excited. This very much impressed my five-year-old mind. I thought, "I'd like to do that". And it never left me – from that point on, that was all I wanted to be. Five years later it was the Monkees.' Glenn Tilbrook speaking in 1988 about his inspiration.

Shakin' Stevens ★ ★ ★

♪ **'Hot Dog'** (1980, no.24)

He came, he saw, he shook. If you ever wondered who had the most Top Twenty hits in the 1980s, then look no further, for it wasn't **Duran Duran** or **Madness** or **Bananarama**, it was this chap – yes, Welsh rock'n'roll karaoke king Michael Barratt. Said by some to be a latter-day Elvis, although if Elvis had started recording in the 1980s, then he'd probably have been a futurist synth-pop pioneer in a white boiler-suit and not an over-earnest, bequiffed chap in faded denim dancing like an uncle at a wedding.

Shaky (as those familiar with his work were allowed to call him) grew up in Cardiff listening to local rock'n'roll bands and took a number of odd jobs to supplement his own stints in The Cossacks, The Olympians and The Denims. After playing Elvis in a West End musical, Stevens tried to launch his solo career, but labels going bankrupt and records flopping meant that he had a, er, shaky start (I'm sorry, I'm *sorry*, I will do penance later).

Shaky was a little ahead of his time, to be fair: he was

doing retro before retro was cool. Warbling his way through 'Green Door', 'This Ole House' and other classics, he got the kids up and dancing when they hadn't heard the originals (much like today's pre-pubescents getting down to a Sugababes song and not realising it's a bootleg of **Gary Numan**). However, I think most of us realised he had gone a little too far in 1985 with his fourth Number One – the video to 'Merry Christmas Everyone' featured Shaky in a *bad* jumper, one which spoke less of a whole lotta shakin' goin' on and more of a nice, quiet sit by the fire in a comfy chair eating Walnut Whips during the Queen's Speech.

But you can't really argue with all those hits – and sixteen albums, too.

✓ Famous Ronnie Corbett joke: 'I've not been so nervous since I found myself in the BBC toilets standing next to Shakin' Stevens.' Ka-boosh. Ah thank yew.

💣 There is a famous and often-repeated moment from Yorkshire TV's regional music show *Calendar Goes Pop*, in which Shakin' Stevens launches himself at a young Richard Madeley, getting him in a headlock. No careers were injured.

♥ You may have thought Shaky was a tribute act and didn't need any more, but he has at least one – a chap called Mark Keeley, who first appeared on *Stars In Their Eyes*, performs as Fakin' Stevens.

⏭ These days, Shaky still performs live. He toured the UK in 1999 and 2000 and performed at the opening of the Welsh Assembly and the open-air Millennium event in Cardiff. He's recently been back in the studio. His website **www.shakin-stevens.com** is being updated but should be the place for all the news on his most recent activities.

_____

Stock, Aitken & Waterman ★★★

♫ **'Roadblock'** (1987, no.13)

Sound of the suburbs... in pastel shirts

I told you I would do penance. Technically, they scrape in here as artists on the strength of the above hit and 'Mr Sleaze', the AA-side to **Bananarama**'s 'Love In The First Degree' in the same year. 'Roadblock' gained a little more publicity than it deserved when **M/A/R/R/S** pinched a bit of it and got into hot water with the lawyers. However, it's their role as producers and Svengalis to a parade of clean-cut youngsters which assures them their place in history – there have been times when I've thought that if I had to invoke their names any more times in this book, it would open up a portal to a dark dimension and the world would be consumed in flame by **Big Fun** and Michaela Strachan.

SAW left a mark on the decade as indelible as that of Mrs Thatcher, Mrs Whitehouse and Mrs McCluskey. Without Mike, Matt and Pete, we'd never have had **Mel & Kim, Bros, Rick Astley** or a whole host of lesser mortals. So, according to how charitable you're feeling, these three gentlemen were either a) slick purveyors of perfectly-honed three-minute singles with a crisp, homogenous pop sensibility, or b) a bunch of plodders whose relentlessly cheesy output all sounded the bloody same.

SAW made music for boys in bomber jackets with gelled flat-tops and their sullen part-time girlfriends with frizzy perms and pastel tops. In other words, the kids hanging round the high streets of Milton Keynes, Ashford and Basingstoke on a Saturday morning with their mum and dad's money in their pockets and little in their heads. They knew what they wanted and SAW gave it to them – music inspired by clubland, but diluted, processed and re-packaged into radio-friendly pop. It was bubblegum, half-chewed and stuck on the wall of a shopping centre next to 'Shaz ♥ Kev'. In the late 80s, the true sound of the suburbs wasn't Paul Weller or **The Smiths** – it was this.

Let's get the grudging praise done, then. Many of their songs have half-decent melodies and some of them even employ good vocalists, notably the aforementioned Mr. Astley – 'Never Gonna Give You Up' is possibly their finest moment. SAW's best quality was the ability to take a dance-floor sound and refashion it in British-suburban mould, to make it as parochial and artificial as fake stone cladding or garden gnomes. And, of course, they started **Kylie Minogue's** career, even if she does sound an awful lot better now. Kylie, unlike others, didn't really need to be squashed through the 'Calrec Soundfield Microphone', a studio gizmo which could make any tone-deaf bit of totty sound like a competent singer. (Yes, we've left the compliments behind now. Keep up.)

They pumped out a sequenced beat, switched on the Linn drum machine and let their starlets sing about the trials of life: boy meets girl, boy dumps girl, girl goes shopping to forget boy, or dances the night away until she meets more fanciable boy. As a microcosm of a particular kind of soulless, 80s suburban life, it was pretty close to the mark. Baked-bean-cans of music, perky ditties to whistle in the bus-shelter before copping off at the local dive. To live and shag and buy garden furniture and die in Ashby-de-la-Zouch.

And it kept coming. And coming. It's almost too horrible to recall, but I'm sure there was a week in 1989 when *everything* in the Top 20 was either yet another brain-dead SAW ditty or a thumping, anodyne house record (fine if you were off your face at a club, but dreadful on the radio).

It was surely round about August 1989 that many people found themselves jumping up and down in front of the radio shouting 'All right, Waterman, all right, we get the point! Please do something else or piss *off!*'

Nobody is quite sure why they went their separate ways. It's rumoured that the split was due to musical similarities.

✔ There is lots more information on SAW activities past and present at **www.cafe80s.freeserve.co.uk** if you feel the urge.

◀» 'Peter [Waterman]'s not involved in songwriting... so he'll just come in and out of the studio. He's very supportive of us, but we don't have to go out with him every night after the studio ... and listen to him talk ...' The diplomatic Keren Woodward from **Bananarama** in 1993.

▶▶ Mr Waterman has continued to do more of the same, most recently with Steps, and was recently a judge on TV's *Pop Idol*.

The Stranglers ★ ★ ★

♫ **'Peaches/Go Buddy Go'** (1977, no.8)

Formed in the early 70s by multi-talented entrepreneur and off-licence manager Jet Black and biochemist Hugh Cornwell. Originally The Guildford Stranglers, they described themselves as 'soft-rock' in an early *Melody Maker* advert. Rode out the punk era, being somewhat older than most of the gobbing and snarling young pretenders, then started to have hits in earnest in the late 70s and early 80s. They had a distinctive sound, but brought a new feel to each hit – the strutting bassline of 'Peaches', the driving keyboards and drums of 'No More Heroes', and a successful rehabilitation of that least rock'n'roll of instruments, the harpsichord, on their biggest hit 'Golden Brown'. Cornwell left in 1990 but the band continued, with muted success.

- The power was cut in the middle of a Stranglers performance at the Roundhouse in 1977, after Cornwell revealed a T-shirt with a four-letter word on it. Apparently GLC performance regulations didn't allow the offending display.

- And it was another electricity-related incident which led to the band's arrest in Nice in June 1980 – they allegedly incited a riot after a generator was not supplied, and the band members were fined in a Nice court later that year.

- 'We've taken rock'n'roll to probably more people than anyone else. We've made asses of ourselves a few times and we've brought a lot of attention to ourselves. We have been quite, uh, an enriching part of the British rock'n'roll culture for several years now. We've been active.' (Bassist Jean-Jacques Burnel interviewed in the *NME* in 1979.)

- 'The priority for me has always been to create, to write, to express and do as many things as possible. To me, speaking out is not a priority any more – I can do that in a song. You might not know about it! I see it as an alternative form of expression. I don't see the point in ranting because I express myself through what I do.' (Hugh Cornwell in *Record Mirror*, 1985.)

Strawberry Switchblade ★★★

♫ **'Since Yesterday'** (1985, no.5)

Started life as a foursome in 1981, but were down to Glaswegian duo Jill Bryson and Rose McDowell by the time they had one of the catchiest hits of the decade. The splendid 'Since Yesterday' is the song, a jaunty melody undercut with some quite dark lyrics. Their strong image certainly helped – two gorgeous girls in polka-dot dresses with mad ribbons and even madder make-up, a bit like a bubblegum-Gothic **Voice of the Beehive**. Hey, it's got a la-la chorus. Just enjoy.

✔ 'Trees and Flowers' was their first single in 1983, and featured Roddy Frame from **Aztec Camera** on guitar.

✔ **www.algonet.se/~akeen/strawberry/index.htm** has some nice pictures.

▶▶ Their last record before they split was a cover of Dolly Parton's 'Jolene'. Since then, Rose McDowall has released two albums - one with Sorrow (*Under the Yew Possessed*) and the other with Spell (*Seasons in the Sun*), both of which came out in 1993.

Swing Out Sister ★★★

♫ **'Breakout'** (1986, no.4)

Founder members were keyboardist Andy Connell and drummer Martin Jackson, formerly of A Certain Ratio and Magazine. For their first single, 'Blue Mood', in 1985, they recruited the lovely Corinne Drewery, instantly recognisable at the time with her glossy raven hair, carmine lips and tight black gloves. Excuse me for a moment… Ahem, yes, the music was nice, too. The splendid, jazzy 'Breakout' was their first hit, followed by 'Surrender', and the debut album *It's Better To Travel* was a Number One.

But 1989's 'You On My Mind' should have been a much bigger hit, and 1994's cover of 'La La (Means I Love You)' was a bit of a last gasp as far as the UK charts went. Where did it all go wrong? You'd think Swing Out Sister had disappeared from the face of the earth, when by rights they should have been at least as big as, say, Simply Red. Well, the record company seemed to lose interest – there's a 1996 *Best Of*, but nobody seems bothered about promoting their new work in the UK, even though their recent albums have been a success overseas.

Shame! The 'Swing Out Sister Come Home' campaign starts here.

✔ If you're a big fan and you're frustrated by their lack of exposure here, then you could do worse than to make friends with someone in Japan. Swing Out Sister were (and still are) huge there – a remix collection, *Another Non-Stop Sister*, was released there in late 1989, followed in 1990 by *Swing 3*, a collection of early B-sides and rarities, then in 1992 by another remix compilation, *Swing Out Singles*, and a live album, *Live at the Jazz Café*! I'd be interested to know if any of these are actually any good, or if they obey the Diminishing Law Of Remixes (the more you get, the more rubbish they usually are).

✔ As well as their Japanese fanbase, they have something of a cult following in the US and Europe.

✔ **www.swingoutsister.com** for more information.

pause

T

twenty cigarettes and a bottle of
Jameson's as a bribe

Taffy ★★

♫ 'I Love My Radio (My Dee Jay's Radio)' (1987, no.6)

British songstrel whose darkly soulful good looks belied the fact that this was a piece of fluffy pop – still, anything with 'DJ' in the title is probably going to get played on the radio. Harmless but ultimately forgettable, the single is also known as 'I Love My Radio (Midnight Radio)' and was technically an 'indie' hit as it was released on Transglobal. The record, produced by Claudio Cecchetto (see **Sabrina**) made no.3 in the Indie charts. Follow-up 'Step by Step' was no.15 in the indie charts and peaked outside the main Top 40.

Amazingly, 'Step by Step' turned up again in 1998 in remixed form, this time produced by Marc Andrews, with an additional mix by D-Bop. It was released in Japan, Australia, and some European countries. So, young Taffy still has a following out there somewhere.

Talk Talk ★★★

♫ 'Today' (1982, no.14)

Further purveyors of an eponymous single. Singer and instrumentalist Mark Hollis, fresh from studying child psychology at Sussex University, started writing songs at the age of 22. The band Talk Talk was formed with the aid of Mark's brother Ed, who happened to be the manager of Eddie and the Hotrods. A radio session with Kid Jensen and a support slot on **Duran Duran's** tour both helped, and before long they had their first hit on EMI, 'Today'. The sound was synth, lush and multi-layered, with Hollis's voice oddly strangulated, always sounding as if it was trying to blend into the mix rather than articulate the lyrics. The label was trying to get them to be New Romantics – they weren't keen.

Strangely, their anthem 'It's My Life' did better in other

European countries than in the UK; it only made the Top 40 here in a 1990 remixed version. Things went a bit mad with the 1988 album *Spirit Of Eden*, which they didn't support with a tour – fair enough, as it would have entailed taking an orchestra and the Chelmsford Cathedral Choir on the road with them. And those choirboys can be monsters on the tour-bus.

◁ᵛ   'EMI are still trying to cash in on the band. The bleak excellence of the songs featured here... is a testament to Talk Talk's ability to withstand their label's financially-driven wishes. Now, of course, they're powerless to do anything about it.' *NME* review of *The Very Best of Talk Talk*.

The Teardrop Explodes ★★★
♪ **'Reward'** (1981, no.6)

Before that well-known pop eccentric, St. Julian of Copeshire, was offering pronouncements on the mystical qualities of stones and proclaiming the impending death of the world by over-dependence on the automobile (and he might have a point there), this is what he was doing. First of all he was in The Crucial Three, a triad who, true to their name, turned out to be three of the most influential pop names to come out of the North-West: Cope, Ian McCulloch and Pete Wylie. After tryouts in a succession of transient combos, Cope formed The Teardrop Explodes. 'Reward', 'Treason (It's Just A Story)' and 'Passionate Friend' were the hits; Mick Finkler, Paul Simpson and Gary Dwyer were the other partners in crime, with Dave Balfe replacing Simpson just before the 80s began. Three albums ensued, but after the somewhat prophetically-titled EP 'You Disappear From View', the band disintegrated amid the usual personality clashes. Cope embarked on an eclectic solo journey influenced by New Age mysticism, drugs, Neolithic stones and German techno.

Tears for Fears ★★★★★

♫ 'Mad World' (1982, no.3)

Two's a crowd

Roland Orzabal de la Quintana. Ponder on that name. Good, isn't it? Flamboyant, exotic, intriguing. Then try this one: Curt Smith. Short, sharp and businesslike. The contrast would seem to sum up Tears For Fears, the duo whose emergence as individuals in their own right ended in a great schism at the end of the decade. Luckily, they left us with three albums and a baker's dozen of mostly-good hit singles before they went their separate ways.

Following their first taste of success with a five-piece ska band called Graduate, Smith and Orzabal – who had known each other since their school days in Bath named their new experimental synth-pop band Tears For Fears and signed to Mercury after two demos. At first, Orzabal was the songwriter in the background and Smith the pretty-boy singer up front, especially in the video for 'Mad World' where you hardly get to see Roland at all.

Great things began to happen, like supporting **The Thompson Twins** and being voted Best New Act in *Smash Hits*. Orzabal started to get himself noticed more, and also to favour guitars over synths. There were more hit singles, including their biggest, the upbeat no.2 classic 'Everybody Wants To Rule The World' (Roland didn't rate this one much, so he graciously decided it was good enough for Curt to sing) and the anthemic 'Shout'. The second album *Songs From The Big Chair* would eventually go triple-platinum in the UK, despite its brevity – just eight tracks, five of which were released as singles. (There is a hard-to-get-hold of 'Special Edition' with extra tracks, but some pressings which claimed to be this were actually just the standard album.) Big MTV stars, they looked set indeed to conquer the world.

Then what happened? The crunch. The perfectionist Orzabal wanted his band to be Big and Serious. He started getting even more Worried. It seemed to have worked for U2, the point at which they became Very Serious and Very Worried happily coinciding with the point at which they became Very Big. And the obvious way to do it? Shut yourself away in the studio for four years and blow the budget, of course.

The Seeds of Love was Orzabal's album, no doubt about it. It's big, bombastic, Beatles-esque and beautiful, although it has more than its fair share of self-indulgent moments which just scream 'over-produced!' at you, even if you're not quite sure what something over-produced ought to sound like. Orzabal drafted in songwriting collaborator Nicky Holland and bluesy American pianist and singer, the titanically-tonsilled Oleta Adams. Where was Smith in among all of this? As Orzabal rather cattily pointed out in later interviews, Curt only sang on two songs on the second album and one on this. However, Curt and Roland still appeared side by side on the album sleeve – that memorable image of them as the 'sun and rain' in a weather-clock – and on the accompanying tour, they were still very much the two front-men with a backing band. They didn't exactly seem chummy on stage, but they still delivered the goods.

It wouldn't last, though, and Smith departed in 1991. Orzabal continued as Tears For Fears for three more albums and did make some interesting singles, including 'Break It Down Again' in 1993, for which he delivered an outstanding *Top Of The Pops* performance, and 1995's 'Raoul and the Kings Of Spain', which paid tribute to his ancestry.

- *Tears Roll Down* draws together all their hits as a duo, plus excellent bonus track 'Laid So Low (Tears Roll Down)'. Sort of thing you'd find in a big store's '2 for £20' sale – snap it up. Oh, and there's a Universal Germany collection, called *Shout*, which has some of the post-'92 singles on it too. You lucky, lucky Germans.

- It's obligatory in any article about Tears For Fears to mention that they were named after a phrase from Arthur Janov's book *Prisoners Of Pain*, which is concerned with confronting fears in order to eliminate them. This makes you look very clever and intellectual.

- While we're in 'not just a pretty face' territory, I can vouch for the fact that both band members speak French, or at least did at the time of their European concerts in 1989… Smith's was workmanlike, while Orzabal's was superb.

- Ex-**Spandau Ballet** singer Tony Hadley has covered 'Woman in Chains' – I wonder if this is why the first track on Roland's solo album is called 'Ticket to the World'?… Gloria Gaynor's done a version of 'Everybody Wants To Rule The World'…There are some interesting takes on 'Shout', including one by distressingly-pierced Chicago rockers Disturbed. (Curt apparently likes this version and thinks they 'bring out the darkness' in the song…hmm.) 'Mad World' underwent a resurgence in 2003 when Gary Jules' cover stormed to the top of the UK's Christmas Top 40 (trouncing the ghastly Pop Idol crew and just scraping past tongue-in-cheek rockers, The Darkness). The minimalist version – an arrangement of just voice, piano and cello which allows the poignancy of the song to emerge – got the Orzabal seal of approval too. 'It's better than our version,' he affirmed in a BBC Radio interview. Praise indeed.

▶▶| Orzabal released a well-received solo album *Tomcats Screaming Outside* in 2001 (more at **www.rolandorzabal.co.uk**) while Smith formed his own band, Mayfield, in 1998. After years of rumours, Curt and Roland confirmed in late 2003 that they had indeed been working together again, and that their new album would be called *Everybody Loves A Happy Ending*. Aaaaah.

Technotronic ★

♫ **'Pump Up The Jam'** (1989, no.2)

Techno Prisoners

Sometimes, when putting this book together, I have felt like the bringer of necessary but unpleasant bad news. Do people really want to be reminded of faceless boy-bands and sterile dance acts? Well, yes, frankly. The 80s weren't all lacy collars, big coats and mascara, you know. Confront these demons, because I have to confront mine.

In early 1989, I was living in an apartment in the small French town of Barr, near Strasbourg. It was attached to a school and looked out on to a quiet, totally empty patch of waste ground. Apart from the occasional joyrider – and you didn't get too many of them in Alsace – nobody ever ventured within a hundred metres of my window on that side. And then, one Saturday morning – when I really needed a lie-in after a night on the Kronenbourg, and just as the early morning sunlight streamed in through my shutters – it began. BOOM-boom-boom. BOOM-boom-boom. Daaa-da-da-da... 'Puuuump up da jam...'

Allow me to explain. A fairground had, for no readily apparent reason, taken up residence on the waste ground, and would remain there for the next six weeks. The owner appeared to have three songs on the PA which accompanied the rides. Over the next few weeks, these became affectionately known as 'Ride On Bloody Time', 'Another Bastard Day In Paradise' and, yes, 'Pump Up The Sodding Jam'. There was a time when I would have sold my soul to Lucifer if it meant I never had to hear this diabolical record again. There were times – usually about midnight on a Sunday, when I knew I had to get up for a class on Monday morning – when I considered visiting the fairground owner and instructing him, in some very colloquial French indeed, to insert the Technotronic CD somewhere which would give him considerably more than a Gallic *crise de foie*.

What made it even worse was that the French kids I was teaching at the time absolutely loved the stupid record, and would constantly be badgering me to translate the lyrics. Look, the person who wrote them was *Belgian*, for God's sake! How was I supposed to know if he was blathering on about turning up the volume at an impromptu musical session, or if he was just obsessed with his mother's home-made loganberry conserve?

For those of you who really want the facts, Technotronic was the brainchild of American producer and former philosophy lecturer Jan Bogaert, whose unlikely real name was Thomas de Quincy. Given that his namesake was an opium-eater, it seems quite appropriate that he should make records liable to produce bizarre hallucinations. Bogaert – who emigrated to Belgium in the 1980s, and so deserved everything he had coming to him – had as his aim the ultimate fusion of hip-hop and house, although why this should be desirable has never been properly explained.

It's worth a little snigger as we point out that Technotronic had their own '**Milli Vanilli** moment': Zairean model Felly, allegedly the voice behind the records, was hired only for her looks, and the rapping duties were actually performed by one Ya Kid K. (Well, quite.) The Kid only later got the credit for her sterling work.

It hardly seems worth telling you that Technotronic released a number of other records, allegedly different songs but actually all sounding the same, a fact acknowledged by a 'Megamix' in 1990. There was an attempted comeback called 'Recall' in 1995, by which time the target audience had all moved on to the Outhere Brothers and 2 Unlimited. Technotronic, meanwhile, remain one of the few groups it would seem quite reasonable to ban under the Geneva Convention.

Let's leave them, though – we've already spent far longer thinking about their records than the people involved with making them ever did.

▸▸ I don't know where they are today, and I don't care. Ideally, if there were any justice, it would be somewhere in a god-forsaken corner of rural France where they have to lie in bed with a hangover and have shite music blaring at them while they are trying to get to sleep.

Then Jerico ★★
♫ **'The Motive (Living Without You)'** (1987, no.18)

Having perfected a big, stadium-sized sound before they could fill the venues to go with it, late-80s rockers Then Jerico were perhaps a triumph of optimism over their actual material. They weren't bad, but always seemed to languish in the decade's second division, despite being endlessly championed by Janice Long on her Radio 1 show. Mark Shaw was the long-haired, raspy-voiced vocalist (and co-producer) and the band had three more hits – their biggest, 'Big Area', got to no.13.

◀» Of all the wit and wisdom of Mr Shaw over the years, I think my favourite is: 'I really dislike people in uniforms unless they are wearing spiked shoes and fishnets.'

▶▶| After the band split, Mark Shaw performed live in the early 90s as a solo artist, but he resurrected the name Then Jerico in 1997 when he signed a new contract. Go to **www.bdmedia.co.uk/jerico/** for news on their activities since re-forming: charity gigs, TV appearances and much more...

Thompson Twins ★ ★ ★

♫ **'Love On Your Side'** (1983, no 9)

Let's get the obvious out of the way. 'Yes, Mum, there are three of them,' sighed teenagers up and down the land, most of whom had little problem with the concept. Named after the bowler-hatted detectives in the *Tintin* books, they initially recorded as a seven-piece. By the time of their first UK hit, they had slimmed down to the threesome of Tom Bailey, Joe Leeway and the candyfloss-haired fan of outlandish millinery, New Zealander Alannah Currie. Never a favourite with the critics, they nonetheless racked up nine hits in the space of two years.

💣 While working on the second album in 1985, Tom collapsed from nervous exhaustion. The single 'Roll Over' was deleted and the album and planned world tour were put on hold. Nile Rodgers was brought in to finish production duties while Tom had some rest and recuperation.

🔊 'Yeah, there was that thing in the *Daily Mail* that said hats were back in, judging by Lady Di and Alannah of the Thompson Twins! It just shows you what happens if you're in the right place at the right time!' Tom in *Melody Maker* interview, 1983. Alannah was apparently 'embarrassed' to be mentioned in the same breath as Diana.

💣 'You had to know how to get in a window and put locks on properly, and you had to do your own wiring and plumbing... Somebody would come and help you, and you'd do your bit for them – generally get things together, drag old furniture off of rubbish heaps and stuff like that. I mean, nobody had any money. It was quite fun.' Alannah on the politics of squatting in *Rolling Stone*, 1984.

⏭ The hits petered out in the latter half of the decade and Leeway left the band. Bailey and Currie kept the name for a while, but started afresh in 1992, recording as Babble.

Tiffany ★★★

🎵 **'I Think We're Alone Now'** (1988, no.1)

Gosh, how 18-year-old Tiffany Darwisch (or Darwish, depending which source you look at) suffered for her art. Not many people would agree to appear under the hot lights of *Top Of The Pops* wearing a thick mohair jumper. However, she did deliver a live vocal – albeit a slightly raw and croaky one – which was a novelty for the time, and syncopated the chorus just to prove she wasn't miming. And she entertained us with an odd, robotic proto-Vogue kind of dance, which seemed to cause her great distress.

It was a childhood performance in a country and western club – after which Tiffany passed a hat round and collected $235 – which started her on the musical road. So, after that, was Tiffany performing in shopping malls to comment on her marketable 'pop princess' package?... That seems to be the main thing she's remembered for, rather than a slightly dodgy Beatles cover ('I Saw Him Standing There').

The boppy 'I Think We're Alone Now' (a cover of the Tommy James and the Shondells track from the 1960s) hit Number One and the ballad follow-up 'Could've Been' made it to 4, so she must have been doing something right. Tiffany bounced back at the end of the year with a long-running Top 20 single, 'Radio Romance'.

She had a patchy career in the 90s, which included a track on a homelessness benefit album and a successful album in Japan, the aptly-titled *Dreams Never Die*.

- In September 1989, Tiffany obtained an injunction from a Los Angeles judge ordering an obsessed fan from Santa Cruz to keep at least 200 yards away from her at all times. The fan had written her numerous letters, including one in which he claimed 'God wants us to be together'.

- Tiffany's surname is Lebanese in origin, so the English spelling is actually a transcription from the Arabic alphabet.

- That fluffy jumper on *TOTP* sported a picture of Marc Almond from **Soft Cell**.

🔊 'When I was about two, they started making Tiffany lamps and even Tiffany rugs. They even started making Tiffany jewellery. I guess it's just a name that got really popular.' (Tiffany in *Rolling Stone*, 1988)

⏭ Tiffany has a new image and sound with her new album *The Color of Silence*. It didn't have great sales in the USA, despite good reviews, but it has sold very well in Asia. Meanwhile, an appearance in the April 2002 issue of *Playboy* saw Tiffany back in the public eye again...

Tight Fit ★★
♫ **'Back To The Sixties'** (1981, no.4)

When you are 12, 'camp' means this. A cold, unwelcoming sleeping-bag on the iron-hard earth; blackening your slices of Mother's Pride on sticks around glowing embers; fashioning aerial runways out of dangerously frayed rope and bits of hardboard; washing in a stagnant stream; moving your bowels over a fetid pit with only a creaking plank between you and a hideous effluent oblivion. It was a mystery back then why anybody would want to leave the comfort of their home to do this, and it remains one to this day. They say the Scouts make you what you are today, which is true – I left, and became a reasonably well-adjusted human being, while those who stayed in became fiery-eyed lunatics with a penchant for smearing their faces with dogshit and stalking through forests with large knives.

Before university, I wouldn't have known the other kind of camp if it had come prancing up to me in a spangly pink jumpsuit, brandishing an entire fistful of Judy Garland records. All of which is a roundabout way of saying that, as I was only 12 in January 1982, I probably thought 'The

Lion Sleeps Tonight' was just a good, fun record to sing along to, and that the headbands, leopardskin off-the-shoulder tops and shiny trousers of the various members of Tight Fit merely indicated a certain sartorial whimfulness. There are people for whom the phenomenon of camp will always be a closed book, of course, such as ageing relatives who still think Liberace just never found the right girl to settle down with.

Tight Fit's singer was the muscular Steve Grant, although questions were asked as to whether he did in fact lend his vocal talents to the records. The backing vocalists were Denise Gyngell – also famous for her 1984 version of **Kirsty MacColl's** 'You Broke My Heart in Seventeen Places' – and Julie Harris. It's worth mentioning the follow-up, 'Fantasy Island', if only for the fact that it sounded very much like ABBA.

- ✔ But what does the chorus 'a-wim-a-way' actually mean? Sources suggest a traditional Zulu song, 'Mbube Wimoweh' (literally meaning 'the lion sleeps') somehow got abbreviated to 'Wimoweh'. The song, after a name change, found its way into the public consciousness via the versions from the Tokens in 1961/62 and Dave Newman in 1972, paving the way for Tight Fit's 1982 interpretation. The public held its breath in 1992, but no new recording was forthcoming... we just got 2 Unlimited instead.

- ♥ In 2001, it came back again: 'The Lion Sleeps Tonight' was sampled in a 'song' (I use the word loosely) entitled 'You All Dat' by the Baha Men. I've not heard it, but I'm happy to be prejudiced against it on the basis of the title alone.

Tanita Tikaram ★★★

♬ 'Good Tradition' (1988, no.10)

Young, intriguing singer-songwriter who seemed to emerge from nowhere in 1988. Her first hit was the sharp-edged, folk-pop song 'Good Tradition', its acerbic lyric about family life wrapped up, **Beautiful South**-style, in a feelgood tune. Later that same year, 'Twist In My Sobriety', with its haunting sax refrain, was her second and last hit; it was probably more representative of the mellow, thoughtful debut album *Ancient Heart*. Further such commercial success seemed to elude Tanita in the 90s – strangely, as she had seemed on the brink of mega-stardom – but critical acclaim continued for her subsequent albums.

Although strikingly beautiful, she did have a perpetual air of resentment about her, which can perhaps be explained by the fact that she was born in Germany and grew up in Basingstoke. She could seem terribly earnest, but she's worth including if only to remind ourselves that there was still room for an off-the-wall singer with a guitar in those awful bleepy years at the end of the decade. And if it wasn't for her, we wouldn't have the likes of Kate Rusby and Thea Gilmore.

✓ Tanita's brother is actor Ramon Tikaram who appeared in *This Life*. Ramon used to be referred to as 'Tanita's brother', but now Tanita is 'Ramon Tikaram's once-famous sister'. Ah, the vagaries of fame.

✓ Tanita once admitted in an interview that she had made up the lyrics to 'Twist In My Sobriety' purely on the basis of what sounded good, without giving much thought to the meaning. A touch of the **Nik Kershaws**?

Timbuk 3 ★★
♫ 'The Future's So Bright I Gotta Wear Shades' (1987, no.21)

Novelty value

What were this pair of one-hit wonders from Austin, Texas singing about, then? I always took it to be some sort of acerbic comment on the imminent prospect of nuclear war destroying the dreams of youth. But what do I know?...

Timbuk 3, for the record, were Pat and Barbara MacDonald, and their debut album, aptly, was called *Greetings From Timbuk 3*. They developed a cult following around their subsequent albums *Eden Alley*, *Edge of Allegiance* and *Big Shot In The Dark*.

The Timelords ★★
⊛ The Justified Ancients of MuMu, The KLF
♫ 'Doctorin' the TARDIS' (1988, no.1)

Who were these sinister, caped and hooded figures, swinging their guitars in unison to the beat of Gary Glitter's 'Rock and Roll' and the sampled Delia Derbyshire arrangement of Ron Grainer's *Doctor Who* theme? None other than the KLF, of course, those jovial sponsors of the British mutton industry who liked to chuck the odd fiver on the fire when things were getting a bit parky in the studio.

Also known as the Justified Ancients of MuMu, alias Bill Drummond and Jimmy Cauty, here they appeared as a one-hit wonder in one of their more bizarre incarnations. Quite why they did this record is a mystery, but it was quite fun at the time... the sublime clubland joys of '3am Eternal' and 'What Time Is Love' were still a couple of years off, and this really has to be put down as a novelty record.

The publicity had to be seen to be believed, with the creative input being credited to a battered police car going under the name of 'Ford Timelord'. They wanted the car to perform on *Top Of The Pops* but this pleasure was denied us, so we got the duo themselves, caped and hatted, accompanied by a home-made Dalek which looked nothing like the real thing – it wasn't even the right shape. Maybe this was the point...

It's fair to say the *Doctor Who* aspect of the song was smuggled in through the back door (not an unfamiliar concept to many *Who* fans). It didn't do much to raise the public interest in the TV show, which at the time was going through an interesting but difficult creative realignment. But this is the only record from the 80s on which you will find a Dalek grating 'Dosh, dosh, dosh, loadsamoney!' And for that, we should be truly grateful.

✔ The title, lest there should be any doubt, is a genial play on 'Doctorin' the House', which had been a hit for Coldcut featuring **Yazz** earlier in the year.

Toto Coelo ★★

♪ **'I Eat Cannibals Part 1'** (1982, no.8)

Another of those half-remembered one-hit wonders. Garishly-garbed quintet, who looked as if they were halfway between dancing with Mr Hopwood at the *Grange Hill* school disco and going to see the *Rocky Horror Show*. They were named after a Latin expression meaning 'entirely' or 'utterly', but someone obviously assumed along the way that this wouldn't be understood across the Atlantic and so they were known in America as 'Total Coelo'... To which my response is, 'Like, duuuh.'

The band didn't ever get round to a full album, although

a retrospective, *I Eat Cannibals And Other Tasty Trax*, appeared for some reason in 1996. It includes 'Dracula's Tango', their only other song to come anywhere near the charts, and the **Bananarama**-esque 'Milk From The Coconut' and 'Man O' War'.

✔ Like many other 80s icons, they are namechecked on the Saint Etienne song 'Fake '88', which is on *Sharks Patrol These Waters – The Best Of Volume Too*. I have now won a bet by getting a Saint Etienne reference into a book about the 80s. Haha.

✔ Lead singer Anita Mahadervan, later Anita Chellamah, became a member of The Cherry Bombz and later a TV presenter.

✔ And *Blockbusters* host Bob Holness' daughter Rosalind was in the band. This is actually true, unlike any of the other music-related rumours involving Bob (specifically those relating to 'Baker Street' and saxophones). It must have run in the family, as Bob's other daughter Carol was also a singer, going under the name of Nancy Nova.

Toyah ✦ ✦ ✦

♪ **'Four From Toyah EP'** (1981, no.4)

Probably somewhat tainted by continually being cited as Adrian Mole's favourite singer, Toyah Wilcox certainly had one of the most distinctive images of the early 1980s, best described as glamorous punk. Combining acting and singing from the start, she appeared, among many other things, in Derek Jarman's *Jubilee* and a West End production of *Cabaret* during which the musicians went on strike and the cast had to sing unaccompanied.

Chart success came with 'It's A Mystery' (the lead track on the EP), 'I Want To be Free' and 'Thunder in the Mountains', which would turn out to be her biggest three hits. Her combination of lisping girly charm and rather scary punkish growling earned her the title of Best Female Singer in the Rock and Pop Awards 1982.

▶▶ She's recently turned to presenting duties on programmes such as *The Heaven and Earth Show*, has been in the Dictionary Corner slot on *Countdown* (that would have been fun in 1982) and has been back on the road with the 'Here and Now' tour. It's generally agreed that she's more gorgeous these days than ever.

_____

T'Pau ★★★

♪ **'Heart and Soul'** (1987, no.4)

It's that big hair, big sound time again

Here was flame-haired temptress Carol Decker, dressed up like the head of an international marketing company. Carol, guitarist Ronnie Rogers and their solid backing band of moody blokes almost didn't make an impact on the charts, but when 'Heart and Soul' did well for them across the Atlantic, British radio stations began to take notice. Its semi-rap verse and full-throttle chorus sounded good on the radio and secured them a top 5 hit.

Purveyors of chunky, melodic Shropshire rock, the band were apparently made to smooth out their sound for a recording contract – those who attended early gigs in the pubs and clubs of Shrewsbury testify to the thundering of speakers and rattling of glasses.

Massive Number One single 'China In Your Hand'

sealed their place in history and committed the unforgivable sin of keeping 'Fairytale Of New York' by **The Pogues** and **Kirsty MacColl** off the top slot. Three albums followed – *Bridge of Spies*, *Rage* and *The Promise* – before they split quietly in the 90s.

Carol Decker re-launched the band in 1997 with a new line-up, a tour of Brannigan's nightspots (aiming at the thirty- and fortysomething lager-and-lime set, then!), some new material and another album, *Red*. There was also a re-working of 'Heart and Soul' with a more pop-dancey sound, making T'Pau part of that select band of 80s artists who have recorded covers of their own hits.

● An enthusiastic fan managed to break into Carol's dressing-room and leave a small, er, deposit of his affection on a dress she was due to wear for the 'China In Your Hand' video. She doesn't seem to have let the incident affect her unduly...

✔ You have to wonder how well *Rage* sold in France, given that it would be the equivalent of an album called *Rabies* over here. (T'Pau might not be as MOR as some people think, but they were never *that* dangerous.)

✔ The band were named after a character from *Star Trek*, which is OK to know. The character was actually a Vulcan High Priestess who first appeared in the classic episode 'Amok Time'. Probably too much information. Let's move on.

✔ The lyrics for 'Heart and Soul' and 'Valentine' on the *Bridge of Spies* album sleeve and CD booklet are not always accurate – they apparently come from the original demo versions of these songs and were printed by mistake.

▶▶ T'Pau took part in 2001's 'Here And Now' arena tour of 80s artists. Ms Decker was also spotted in a cameo appearance on Channel 4's *Trigger Happy TV*, being 'introduced' to the neighbourhood by prankster Dom Joly.

▶▶ Carol has now decided to take a break from the new incarnation of T'Pau, and rumours of a live album are yet to be confirmed, but she's happy to play the nostalgia game on shows like *Class Of...*

Transvision Vamp ★★★

♫ **'I Want Your Love'** (1988, no.5)

If it's trashy, ragged, sex-on-legs indie goddesses you're after, they came no better than Vamp frontperson Wendy James, the kind of girl your mother warned you about. Mouthy, pouting and flouncing, she seemed to say 'come hither' and 'fuck off' with the same expression.

The band consisted of post-**Madonna** prima donna Wendy, guitarist/songwriter Nick Christian Sayer, keyboardist Tex Axile (real name Anthony Doughty), bassist Dave Parsons and drummer Pol Burton. They affected a kind of punk sensibility married to a strong commercial nous, and every bit of spontaneous scandal was as carefully placed as their guitar-solos. The fact that they were despised by rock journalists just made them more interesting, given the kind of stuff the trendy music press were known to champion.

A pop myth has grown up – the Vamp seem to attract them – about how Wendy first got together with Nick Christian Sayer. Did he discover her, as the story goes, working as a backing singer for Patti Smith? Well, in a way – singing Patti Smith songs to backing tapes in a basement drinking club in Brighton, more like it. And then all kinds of stories abound about their 1986 signing to MCA and the release of debut album *Pop Art*. There's the alleged hiring of the other three band members from a street graffiti gang, and the change of staff at the record company resulting in the band being told to remix the whole album…It all makes for good copy.

Publicity undeniably played on the filthy charms of Ms J, who perfected the art of sounding as if she was really annoyed at being woken up at 3am to do the vocal and had been given twenty cigarettes and a bottle of Jameson's as a bribe. 1989 brought the anthemic dancefloor-rock of 'Baby I Don't Care' (which features one of the best screams ever committed to vinyl), followed by further top 20 hits 'The Only One' and 'Landslide of Love'. The latter is a great pop composition, sounding like **Blondie** haunted by Spector and graced with a heartfelt, near-to-cracking-point vocal from Wendy. The album *Velveteen* went to Number One – as well as the singles, it featured the epic, sprawling title track and the journalist-bashing 'Kiss Their Sons'. And Wendy on the cover, looking raggedly alluring.

They were helped along the way by Wendy's little man-ufactured controversies, which included having a dig at **Kylie Minogue's** alleged paucity of talent and an airborne snog-and-fumble with **Jason Donovan** (ooh, *so* late 80s). This would have been so much more interesting the other way round. After she was accused of revealing more flesh than was healthy for the nation's adolescents, Wendy took to dressing in a suit and tie for a while. Boo.

Things began to fall apart when the UK release of their third album *Little Magnets Versus the Bubble of Babble* was delayed – it emerged in 1991 to general disappointment, and the band split soon after. Wendy re-surfaced complete with 'classy serious artist' look for a brief solo career, of which the quality high-point was the jaunty Elvis Costello-penned single 'London's Brilliant' in 1993.

✔ Ever wondered about the missing link between Transvision Vamp and Malcolm McLaren? It's the Vamp's keyboard player Tex Axile, who played in former **Bow Wow Wow** and **Adam and the Ants** member Matthew Ashman's last band, Max.

◀» Wendy cites their influences in the original *Pop Art* press release: 'Prince, **The Jesus & Mary Chain**, Sinead O'Connor, Nick Cave, **The Pogues**. But we don't copy or steal from the past, and I don't see the point in rehashing what's been done. A great band should acknowledge its influences, then strive to make something original out of them.'

◀» 'Does my voice get sore from all the bawling I do in this song ['Baby I Don't Care']? Oh no, my voice is tough. Do I use honey and lemon? No, honey and lemon is a bit of a fallacy. What I do use is royal jelly with a bit of ginseng mixed in it.' (Wendy in *Smash Hits*, September 1989)

▶▶ Tex Axile has done solo albums, co-owns a bar and is said to be filming a documentary. Pol Burton has been in bands called Angora and Tom Patrol. Dave Parsons is now part of exported grunge-rockers Bush. Nick Sayer tried to write some new songs with Wendy around 1997, which came to nothing; apparently he's more into stuff like Radiohead these days and has no further plans to perform.

▶▶ Ms J herself is lying low. So, a free signed copy to the person who gives me her telephone number.

———————————

A Tribe of Toffs ★★
♫ 'John Kettley (Is A Weatherman)' (1988/89, no.21)

Back in the happy days when Simon Mayo used to do the Radio 1 Golden Hour, you would probably have got four points for name-checking this lot, but only if you remembered the brackets in the title. This is something defiantly silly, very much of its time, and worth giving three minutes of your life to.

Over the Christmas and New Year of 1988-89, things got a little too earnest, what with Cliff Richard's 'Mistletoe and Wine' at Number One and **Kylie** and **Jason** crooning 'Especially For You'. We can't emphasise enough, then, how refreshing it was to find in the charts at the same time a bunch of lads who seemed to be taking the business rather less than seriously. Their hit, a breezily unpolished ditty, owes a debt to the legendary **Half Man Half Biscuit** with its jaunty amateurishness and wry asides about less-than-stellar contemporary icons. Half the celebs mentioned here have long since faded into obscurity – this just adds to the charm, though, especially if you have fond memories of former Children's BBC presenters Simon Parkin (he's 'always larkin'' according to the song) and Andy Crane (who has 'got no brain').

Why can't more pop music be this much fun?

pause

425

U

unwritten rules of the pop charts

UB40 ★★★

All right, so everybody needs a distinctive sound. There are times, though, when taking a risk with a little diversity wouldn't have gone amiss. Seen at first as a protest band and associated with the early 80s ska revival and 'Two-Tone' movement, the unfeasibly over-populated reggae band UB40 had two no.2 albums on their own DEP International label. Hit single 'One In Ten' is invariably trotted out, along with **The Specials**' 'Ghost Town', as a Zeitgeist-grabbing, Thatcher-bashing soundtrack to the social unrest of 1981. Number One single 'Red Red Wine' stands out as something special, as do their two duets with Chrissie Hynde, 'I Got You Babe' and 'Breakfast In Bed'. Generally speaking though, with each UB40 release you knew what you were going to get. Expecting a little diversion into thrash-punk or experimental jazz, perhaps? Nope, it's just more reggae-lite with a social conscience.

Ooh, but there was a brief moment of excitement in the early 90s when dance gurus 808 State remixed 'One In Ten' kicking it into the charts for a new generation. Sadly, UB40 seem to have thought the prospect of a new dance-orientated direction was a little too much like fun, and so it was back to the plodding reggae for subsequent releases, beginning with the huge and dreary 1993 chart-topper '(I Can't Help) Falling In Love With You'.

💣 In 1981, UB40 played benefit gigs for those arrested in the inner-city riots. This led to the group being banned from playing venues in some cities.

✔ The band was formed by brothers Ali and Robin Campbell and they took their name from the number of the Unemployment Benefit attendance card.

- As well as having three UK Number Ones in their own right, the Campbell brothers guested on Pato Banton's cover of The Equals' 'Baby Come Back' in 1994.

Tracey Ullman ★★

♪ **'Breakaway'** (1983, no. 4)

Have you noticed how the *Guardian* has adopted the toe-curlingly PC habit of calling lady thesps 'actors' now? So, it's 'Kate Winslet, actor'. And presumably 'as the actor said to the bishop'. And 'my daughter, what a little actor'. If I were living on Planet *Guardian*, I'd presumably be forbidden from giving Ms Ullman her usual title of 'comedienne', which is such a wonderfully British, retro and holiday-camp kind of word. The singer, *actress* and comedienne with the tousled hair and fixed grin first came to prominence in the 1980s hit-and-miss sketch show *Three Of A Kind*. You may recall that her fellow participants were Lenny Henry and David Copperfield. Tracey, after a bit of dabbling in music, went to America for fame and fortune; Lenny became Mr Dawn French and a pillar of the comedy and charity community, while David returned to his other hobbies of flying across theatres on hidden wires and making the Statue of Liberty disappear. Oh, all, right, no – he wasn't *that* David Copperfield at all. You weren't fooled, were you? This one was considerably less bronzed and rather more Northern.

'They Don't Know' was a **Kirsty MacColl** song, and so you'd have to do something really defiantly stupid to cock it up. She didn't. 'Move Over Darling' and 'Sunglasses', well, they were OK. I'm just assuming here that you're not going to rush out and buy Tracey's greatest hits. I think we'll move on, as we still have others to address. (Or adder, as the *Guardian* would say.)

> ● Remember Tracey and friends with bouncy *Grange Hill* hairstyles, miming into hairbrush microphones on *Top Of The Pops* for 'Breakaway'?

Ultravox ⊘ Ultravox!, U-Vox ★ ★ ★ ★
♪ **'Sleepwalk'** (1980, no.29)

It's one of the unwritten rules of the pop charts that many of the best songs peak at no.2. Just look at the roll-call of silver medallists over our decade: 'Golden Brown', 'Denis', 'Fairytale of New York', 'Girls Just Want To Have Fun', 'Song For Whoever'... and that's just the tip of the iceberg. Perhaps the most famous case is 'Vienna', synth-pop's very own 'Bohemian Rhapsody'. This epic (i.e. it's very long and pompous and has twiddly bits) was held off the top slot in 1981 by – surely you know this – 'Shaddap You Face' by the Joe Dolce Music Theatre. Mr Dolce does not feature elsewhere in this book. However, it is also worth mentioning that the Midge Ure of the 'Vienna' era sported a silly Sparks moustache and a laughable leather cap with a chain half-throttling him, which is just as embarrassing as being kept off Number One by a crap comedy record.

Ultravox continued to churn out the hits, upping the rock factor as the decade went on. Notable highlights included the nuclear-angst anthem 'Dancing With Tears In My Eyes' and 'All Stood Still'.

✔ In the band's 'exclamation mark' period they were fronted by John Foxx. Midge Ure, (born James Ure in 1953 in Glasgow) joined after being in Slik and **Visage**. The U-Vox incarnation came later, after Midge and drummer Warren Cann had both left.

✔ On the video for 'Love's Great Adventure', Midge's

macho hurtle through the jungle is undercut when he stops to pause for breath – a rare moment of humour from a band who had seen nothing amusing in big shades, pointy sideburns and orange snoods.

✔ Fans from all over the world get together at popular gatherings called 'Voxgates'.

◀» 'Yet, despite their wanton plagiarism and less clear-ly defined ideas, *Vienna* will probably be the album that makes Ultravox, because, unfettered [by] Foxx's commitment, they're free to compromise themselves a touch to suit contemporary tastes. Ultravox of today fall somewhere between Midge Ure's hard rock poise and their old art school pose. Less aloof and more willing, their obsession with style fits present tastes.' *NME* review of the *Vienna* album, July 1980. The album stayed on the UK charts for 72 weeks.

▶▶ Midge Ure had a leading role in **Band Aid**, of course, and carved out a successful solo career, most notably with the melodic but grammatically suspect 'If I Was'. There have been attempts to revive Ultravox with other singers, but the results haven't set the world alight.

U2 ★★★★★

♪ **'Fire'** (1981, no.35)

They Four
The restraint in their choice of moniker was not evident in the world-bestriding ambitions of these rock colossi. There can be few bands who have attracted more attention in the

432

last twenty years. A constant hunger for re-invention and a willingness to experiment have been their strengths, while a bombastic self-importance may yet be their downfall.

The quartet comprises Paul 'Bono' Hewson, David 'The Edge' Evans, Adam 'Adam' Clayton and Larry 'Larry' Mullen. Bono took his name after he happened to see a billboard advertising a hearing-aid shop in Dublin called Bono Vox. The Edge, well, he was called that because of his daredevil habit of standing right on 'the edge' of stages during performances, rocking dangerously on the balls of his feet as he teased out those soaring arpeggios and threatening, with every deft flick of a chord-change, to go hat-over-boot into the baying hordes in rows A to E. (Oh, of course he wasn't. Don't be ridiculous. It's some old cobblers about his being at the 'edge' of guitar genius, or something.) The line-up has stayed consistent since they first formed in 1976 with the not-very-amusing comedy punk name of Feedback. Although all of them have at some point veered off into side projects, the foursome have remained a unit and it is hard to imagine U2 without all its members present and correct.

In the 1980s, they began with hard-edged rock like 'Out Of Control' and 'A Celebration' and ended up doing heartfelt and soaring string-backed epics like 'With Or Without You', heartfelt and soaring string-backed epics with interesting key-changes like 'The Unforgettable Fire' and very long, heartfelt and soaring string-backed epics with show-off twiddly bits like 'All I Want Is You'. Their musical dexterity was always offset by an almost terrifying seriousness – this was undercut by The Edge's silly hat, Bono's ridiculous mullet, Larry's resemblance to a resentful dustman and Adam's little round 'I'm the intellectual one, me' glasses. Oh, and in case anybody forgot that they were Irish – and, therefore, had a congenital need to show the rest of the world how much they had suffered – they recorded a song called

'Sunday Bloody Sunday'. It wasn't a soaring string-backed epic. It was a very worried and serious Political Song, which you could tell straight away because it had a drum intro which sounded like a sequence of gunshots. A decade later, Alan Partridge would muse on the lyrics' apt encapsulation of the hollow boredom of mowing the lawn and reading the paper. I do sometimes wish he had been right.

Live Aid, the one place in the world where you could be right-on for a day and everybody would love you, seemed tailor-made for them; few can forget Bono's 'spontaneous' dragging of a girl out of the audience during the very worried, heartfelt and soaring string-backed epic, 'Bad'. The apogee of the 'serious' U2 came with their best album, 1987's *The Joshua Tree*, a very listenable collection of songs with a good balance of passion and restraint. The same could not be said of *Rattle And Hum*, a sprawling, self-indulgent opus inside which there is a fantastic nine-track album kicking and screaming to get out.

It had to end somewhere: there is only so much mileage you can get from standing among the cacti looking constipated and coming on all globally-aware. The 90s gave us the new, 'ironic', multi-media U2, the eclectic albums *Achtung Baby* and *Zooropa* showcasing a band who surfed the shortwave for soundbites, deconstructed post-Communist Europe beneath swinging Trabant mobiles and had onstage telephone conversations with Salman Rushdie (in 1993, when mobile phones were the size of small housebricks and were still a novelty).

The *PopMart* tour went even further. Someone, somewhere decided it would be a great idea if the band all emerged on to the stage from a giant lemon – one night, however, the lemon failed to open and U2 had to sidle somewhat sheepishly out of the wings. At last, they had become Spinal Tap; their 'Jazz Odyssey' is now surely only two albums away.

- ✔ Larry and Adam worked together as a duo to rejig the *Mission: Impossible* theme as a thumping bass-heavy dance track for the 1996 film. They were going to be 'U1' – presumably as they were the two who didn't yet have comedy nicknames and they needed to redress the balance – but better judgment prevailed.

- In 1987, the band withdrew their official endorsement of Eamon Dunphy's book *Unforgettable Fire: The Story of U2* after their unsuccessful attempts to change some allegedly inaccurate portions of the text.

- In 1989, Adam Clayton was arrested in Dublin for possession of marijuana and intent to supply. His conviction was waived in return for a donation to a women's refuge.

- Among the covers worth mentioning are Irish girl-band Bellefire's pretty 2002 version of 'All I Want Is You', after which they were dropped by their label – come on, guys, it wasn't that bad! It certainly knocked the spots off The Chimes' take on 'I Still Haven't Found What I'm Looking For' in 1990, which turned the slow-building rock classic into an insipid soul/R&B dirge. We must mention the **Pet Shop Boys**' inspired reworking of 'Where The Streets Have No Name' in 1991. And, of course, who could forget Clivilles and Cole's dance version of 'Pride (In The Name Of Love)' from 1992?... Oh, you had.

pause

V

vibrant and loveable

Visage ★★★

♫ **'Fade To Grey'** (1980, no.8)

Steve Strange, alias Steve Harrington, was a part-owner of the famous New Romantic hangout, the Blitz Club in Covent Garden. Strange and partner-in-crime Rusty Egan wanted to create music to dance to, and, it being the early 80s, this obviously involved wearing ridiculous amounts of make-up, poncing about quite a lot and getting sliced by dodgy electronic effects in the videos. Band members Billy Currie and Midge Ure escaped to **Ultravox**, leaving Visage to enter the Top 20 a few more times with some weaker tunes. 'Damned Don't Cry' is pretty good, though.

✔ In 2000, Steve Strange was given a three-month suspended sentence for stealing a Teletubby doll, of all things.

◄)) 'I know you'll probably think this is very naive, but at 17 a boy comes from the valleys, all of a sudden 'Fade to Grey' goes off and there's a limousine on hand 24 hours a day. You're staying at the Hilton, you're travelling first class. All I wish was that I was told, "You're paying for that, Steve, it's not all it's cracked up to be"... You think, wow, this is going to go on forever... But when things do go wrong and your album isn't going into the top five and you're not having a Number One worldwide, it's quite degrading, because the limousine isn't a limousine anymore. You're lucky if it's a fucking taxi.' Steve Strange interviewed in the *Guardian* in May 2000.

Voice of the Beehive ★★★

♫ **'Don't Call Me Baby'** (1988, no.15)

Exuberant tales of domestic woe

Californian sisters Tracey Bryn and Melissa Brooke Belland livened up the straight-faced and boyish indie scene of the late 80s, and yet they still came out of it undervalued and in need of escape. Tracey and Melissa had come over to London and stayed, and after their early demos received a favourable hearing at Food Records, they and their backing band – guitarist Mike Jones and former **Madness** members Mark Bedford and Daniel Woodgate, on bass and drums respectively – put out their first single 'Just A City'. A deal with London Records followed and the band acquired Martin Brett as a new bassist.

When the vibrant and loveable indie anthem 'I Say Nothing' jangled on to the airwaves in the Autumn of 1987, there wasn't much like it around, certainly not on daytime Radio 1, so there was a bit of a buzz about it (sorry). For a while, it seemed that a breath of fresh air was to sweep through the moribund charts.

However, record-buyers didn't initially take to the Beehive girls in their droves. Both the first single and the thunderously harmonic 'I Walk The Earth' peaked outside the Top 40, and they had to wait until the Spring of 1988 before 'Don't Call Me Baby', admittedly their most agreeable melody, gave them their first and biggest hit. 'I Say Nothing' was re-released and managed to do better second time around, while *Let It Bee*, despite the groanworthy title, did good business in the album charts, peaking at no.13. It's a very listenable album, covering a huge range: 'Beat Of Love' is a sideways look at relationships turning sourly into violence and 'Man In The Moon' is a wry depiction of the perfect man, while 'There's A Barbarian In The Back Of My Car' rocks to the sound of more turbulent male-female interaction. And it's all infused with harmonic vocals, big crunchy guitars and great drumming.

The playfully-titled *Honey Lingers* followed in 1991, a more diverse collection, with the standout track an upbeat cover of The Partridge Family's 70s hit 'I Think I Love You'.

In 1993, Tracey sang with Jimmy Somerville on one of the many versions of 'Gimme Shelter' put together by Food and EMI to raise money for a homelessness charity. 1995's *Sex and Misery* was the final album, by which time the girls had decided to go it alone as a duo, polished their sound and found more success in the US than over here.

- On 'I Say Nothing', the reference to 'I get it every night' was bowdlerised for the single re-release to 'I see him every night', although they continued to sing an even ruder version in live shows!

- The music paper *Sounds* gave away a free EP in October 1987, which included an early version of 'What You Have Is Enough' as well as tracks from **The Primitives**, The Soupdragons and The Band Of Holy Joy.

- The girls' father, Bruce Belland, was a member of 50s group The Four Preps. The sisters appeared in TV commercials as children.

- Tracey and Melissa's first recording experience came when they sang backing vocals on Bill Drummond (of the KLF)'s first solo album, *The Man*. They were billed as 'Voice Of The Beehives'.

- The sleeve notes of the 12" of 'I Say Nothing' hint that they came perilously close to being 'Voice of the Grapefruit', while it's known that The Fashion

Dont's, Down Worm and The They Monster were also considered as names at various times.

✓ Some clues as to the mood surrounding the final album can be gleaned from its original title: *Disastrous Relationships, Disillusionment, Depression & Death*.

▶▶❘ Tracey and Melissa now live in Laguna Beach: Tracey writes and illustrates children's books while Melissa designs statues and sculptures. 'Woody' Woodgate, meanwhile, has returned to the **Madness** fold.

pause

white teeth and designer stubble

The Waitresses ★★

There will come a time, usually around the first week in December, when you realise you're heartily sick of the state-imposed soundtrack to Christmas. Endless spins of bloody John and Yoko whining on. Cliff Richard again. Boy-bands doing their slush-pappy ballads-with-bells. That man from Wizzard who, for some inexplicable reason, wishes it would be Christmas Every Sodding Day, and so has evidently never had to stand in a supermarket queue behind some pudgy slapper in a shell-suit buying six crates of lager and a ton of fags while her scabby kids in Santa hats run riot, stuffing their mouths with chocolate they haven't paid for.

Thank goodness, then – and the little baby Jesus, if you are so inclined – for 'Fairytale of New York', and for Jona Lewie and for the Waitresses. If you feel like saying 'bah, humbug', then 'Christmas Wrapping' is a perky little ditty which will restore your faith in humanity. At least, until that trip to Tesco to get those walnuts for Auntie Gladys.

It may come as a surprise to know that the song was never a UK Top 40 hit – so technically we can't list it above, despite the fact that it has brightened up the dire Yuletide playlists of several radio stations for the past 15 years. Oh, and the Ohio-based band were also nearly famous for 'I Know What Boys Like', which was almost a hit in the USA.

🔊 Writer and co-producer Chris Butler: 'The song ("Christmas Wrapping") was a total goof. Our independent label gave us one week to come up with a Christmas song for an album they were recording. We gave them the song and forgot about it, until one day my wife heard it on the radio.'

💙 It was covered by the Spice Girls. Please don't let that put you off...

Wang Chung ★★

♪ 'Dance Hall Days' (1984, no.21)

A one-hit wonder, but a popular one, especially if you were ever cool on craze…and America rather took to them. Starting life as Huang Chung in 1980, they were Jack Hues, Nick Feldman and Darren Costin. They were among the acts for the very first 'Rock on the Tyne' festival in 1981, supported **Toyah,** and became the first UK act to be signed to the American label Geffen. Hues and Feldman became a duo in 1986, having success in the US with the album *Mosaic* – the single 'Everybody Have Fun Tonight' was a no.2 hit. By this time, it's fair to say, they looked like a pair of supporting characters from *Miami Vice.*

▶▶ After going their separate ways for other projects, the Hues-Feldman duo re-formed for some tours in the late 90s. Jack is now writing and producing; Nick is an A&R man for Sony and Darren is an engineer.

The Weather Girls ★★

♪ 'It's Raining Men' (1984, no.2)

Actually first released in 1983 and a hit on its re-entry into the charts the following year. One of the better-remembered one-hit wonders of the decade, probably for several reasons: it features the vocal talents of Martha Wash and Izora Rhodes, it was covered and taken to Number One by Lady Geraldine of Halliwell, and it has been adopted as a gay anthem. This record has something in common with Graham Norton, cute screen-savers and the re-emergence of the asymmetric striped top: all likeable at first, then rapidly more irritating with each successive appearance.

- ✔ Izora was apparently a musical prodigy at the age of 4; her teachers and her mother expected her to be a concert pianist and she studied music at the San Francisco Conservatory.

- 📢 Izora: 'Anybody who, like me, belongs to the old school, will again and again practise basics to improve all-round mastery – no matter whether this applies to playing the piano or to singing. We therefore practise two or three times per week, putting in eight hours each time. Perfection can only be reached through practising.'

Westworld ★ ★

♫ **'Sonic Boom Boy'** (1987, no.11)

A few bands have this one particular recurring myth attached to them, but it was Westworld in the version I heard, and it goes like this. Band turns up at record company HQ, asks for a meeting, gets given the cold shoulder – and so sets up in the foyer with two guitars and a beat-box and starts to play. Jaded record company exec is hauled out of a meeting to come and hear them, thinks they are fantastic and the label signs them on the spot. Yes, well, that's how the feelgood ITV drama version would go, probably with Robson Green as the easily-impressed A&R man…

Westworld, named after the 1973 film in which robots go on the rampage at a theme park, were founded by Bob 'Derwood' Andrews from Generation X. A punky feel within a light indie-pop framework was the order of the day. The single 'Sonic Boom Boy' looks back even further, as it is driven by a 50s-ish rock'n'roll guitar riff beneath the vocal histrionics of American singer Elizabeth Westwood. It has a lot of likeable energy, as does most of the debut album *Where*

The Action Is, although some of the more experimental rap/dance crossover meanderings don't quite work.

They had potential, but sadly Westworld were not to be chart regulars, with 'Ba-Na-Na-Bam-Boo' just scraping into the Top 40 and the atmospheric 'Silver Mac' stalling just outside. They did manage to get to three albums, somehow.

▸▸┃ Bob and Elizabeth later formed the band Moondogg, who released the albums *Fat Lot Of Good* and *God's Wallop*.

_____

Wet Wet Wet ✭✭✭✭

♪ **'Wishing I Was Lucky'** (1987, no.6)

Known to their detractors by a number of cruel and rather obvious derivatives of their name, this Scottish quartet were popular exponents of the 'blue-eyed soul' area of commercial songwriting. Fronted by Marti Pellow (born Mark McLaughlin) they had three Top 10 hits in 1987 which saw them prancing in denim and beaming winsome Colgate smiles at the camera. The following year they were at Number One with a charity song, a cover of the Beatles' 'With A Little Help From My Friends', a perky and poppy version which has a lot more going for it than the dreary histrionics of the Joe Cocker cover. Nobody played the **Billy Bragg** version of 'She's Leaving Home' on the alternative A-side.

Perhaps too wholesome for their own good, they looked to be on the downslide in the early 90s, but stormed back with the unexpected chart-topper 'Goodnight Girl' and, two years later, a residency at the top of the charts to rival Bryan Adams when 'Love Is All Around' featured on the sound-track to *Four Weddings And A Funeral*. Pellow grew his hair and acquired a drug habit, both of which are not good indicators for members of former boy-bands. But they seemed to survive, perhaps by acknowledging that their former audience of screaming teenage girls had now matured into women with lots of make-up, white stilettos and sports cars.

✔ They had a Silly Punk Name! Only a few years late, but the first incarnation of the band in 1982 played Clash cover versions and were known as The Vortex Motion.

◀)) Marti said his permanent smirk was 'a complete nervous reaction. People bite their nails, I have this fucking perma-grin. For me it was always about music, but it was falling upon deaf ears because of my looks. We were writing great pop songs and that wasn't being appreciated.'

▸▸| Marti Pellow now has a solo career, and you can read all about the ups and downs of his post-Wet years at **http://martipellow.cjb.net**

We've Got A Fuzzbox And We're Gonna Use It ★★★ ⦿ Fuzzbox
♬ **'Love is The Slug'** (1986, no.31)

Surely the winner of the 'least catchy name' award – as, to be fair, this bunch of lively females seem to have realised when they shortened it. Presumably they looked around and noticed that **New Order** didn't get where they were today by being called We Own A Big Scary Drum Machine Which We're Going To Switch On While We Leave The Stage, or that **U2** might not have flourished had they been known as Yes, Let's All Pose Wearing Silly Cowboy Hats.

Fuzzbox's singer was Vickie Perks, credited as Vic – she

obviously didn't have this 80s name thing sussed, or she would surely have been Vikki. The band also featured guitarist/vocalist Maggie Dunne (credited as Magz, so she had the right idea), her sister Jo on bass and drummer Tina O'Neill. They were, if you can imagine this, a kind of missing link between The Slits and **Bananarama**, or alternatively a sort of cut-price, cartoon **Bangles**. Daft punk outfits were the order of the day. Much hair-gel was in evidence suspending both fringes and disbelief, plus assorted ribbons, glitter, mascara and 'comedy' star-shaped sunglasses, all of which made them resemble the feisty younger sisters of **Sigue Sigue Sputnik**. They got a career boost by being included on the now-legendary C-86 sampler tape from the *NME* in 1986, and their debut, the 'Rules and Regulations EP' (comprising 'XX Sex', 'Do I Want To', 'Rules and Regulations' and 'She') hovered just outside the Top 40.

They later returned, sleek and transformed after having honed a more commercial sound for the album *Big Bang*. Vickie, in particular, showed that she had been hiding her light under a bushel and emerged as a goddess in a blue PVC dress who liked to simulate pleasuring herself with the microphone stand. (Well, we assume she was simulating.) They famously defended their re-invention by asserting that every band in history had sold themselves with sex, 'except **Marillion**'. Fuzzbox even had a few hits then, such as the exuberantly silly 'Pink Sunshine' and the Gerry Anderson homage 'International Rescue' – but they split in 1990 when the perky Vickie, bless her, left for a solo career.

☊ The 15-track compilation *Fuzz & Nonsense* features acoustic versions, demos and remixes of their best-known songs – or, if you're feeling very brave, you could try the 31-track *Rules And Regulations To Pink Sunshine*, which has even more, plus live versions. Perhaps one for hardened fans only. There really should, if only for comedy value, be a box set, entitled *We've Got A Fuzz Box Set*. There isn't, but I wanted to shoehorn a feeble joke in anyway.

▶▶ Maggie Dunne joined Babes in Toyland as bassist, but she and Jo were recently reported to be back together as Fuzzbox and recording a new album. Vickie, meanwhile, re-appeared as 'Vix Fuzzbox' and has worked in drama and dance as well as collaborating with Glenn Tilbrook of **Squeeze** and Hugh Cornwell of **The Stranglers** and promoting various charities.

Wham! ★★★★★

♫ **'Young Guns (Go For It)'** (1982, no.3)

Street credibility?

Pop and entertainment fashions had suffered in the terrible, technicolour 70s, blighted by designers like kids with new paintboxes trying out every hue together. The early 80s, by contrast, were so full of chrome, cream and industrial beige that they could have been entirely filmed in black-and-white. It sometimes seemed like a monochrome world full of riots and unemployment, where a packet Vesta curry was an exotic meal and, lest we forget, digital watches were the height of technology and fashion and your parents' TV set still took half a minute to warm up.

Into this pale world came two exuberant young gentlemen in multi-coloured shirts, **George Michael** and Andrew Ridgeley, who looked as if they had got their tans somewhere rather more exotic than the dole queue in Basildon. Even their band name had a compulsory exclamation-mark. And whispers had it that the new symbol of a brighter Britain – Princess Di herself – was a big fan. George'n'Andrew lounged by poolsides in their videos and bared their tanned torsos (with varying degrees of homoeroticism). They sang about being young, about going for it, about getting drinks for free and taking pleasure in leisure. How could they fail? This was rainswept, pre-Lotto Britain, where almost nobody had swimming-pools, beer was weak and over-priced and quite a few people were beginning to wonder why they'd voted Conservative. The nation was missing a feelgood factor, and Wham! were going to provide it.

Well, naturally it wasn't that straightforward. Wham! were not universally loved, and they had their brickbats like other boy-bands before and since. Some critics wondered what Andrew actually did; it was rumoured that, although he liked to take a guitar on stage, the roadies would always unplug it without him noticing (probably the best arrangement all round). But teenage girls up and down the land fell in love with George's white teeth and designer stubble and Andrew's, um... um... Andrew's charisma. That must have been it.

A few basic facts: George and Andrew met at school in Bushey in the 1970s, and were in a ska band called The Executive for a while. As Wham! they were originally on independent label Innervision, but, in a deal which cost them some royalties but ultimately proved fruitful, they moved to Sony's Epic label and had a huge hit with 'Wake Me Up Before You Go Go'. The subsequent album *Make It Big* did what it said on the sleeve.

With hindsight, it's difficult to *dislike* Wham! with any great passion (there were far worse 80s bands) although it's easy to see how much of their career was built by hyping what was, at best, an arguable amount of talent, most of it contained within George. Well, all right, all of it.

🙢 Wham! split in 1986, allegedly as a protest at manager Simon Napier-Bell's business interests;

George's solo career was already well under way. Their farewell performance was at Wembley Stadium in front of an audience of 72,000 fans.

✔ Their long-serving backing singers were **Pepsi & Shirlie**, who later became chart stars in their own right.

🔊 'I was at home a few weeks ago and it was really strange. I walked down to the bottom of the garden – the first time for three years – and I looked over the fence. There's a farm next door and all this countryside and it looked exactly how I remember it as a kid. And I was getting really kind of reflective and I was thinking of all the things that have happened over the past five years and how it didn't really matter... how small it was in relation to all this. The insignificance of man next to nature and all that. And it just felt nice, how you could just stand there and nothing had really changed... And, suddenly, I heard this noise. It was tittering coming from behind the neighbours' bushes. I looked down and there were all these kids there with cameras, all trying to take my picture. I just thought 'don't kid yourself' and went back inside... Yes, it is weird being in Wham! sometimes.' George Michael interviewed in 1985.

🔊 Andrew Ridgeley: 'I have no real ambition, motivation, aspirations career-wise. Let's say I don't have any real ambition to be anything other than what I am now and to do what I do within the music industry, which isn't an awful lot these days but it suits me. There's really nothing else I can do; certainly nothing I really want to do. And for the moment that suits me but things may change, it's very difficult to say.' (Interviewed in *Hello*, 1992)

❤ Here's two tribute acts in one: as the name suggests, Wham!Duran (**www.whamduran.com**) are a tribute band performing both **Duran Duran** and Wham! songs. Let's hope they don't split due to musical differences. (And imagine being in a Wham! tribute band and having to be Andrew…)

▶▶ George is dealt with elsewhere, but Andrew's solo career consisted of an album called *Son Of Albert*, preceded by a not-quite-hit single 'Shake' in 1990, which had a surprisingly hard-edged rock/funk sound. Otherwise, as is well-documented, he married Keren from **Bananarama** and enjoys himself racing (and crashing) cars and living the surfing life in Cornwall. Respect, somewhat grudgingly, is due.

Whitesnake ★★★

♪ **'Fool For Your Loving'** (no.13, 1980)

The name alone is enough to make you turn into Beavis and Butthead. 'Hur, hur. He said, like, "snake". Hur, hur.' Album titles *Ready An' Willing*, *Come An' Get It* and *Slide It In* leave one in little doubt, though – Whitesnake were obviously closet Delia Smith fans and wanted to share their delight in the joys of preparing oven-baked scones.

Anyway, here was the proof that 1987's pop stars weren't all clean-cut bequiffed chaps, frizzy floozies in puffball skirts and pale youths in baseball caps. Easy-listening metal outfit Whitesnake had their two biggest hits in this year, despite the fact that their singer, the distinctly Robert Plant-like David Coverdale, had just had an operation for a deviated septum. 'Ouch' barely covers it.

'Is This Love' and the reworked 'Here I Go Again' both made no.9. The first, like most romantic ballads by heavy-rock acts, can only make you think of Spinal Tap's Nigel Tufnell and his majestic moment of melody, 'Lick My Love Pump'. The other, a tougher affair which is actually quite fun to listen to, had already been a US chart-topper five years before. The band had worked their way through many producers to get so far, not to mention several different members (some of whom may actually have exploded). But at last they were in the Top 10.

No amount of crossover appeal, though, can disguise the fact that Mr Coverdale had girly hair. And quite apart from that, he decided to devote his life to R'n'B and divorced a foxy minx called Tawny Kitaen (*sic*). Just how much better did he think it was going to get?

Kim Wilde ★ ★ ★

♬ **'Kids In America'** (1981, no.2)

From the pulsating bass and drawling vocal of 'Kids In America' to the laid-back melody of 'Love In The Natural Way', Kim is one of those who define the decade, and she even had a US chart-topper with 'You Keep Me Hangin' On' in 1986. Two facts everyone seems to know about Kim: she's Marty Wilde's daughter and she had more hits than any other female singer in the 1980s. Kate Bush was robbed, is all I can say.

Kim's tunes were great, produced by brother Ricky and co-written by Ricky and Dad, but on the early work you can almost hear the tape creaking as they double-track her one more time. Her late-80s work is slightly more redolent of depth and maturity, like the powerful 'You Came' and the lush 'Four-Letter Word'. And we shall pass diplomatically over 1987's 'Rockin' Around the Christmas Tree'…

▶▶ Kim must have got a good deal on that portrait in the attic; either that or she's living testament to the power of vegetables and Oil Of Ulay/Olay (other anti-ageing products are available) because she still today, as a woman of a certain age, has the power to render grown men speechless with desire, only able, once they have put their tongues back in, to string together the word *hubba* and the other word, *hubba*. You get the idea. Kim has moved into the more leisurely pursuits of gardening. She now dispenses tips on greenfly and soil composition in the *Radio Times*, with a touch of the surreal to match anything *Viz* could have come up with.

The Wonder Stuff ★★
♫ 'It's Yer Money I'm After Baby' (1988, no.40)

One of those indie acts who gradually sneaked into the charts when no one was looking at the end of the 80s. They went on to bigger things in the 90s, but swaggering lead singer Miles Hunt was possibly the only pop star to have long hair and still be cool in 1988. How he got away with it is still a mystery, but we're glad he did.

They were a guitar band with strong melodies and a distinct folky element, particularly on 'Golden Green', a no.33 hit which deserved to do much better. 'Don't Let Me Down Gently' was the first Wonder Stuff song to imprint itself on the public consciousness, a wryly anthemic, summery song (released in the autumn – oh, well) which scraped into the Top 20.

At the start of the 90s, 'The Size of a Cow' got them Top Five recognition and they even kept credibility intact during a Number One with Vic Reeves, a remake of the Tommy Roc 60s classic 'Dizzy'. America never clasped them to its rugged bosom, though, which probably hastened their split in 1994. They left behind just enough hits for a collection, called *If The Beatles Had Read Hunter*.

'We look at ourselves like bands like **The Cure** and R.E.M. and **New Order**, not in success stakes, but in the sense that those bands have just done what the fuck they like. They've made records to please themselves over the course of ten years or more. We're dead comfortable with that and it looks like we're gonna be around for a while now, doesn't it? We're pleased with what we've got and I'm very very grateful as well.' (Miles interviewed in 1993, a year before the band split up.)

A newly-shorn Miles formed the group Vent, which had to become Vent 414 after legal problems. There was a brief series of Wonder Stuff reunion gigs in 2000, but Miles now has a new band, The Miles Hunt Club, and you can read all about it at **www.themileshuntclub.com** – where else?

Other members Malc Treece, Martin Gilkes and Paul Clifford formed the short-lived WeKnow WhereYouLive in 1995. (Short-lived because they had a name almost as silly as **We've Got A Fuzzbox And We're Gonna Use It** ?) Clifford and Gilkes are now in record management, while Treece has been back playing with old Miles Hunt again.

pause

X marks a quirky little spot

XTC ★★★

So here they are – the people who would be the lone occupiers of all antepenultimate sections of alphabetical music books, were it not for the more obscure delights (which we won't dwell on here) of X-Ray Spex and X-Mal Deutschland. Our X marks a quirky little spot in the history of pop, one which could have been a great deal bigger.

Led by Andy Partridge, the band was formed in 1977 and were linked to the 'new wave' movement on the release of their album *White Music*. Success gradually built up and they seemed to be heading for hugeness, but then the stress of performance got the better of Andy in 1982 and he collapsed on stage in Paris. He was later found to have a stomach-ulcer and put it down to a fear of performing live in front of an audience.

As well as rehabilitating the uncool name Nigel in their lively 1979 hit, they provided us with possibly one of the best pop-songs of the decade in 'Senses Working Overtime' (and let's face it, at the age of 12 you probably did wonder about the difference between a lemon and a lime). Looking at old XTC performances now, they seem to have dated far less than some of their contemporaries – the smart, minimalist style of dress probably helped in that regard.

After Partridge decided not to play live again, the band were out of the charts for most of the decade. Tensions with the record company ensued and recordings came out under a number of aliases, including The Three Wise Men and The Dukes Of Stratosphear.

However, Andy did get around the USA in 1989 to promote *Oranges And Lemons*, meeting his stage-fright halfway by sticking to acoustic performances at radio stations.

- ✔ The 1981 single 'Respectable Street' was banned from BBC airplay because it mentioned Sony by name.

- ✔ The 1986 album *Skylarking* was re-pressed to include 'Dear God', a track not originally on the album but which was receiving airplay as a B-side.

- ✔ And the Silly Punk Name was: The Helium Kidz.

pause

you have to admire ambition

Yazoo ★★★

♫ 'Only You' (1982, no.2)

Early experiments should often be disregarded if you don't wish to suffer great disillusionment. Fans of Alanis Morrisette, for example, draw a veil over her former bubble-permed incarnation, Tori Amos's time as a fledgling grunge-rocker is usually forgiven and forgotten, and even **Kylie** aficionados are prepared to admit she wasn't doing herself any favours in the early days. **Alison Moyet**, however, has been consistently good from the beginning, her voice coming through strongly no matter what the instrumental style, and her collaboration with Vince Clarke stands up very well. Classic singles 'Don't Go', 'Nobody's Diary' and 'Situation' are still well-remembered today, despite being afflicted in the early 90s by the blight of unnecessary remixing.

'Only You' is probably more famous in the *a cappella* version by the Flying Pickets, who for some reason don't feature in this book. However, they couldn't outdo Yazoo's performance of the song on *Cheggers Plays Pop*, which featured starring roles for Alison's excessive blusher/ frilly black dress look, and Vince's winning quiff-and-comfy-grey-cardigan combination.

- The name Yazoo already belonged to a record company in the US, so for their career across the Atlantic, the band had to be known as Yaz (not to be confused with Yazz).

- Alison was previously a singer in bands called The Vicars and The Screaming Abdabs.

Yazz ★★

♫ **'Doctorin' The House'**

(1988, no.6) (Coldcut featuring Yazz and the Plastic Population)

Yasmin Evans – big tall woman in a leather jacket with a scary blonde buzzcut. You remember. After she had guested on the Coldcut single, it was something of a relief to hear the chart-topper 'The Only Way Is Up' in mid-1988 – a song you could dance to which was also blessed with a tune. The title perhaps betrays a touchingly naïve grasp of the dynamics of chart performance – a brief glance down the list of hits shows that, unfortunately, the usual law of diminishing returns prevails, although 'Fine Time' was pleasant enough. And just as the Miami Sound Machine were airbrushed out of Gloria Estefan's history, so the Plastic Population were cruelly abandoned by Yazz. Such is showbiz. Attempted chart comeback in 1993 was scuppered by hitching her star to Aswad, but the reggae combo then had the last laugh by plunging back into the Top 5 the following year.

✔ Yazz was apparently once quoted as saying she'd pose topless if it would help bring about the end of apartheid. Well, you have to admire ambition.

🔊 'We were a bit hardcore with Yazz. We'd say "do a lead vocal, two backing vocals and, no, you can't come to the mix." It caused problems because she had a wonderful voice and ideas about what she wanted to do with it, whereas we'd already decided what we were after.' (Jonathan Moore of Coldcut.)

Yello ★★

♪ **'The Race'** (1988, no.7)

Wacky Swiss synth-pop pioneers. They had threatened the charts a few times before their motorsport-inspired techno epic stormed into the charts across Europe in 1988, proving that there could be a few good things about this dance music revolution after all. The wonderfully-named Dieter Meier and Boris Blank were contemporaries of **Kraftwerk**, and had early acclaim for albums *Solid Pleasure* and *Claro Que Si*. The song 'Oh Yeah', from 1986, featured in the films *Ferris Bueller's Day Off* and *The Secret Of My Success*, and was later used for a chocolate bar advert.

By the time they made their 1988 breakthrough, Meier's disillusionment with contemporary music was showing, something of which British audiences got a little taste when he appeared on Radio 1's review show *Singled Out* to give just about everything a pasting. **Mike and the Mechanics'** 'The Living Years', in particular, got short shrift for Mr Rutherford's simultaneous tugging on the heart-strings and the purse-strings of the nation... Herr Meier loved **Tanita Tikaram's** 'Twist In My Sobriety', though. Yello continue to plough their own strange furrow. If you must have a Swiss duo, they're a better bet than Double.

✔ To link with the 1997 album *Pocket Universe*, Meier created a multimedia show for the Planetarium of the Deutsches Museum in Munich.

▶▶ **www.yello.ch** is their official virtual home, where you can find all the information on their current activities, join the Friends Of Yello or access the Soundstation.

Paul Young ★★★
♫ **'Wherever I Lay My Hat (That's My Home)'** (1983, no.1)

Young Paul was a Vauxhall car factory apprentice when he formed his first band, and had his first taste of showbiz when his group Streetband were signed. Subsequently he became vocalist for the hard-gigging Q Tips, then started out as a solo artist in 1982.

'Love Of The Common People', actually his debut single, flopped at first, only becoming a hit later on the back of his chart-topper. Things went crazy then, with the album *No Parlez* getting world sales of 7 million and more hits stacking up. People seemed to have taken Paul's cheerful grin and soulful voice to their collective bosom. Actually, the voice gave him a bit of trouble over the years, and he was ordered to rest it for a couple of months in 1984 (by a doctor, we hasten to point out). He was back on form for a UK tour the same year, although his time off appeared to have been spent carefully nursing a mullet to full growth. Live Aid saw him duetting with **Alison Moyet**.

● 'It's Christmas time…' Yes, Paul had the honour of delivering the opening line on the **Band Aid** single.

✔ His backing singers, for a period up to and including the 1984 single 'I'm Gonna Tear Your Playhouse Down', were two girls called Maz and Kim, known collectively as The Fabulous Wealthy Tarts.

◀» On his shyness: 'I was very, very shy. I had a bad stutter when I was a child, and I'm sure one made the other worse. The best thing to happen in that respect was joining a band.'

◀» On his voice problems: 'I hadn't damaged my throat

or had any operations but there was constant speculation about that and it just got pushed out of all
proportion. Then it becomes a mental block because
everybody is saying you have problems and it's really difficult to rise above that. In retrospect, I would-
n't have done such a back-breaking schedule for
those first few years.'

▶▌ Paul still appeared in the charts from time to time in
the 90s, most notably his duet with Zucchero,
'Senza Una Donna'. He performed 'Radio GaGa' at
1992's Freddie Mercury tribute concert – perhaps
not the obvious choice – and was last seen fronting
a Tex-Mex band called Los Pacaminos. If you're
dedicated, you'll find the Paul Young Fan Database
at **www.angelfire.com/on/lisag/paul.html** a useful resource.

pause

Z

Zen-like inevitability

ZZ Top ★★

Zany, hirsute Texan rockers who have been going since 1969. Zen-like inevitability means they will always be last in books like this (at least until Belgian techno duo ZZZ have their first Top 40 hit). Zingy blues-rock sound has been updated over the years by throwing synthesisers into the mix, but essentially they haven't changed much. Zestful wackiness has prevailed, as evidenced by their naming their 1972 gig 'ZZ Top's First Annual Texas Size Rompin' Stompin' Barndance Bar-B-Q festival', and, in 1987, announcing that they had booked themselves as 'House Band' on the first passenger Space Shuttle to the Moon. Zealously crazy men, but not for the pogophobic.

✔ Zooming on: their names are Billy Gibbons, Dusty Hill, and – wait for it – Frank Beard, who, obviously, is the one without the beard.

✔ Zenith of Dusty Hill's craziness came when he accidentally shot himself in the stomach in January 1985. Zippily, he recovered.

✔ Zeroing in on the origin of the name: a) it came from the two brands of cigarette paper, Zig-Zag and Top; b) it's a tribute to the blues legend Z.Z. Hill; c) Gibbons saw the two words together on a dilapidated billboard.

pause

Appendix 1: 'Especially For You'

For those who like lists and statistics, here are a few of those relevant to the 1980s. They've all been checked from several sources, so there shouldn't be any arguments. Again, artists who have a separate entry elsewhere are referenced in **bold type**.

✓ The first Number One of the 80s was Pink Floyd's 'Another Brick In The Wall (Part II)', hanging over from 1979, while the last was the reworking of 'Do They Know It's Christmas' by Band Aid II. See Appendix L3 for a full list.

✓ Fourteen singles went straight in at the top in the course of the decade, including three by **The Jam** ('Going Underground/Dreams of Children', 'A Town Called Malice/Precious' and 'Beat Surrender'), both versions of the **Band Aid** hit and two other charity singles, 'Let It Be' by Ferry Aid and the Hillsborough stadium disaster single, 'Ferry Cross the Mersey'. No singles went straight in at Number One during either 1986 or 1988.

✓ **Madness** were the band who spent the most weeks on the chart, clocking up 218 weeks in the Top 75 during the 80s.

✓ The biggest-selling single of the decade was 'Do They Know It's Christmas' by **Band Aid**, which sold over 50 million copies (3 million in the UK).

✓ The single which had the longest run at Number One in the 80s was 'Two Tribes' by **Frankie Goes To Hollywood**, which spent 9 weeks at the top in 1984.

- John Lennon's 'Just Like Starting Over' bounced back up the charts to Number One in the week after his death. **St Winifred's School Choir** then stepped in and prevented Lennon having a straight run of three Number One records – the lovely children were knocked off the top by 'Imagine', which in turn was replaced by 'Woman'. This remains the only case of an act replacing itself at Number One, and was the only instance of two consecutive posthumous Number Ones until 2002 (when Aaliyah was succeeded by George Harrison).

- The act with the shortest name to have a hit in the 80s was M, whose 1979 hit 'Pop Muzik' was remixed and re-entered the chart in the summer of 1989.

- In 1989, 50 leading music journalists were asked to choose the most over-rated artists of the decade. The result was: 1) **The Smiths** 2) **Bros** 3) **U2** 4) Elvis Costello 5) Bruce Springsteen.

- The first British female singer to top the album charts was Kate Bush with *Never For Ever* in 1980.

- The winners of the **Best Male Artist, Best Female Artist, Best Group** and **Best Newcomer** categories at each of the annual BPI Awards (Brit Awards from 1988) were as follows:

1982   Cliff Richard, Randy Crawford, **The Police, Human League**

1983   Paul McCartney, **Kim Wilde, Dire Straits, Culture Club**

1984	David Bowie, Annie Lennox, **Culture Club, Paul Young**
1985	**Paul Young, Alison Moyet, Wham!, Frankie Goes To Hollywood**
1986	Phil Collins, Annie Lennox, **Dire Straits, Go West**
1987	Peter Gabriel, Kate Bush, **Five Star, The Housemartins**
1988	**George Michael, Alison Moyet, Pet Shop Boys, Wet Wet Wet**
1989	Phil Collins, Annie Lennox, **Erasure, Bros**

✔ And the most outlandish album title of the decade? It's got to be a toss-up between **Bow Wow Wow's** *See Jungle! See Jungle! Go Join Your Gang! Yeah, City All Over! Go Ape Crazy!* and the **Happy Mondays'** *Squirrel And G-Man Twenty Four Hour Party People Plastic Face Carnt Smile (White Out)*…Unless anyone out there knows of a sillier one?

Appendix 2: 'Too Good To Be Forgotten'

The ones that got away: some of the greatest singles of the 1980s which should have been big hits, and weren't. Wouldn't you gladly have sacrificed 'Agadoo', 'Pump Up The Jam' or 'Swing The Mood' for one of these to have had a chance?

- **The Cure** 'Charlotte Sometimes' (1981, no.44)
- **A Flock of Seagulls** 'I Ran' (1982, no.43)
- Care 'Flaming Sword' (1983, no.48)
- **The Adventures** 'Another Silent Day' (1984, no.71)
- **New Order** 'Bizarre Love Triangle' (1986, no.56)
- **The Icicle Works** 'Who Do You Want For Your Love?' (1986, no.54)
- **Half Man Half Biscuit** 'Dickie Davies' Eyes' (1987, did not chart)
- House of Love 'Shine On' (1987, did not chart; 1990, no.20 re-recorded)
- **Voice of the Beehive** 'I Walk The Earth' (1988, no.42)
- **The Proclaimers** 'Make My Heart Fly' (1988, no.63)
- The River Detectives 'Chains' (1989, no.51)
- Cry Before Dawn 'Witness For The World' (1989, no.67)
- Frazier Chorus 'Dream Kitchen' (1989, no.57)
- 1927 'That's When I Think Of You' (1989, no.46)

If you would like to make a case for any others, please e-mail to **dan80s@hotmail.com**, and the most deserving will get a mention in the paperback edition.

Appendix 3: 'Numero Uno'

The Number Ones of the 1980s

15/12/79	**Pink Floyd** Another Brick In The Wall (Part II)	**5 weeks**
19/1/80	**Pretenders** Brass In Pocket	**2 weeks**
2/2/80	**Special AKA** Special AKA Live! (EP)	**2 weeks**
16/2/80	**Kenny Rogers** Coward Of The County	**2 weeks**
1/3/80	**Blondie** Atomic	**2 weeks**
15/3/80	**Fern Kinney** Together We Are Beautiful	**1 week**
22/3/80	**The Jam** Going Underground / Dreams of Children	**3 weeks**
12/4/80	**The Detroit Spinners** Working My Way Back To You	**2 weeks**
26/4/80	**Blondie** Call Me	**1 week**
3/5/80	**Dexy's Midnight Runners** Geno	**2 weeks**
17/5/80	**Johnny Logan** What's Another Year	**2 weeks**
31/5/80	**M★A★S★H** Theme from M★A★S★H (Suicide Is Painless)	**3 weeks**

Date	Artist / Title	Weeks
21/6/80	**Don McLean** Crying	**3 weeks**
12/7/80	**Olivia Newton-John & ELO** Xanadu	**2 weeks**
26/7/80	**Odyssey** Use It Up And Wear It Out	**2 weeks**
9/8/80	**ABBA** The Winner Takes It All	**2 weeks**
23/8/80	**David Bowie** Ashes To Ashes	**2 weeks**
6/9/80	**The Jam** Start	**1 week**
13/9/80	**Kelly Marie** Feels Like I'm In Love	**2 weeks**
27/9/80	**The Police** Don't Stand So Close To Me	**4 weeks**
25/10/80	**Barbara Streisand** Woman In Love	**3 weeks**
15/11/80	**Blondie** The Tide Is High	**2 weeks**
29/11/80	**ABBA** Super Trouper	**3 weeks**
20/12/80	**John Lennon** (Just Like) Starting Over	**1 week**
27/12/80	**St. Winifred's School Choir** There's No One Quite Like Grandma	**2 weeks**
10/1/81	**John Lennon** Imagine	**4 weeks**

7/2/81	**John Lennon** Woman	**2 weeks**
21/2/81	**Joe Dolce Music Theatre** Shaddap You Face	**3 weeks**
14/2/81	**Roxy Music** Jealous Guy	**2 weeks**
28/3/81	**Shakin' Stevens** This Ole House	**3 weeks**
18/4/81	**Bucks Fizz** Making Your Mind Up	**3 weeks**
9/5/81	**Adam and the Ants** Stand And Deliver	**5 weeks**
13/6/81	**Smokey Robinson** Being With You	**2 weeks**
27/6/81	**Michael Jackson** One Day In Your Life	**2 weeks**
11/7/81	**The Specials** Ghost Town	**3 weeks**
1/8/81	**Shakin' Stevens** Green Door	**4 weeks**
29/8/81	**Aneka** Japanese Boy	**1 week**
5/9/81	**Soft Cell** Tainted Love	**2 weeks**
19/9/81	**Adam and the Ants** Prince Charming	**4 weeks**
17/10/81	**Dave Stewart & Barbara Gaskin** It's My Party	**4 weeks**

14/11/81	**The Police** Every Little Thing She Does Is Magic	**1 week**
21/11/81	**Queen & David Bowie** Under Pressure	**2 weeks**
5/12/81	**Julio Iglesias** Begin The Beguine (Volver A Empezar)	**1 week**
12/12/81	**Human League** Don't You Want Me	**5 weeks**
16/1/82	**Bucks Fizz** The Land Of Make Believe	**2 weeks**
30/1/82	**Shakin' Stevens** Oh Julie	**1 week**
6/2/82	**Kraftwerk** The Model /Computer Love	**1 week**
13/2/82	**The Jam** A Town Called Malice/Precious	**3 weeks**
6/3/82	**Tight Fit** The Lion Sleeps Tonight	**3 weeks**
27/3/82	**The Goombay Dance Band** Seven Tears	**3 weeks**
17/4/82	**Bucks Fizz** My Camera Never Lies	**1 week**
24/4/82	**Paul McCartney with Stevie Wonder** Ebony And Ivory	**3 weeks**
15/5/82	**Nicole** A Little Peace	**2 weeks**
29/5/82	**Madness** House Of Fun	**2 weeks**

12/6/82	**Adam Ant** Goody Two Shoes	**2 weeks**
26/6/82	**Charlene** I've Never Been To Me	**1 week**
3/7/82	**Captain Sensible** Happy Talk	**2 weeks**
17/7/82	**Irene Cara** Fame	**3 weeks**
7/8/82	**Dexy's Midnight Runners with The Emerald Express** Come On Eileen	**4 weeks**
4/9/82	**Survivor** Eye Of The Tiger	**4 weeks**
2/10/82	**Musical Youth** Pass The Dutchie	**3 weeks**
23/10/82	**Culture Club** Do You Really Want To Hurt Me	**3 weeks**
13/11/82	**Eddy Grant** I Don't Wanna Dance	**3 weeks**
4/12/82	**The Jam** Beat Surrender	**2 weeks**
18/12/82	**Renee and Renato** Save Your Love	**4 weeks**
15/1/83	**Phil Collins** You Can't Hurry Love	**2 weeks**
29/1/83	**Men at Work** Down Under	**3 weeks**

19/2/83	**Kajagoogoo** Too Shy	2 weeks
5/3/83	**Michael Jackson** Billie Jean	1 week
12/3/83	**Bonnie Tyler** Total Eclipse Of The Heart	2 weeks
26/3/83	**Duran Duran** Is There Something I Should Know	2 weeks
9/4/83	**David Bowie** Let's Dance	3 weeks
30/4/83	**Spandau Ballet** True	4 weeks
28/5/83	**New Edition** Candy Girl	1 week
4/6/83	**Police** Every Breath You Take	4 weeks
2/7/83	**Rod Stewart** Baby Jane	3 weeks
23/7/83	**Paul Young** Wherever I Lay My Hat (That's My Home)	3 weeks
13/8/83	**KC & The Sunshine Band** Give It Up	3 weeks
3/9/83	**UB40** Red Red Wine	3 weeks
24/9/83	**Culture Club** Karma Chameleon	6 weeks

5/11/83	**Billy Joel** Uptown Girl	5 weeks
10/12/83	**Flying Pickets** Only You	5 weeks
14/1/84	**Paul McCartney** Pipes Of Peace	2 weeks
28/1/84	**Frankie Goes to Hollywood** Relax	5 weeks
3/3/84	**Nena** 99 Red Balloons	3 weeks
24/3/84	**Lionel Richie** Hello	6 weeks
5/5/84	**Duran Duran** The Reflex	4 weeks
2/6/84	**Wham!** Wake Me Up Before You Go Go	2 weeks
16/6/84	**Frankie Goes to Hollywood** Two Tribes	9 weeks
18/8/84	**George Michael** Careless Whisper	3 weeks
8/9/84	**Stevie Wonder** I Just Called To Say I Love You	6 weeks
20/10/84	**Wham!** Freedom	3 weeks
10/11/84	**Chaka Khan** I Feel For You	3 weeks
1/12/84	**Jim Diamond** I Should Have Known Better	1 week

Date	Artist / Song	Weeks
8/12/84	**Frankie Goes to Hollywood** The Power Of Love	**1 week**
15/12/84	**Band Aid** Do They Know It's Christmas	**5 weeks**
19/1/85	**Foreigner** I Want To Know What Love Is	**3 weeks**
9/2/85	**Elaine Paige/Barbara Dickson** I Know Him So Well	**4 weeks**
9/3/85	**Dead or Alive** You Spin Me Round (Like A Record)	**2 weeks**
23/3/85	**Philip Bailey & Phil Collins** Easy Lover	**4 weeks**
20/4/85	**USA for Africa** We Are The World	**2 weeks**
4/5/85	**Phyllis Nelson** Move Closer	**1 week**
11/5/85	**Paul Hardcastle** 19	**5 weeks**
15/6/85	**The Crowd** You'll Never Walk Alone	**2 weeks**
29/6/85	**Sister Sledge** Frankie	**4 weeks**
27/7/85	**Eurythmics** There Must Be An Angel (Playing With My Heart)	**1 week**
3/8/85	**Madonna** Into The Groove	**4 weeks**

31/8/85	**UB40 & Chrissie Hynde** I Got You Babe	1 week
7/9/85	**David Bowie & Mick Jagger** Dancing In The Street	4 weeks
5/10/85	**Midge Ure** If I Was	1 week
12/10/85	**Jennifer Rush** The Power Of Love	5 weeks
16/11/85	**Feargal Sharkey** A Good Heart	2 weeks
30/11/85	**Wham!** I'm Your Man	2 weeks
14/12/85	**Whitney Houston** Saving All My Love For You	2 weeks
28/12/85	**Shakin' Stevens** Merry Christmas Everyone	2 weeks
11/1/86	**Pet Shop Boys** West End Girls	2 weeks
25/1/86	**A-Ha** The Sun Always Shines On TV	2 weeks
8/2/86	**Billy Ocean** When The Going Gets Tough, The Tough Get Going	4 weeks
8/3/86	**Diana Ross** Chain Reaction	3 weeks
29/3/86	**Cliff Richard & The Young Ones** Living Doll	3 weeks

19/4/86	**George Michael** A Different Corner	3 weeks
10/5/86	**Falco** Rock Me Amadeus	1 week
17/5/86	**Spitting Image** The Chicken Song	3 weeks
7/6/86	**Doctor & The Medics** Spirit In The Sky	3 weeks
28/6/86	**Wham!** The Edge Of Heaven	2 weeks
12/7/86	**Madonna** Papa Don't Preach	3 weeks
2/8/86	**Chris de Burgh** The Lady In Red	3 weeks
23/8/86	**Boris Gardiner** I Want To Wake Up With You	3 weeks
13/9/86	**Communards** Don't Leave Me This Way	4 weeks
11/10/86	**Madonna** True Blue	1 week
18/10/86	**Nick Berry** Every Loser Wins	3 weeks
8/11/86	**Berlin** Take My Breath Away (Love Theme From *Top Gun*)	4 weeks
6/12/86	**Europe** The Final Countdown	2 weeks

20/12/86	**Housemartins** Caravan Of Love	**1 week**
27/12/86	**Jackie Wilson** Reet Petite	**4 weeks**
24/1/87	**Steve 'Silk' Hurley** Jack Your Body	**2 weeks**
7/2/87	**George Michael & Aretha Franklin** I Knew You Were Waiting (For Me)	**2 weeks**
21/2/87	**Ben E. King** Stand By Me	**3 weeks**
14/3/87	**Boy George** Everything I Own	**2 weeks**
28/3/87	**Mel & Kim** Respectable	**1 week**
4/4/87	**Ferry Aid** Let It Be	**3 weeks**
25/4/87	**Madonna** La Isla Bonita	**2 weeks**
9/5/87	**Starship** Nothing's Gonna Stop Us Now	**4 weeks**
6/6/87	**Whitney Houston** I Wanna Dance With Somebody (Who Loves Me)	**2 weeks**
20/6/87	**The Firm** Star Trekkin'	**2 weeks**
4/7/87	**Pet Shop Boys** It's A Sin	**3 weeks**

25/7/87	**Madonna** Who's That Girl	**1 week**
1/8/87	**Los Lobos** La Bamba	**2 weeks**
15/8/87	**Michael Jackson with Siedah Garrett** I Just Can't Stop Loving You	**2 weeks**
29/8/87	**Rick Astley** Never Gonna Give You Up	**5 weeks**
3/10/87	**M/A/R/R/S** Pump Up The Volume	**2 weeks**
17/10/87	**Bee Gees** You Win Again	**4 weeks**
14/11/87	**T'Pau** China In Your Hand	**5 weeks**
19/12/87	**Pet Shop Boys** Always On My Mind	**4 weeks**
16/1/88	**Belinda Carlisle** Heaven Is A Place On Earth	**2 weeks**
30/1/88	**Tiffany** I Think We're Alone Now	**3 weeks**
20/2/88	**Kylie Minogue** I Should Be So Lucky	**5 weeks**
26/3/88	**Aswad** Don't Turn Around	**2 weeks**
9/4/88	**Pet Shop Boys** Heart	**3 weeks**
30/4/88	**S'Express** Theme From S'Express	**3 weeks**

14/5/88	**Fairground Attraction** Perfect	**1 week**
21/5/88	**Wet Wet Wet** With A Little Help From My Friends/ **Billy Bragg with Cara Tivey** She's Leaving Home	**4 weeks**
18/6/88	**The Timelords** Doctorin' The Tardis	**1 week**
25/6/88	**Bros** I Owe You Nothing	**2 weeks**
9/6/88	**Glenn Medeiros** Nothing's Gonna Change My Love For You	**4 weeks**
6/8/88	**Yazz & The Plastic Population** The Only Way Is Up	**5 weeks**
10/9/88	**Phil Collins** A Groovy Kind Of Love	**2 weeks**
24/8/88	**The Hollies** He Ain't Heavy, He's My Brother	**2 weeks**
8/10/88	**U2** Desire	**1 week**
15/10/88	**Whitney Houston** One Moment In Time	**2 weeks**
29/10/88	**Enya** Orinoco Flow (Sail Away)	**3 weeks**
19/11/88	**Robin Beck** First Time	**3 weeks**
10/12/88	**Cliff Richard** Mistletoe And Wine	**4 weeks**

| 7/1/89 | **Kylie Minogue/Jason Donovan** | |
| | Especially For You | **3 weeks** |

28/1/89	**Marc Almond/Gene Pitney**	
	Something's Gotten Hold	
	Of My Heart	**4 weeks**

| 25/2/89 | **Simple Minds** | |
| | Belfast Child | **2 weeks** |

| 11/3/89 | **Jason Donovan** | |
| | Too Many Broken Hearts | **2 weeks** |

| 25/3/89 | **Madonna** | |
| | Like A Prayer | **3 weeks** |

| 15/4/89 | **Bangles** | |
| | Eternal Flame | **4 weeks** |

| 13/5/89 | **Kylie Minogue** | |
| | Hand On Your Heart | **1 week** |

| 20/5/89 | **Various Artists** | |
| | Ferry 'Cross The Mersey | **3 weeks** |

| 10/6/89 | **Jason Donovan** | |
| | Sealed With A Kiss | **2 weeks** |

14/6/89	**Soul II Soul featuring Caron Wheeler**	
	Back To Life	
	(How Ever Do You Want Me)	**4 weeks**

| 22/7/89 | **Sonia** | |
| | You'll Never Stop Me Loving You | **2 weeks** |

| 5/8/89 | **Jive Bunny & The Mastermixers** | |
| | Swing The Mood | **5 weeks** |

| 9/9/89 | **Black Box** | |
| | Ride On Time | **6 weeks** |

21/10/89	**Jive Bunny & The Mastermixers** That's What I Like	**3 weeks**
11/11/89	**Lisa Stansfield** All Around The World	**2 weeks**
25/11/89	**New Kids on the Block** You Got It (The Right Stuff)	**3 weeks**
16/12/89	**Jive Bunny & The Mastermixers** Let's Party	**1 week**
23/12/89	**Band Aid II** Do They Know It's Christmas	**3 weeks**

Acknowledgements: 'Give It Up'

The following, even if they may not have realised it at the time, helped a great deal – whether by lending me CDs, tapes and back copies of *Smash Hits* and *Melody Maker*, arguing the toss about OMD and The Icicle Works, sending me obscure quotes and facts, providing tea, biscuits and cultural enrichment, generally convincing me that I could write the damn thing, or just giving free hugs:

Rachel ('Party Fears Two') and Ellie the Minx ('Sweetest Smile'): Yes, this is what I do in the attic.
Steve & Julia ('I Say Nothing'): Vintage 1987, definitely not a 'table wine'.
La famille Simms ('She Sells Sanctuary'): Special thanks to David for the comments and additional facts. *'Ce n'est pas mieux, mais c'est plus fort.'*
Vicki & Pete ('Panic'): I've not stolen your dialogue for this one, honest!
Julia T. ('Happy Hour'): See, I told you blasting your wall with Joy Division at 2am would have a purpose one of these days.
Chenab ('Down In The Tube Station At Midnight'): Seems long enough even since 1993, no?
Jo & Jason ('Bring On The Dancing Horses'): Are you feeling old yet?
Grant Slater ('A Little Respect'): To be fair, Grant and Siân, NWOBHM needs a book to itself.
Sam Young ('Say Hello Wave Goodbye'): Sorry for the un-PC bits. They might be funny, though.
Mick Ashman ('Life In A Northern Town'): Nope, still haven't found a happy Manchester group...
Caroline Absalom ('Club Tropicana'): 'Golden Oldies Day' was never in the frame, was it?

Thanks also to Richard Lewis ('Ghosts'), Louis Barfe

('The Sun Goes Down (Living It Up)') and Jon Howells ('Planet Earth').

And, last but not least, thanks to my agent Caroline Montgomery ('Fantastic Day') and David Shelley and the staff at A&B ('Promised You A Miracle').

Of course, I'm ultimately responsible for any errors (but if you were a fan of Technotronic, you have only yourself to blame). While every care has been taken in compiling this book, it is possible that some small inaccuracies may have crept in. Especially where I have deliberately invented something for the sake of a cheap gag.

However, if you have noticed any glaring mistakes, I trust you'll be kind enough to write to me at **dan80s@hotmail.com** with a petty, sarcastic and carping little e-mail. I will then have the pleasure of deleting it and sending your address to the mailing list of a persistent Japanese website sending out spurious get-rich-quick chain letters.

That was the Eighties. And if you enjoyed it half as much as I did, then I enjoyed it twice as much as you.

Goodbye.

stop

eject